FOOD FOR DISSENT

FOOD FOR DISSENT

NATURAL FOODS AND THE CONSUMER
COUNTERCULTURE SINCE THE 1960S

MARIA MCGRATH

UNIVERSITY OF MASSACHUSETTS PRESS
Amherst and Boston

Copyright © 2019 by University of Massachusetts Press
All rights reserved
Printed in the United States of America

ISBN 978-1-62534-422-9 (paper); 421-2 (hardcover)

Designed by Jen Jackowitz
Set in Adobe Jenson Pro and Mr Eaves

Cover design by Rebecca Neimark, Twenty-Six Letters
Cover photo by Ben Chang courtesy Weavers Way.

Library of Congress Cataloging-in-Publication Data

Names: McGrath, Maria, 1965–author.
Title: Food for dissent : natural foods and the consumer counterculture since the 1960s / Maria McGrath.
Description: Amherst : University of Massachusetts, [2019] | Revision of author's thesis (Ph. D.)—Lehigh University. 2006. | Includes bibliographical references and index. |
Identifiers: LCCN 2018051826 (print) | LCCN 2018052916 (ebook) | ISBN 9781613766705 (ebook) | ISBN 9781613766712 (ebook) | ISBN 9781625344212 (hardcover) | ISBN 9781625344229 (paper)
Subjects: LCSH: Food habits—United States—History—20th century. | Natural foods—United States—History—20th century. | Consumer movements—United States—History—20th century. | Natural foods industry—United States—History—20th century.
Classification: LCC GT2853.U5 (ebook) | LCC GT2853.U5 M387 2019 (print) | DDC 394.1/209730904—dc23
LC record available at https://lccn.loc.gov/2018051826

British Library Cataloguing-in-Publication Data
A catalog record for this book is available from the British Library.

Portion of this book was adapted from Maria McGrath, "Living Feminist: The Liberation and Limits of Countercultural Business and Radical Lesbian Ethics at Bloodroot Restaurant," *The Sixties* 9, no. 2 (2016): 189–217. Published by Taylor & Francis. Reprinted by permission of Taylor & Francis Ltd; and Maria McGrath, "Recipes for a New World: Utopianism and Alternative Eating in Vegetarian Natural-Foods Cookbooks, 1970–84," *Eating in Eden: Food and American Utopias*, edited by Etta M. Madden and Martha L. Finch, by permission of the University of Nebraska Press. Copyright © 2006 by the Board of Regents of the University of Nebraska.

FOR JOHN.

CONTENTS

PREFACE IX

ACKNOWLEDGMENTS XIII

INTRODUCTION
The Gathering Storm 1
Baby Boomers and Their Discontent

CHAPTER 1
"More Than Just Cheap Cheese" 15
Community, Class, and Consumerism in Countercultural Food Co-ops

CHAPTER 2
Recipes for a New World 53
Vegetarian Opposition in Seventies Natural Foods Cookbooks

CHAPTER 3
"Organic Style" 95
Rodale Press and Mass-Mediated Organics

CHAPTER 4
Dr. Andrew Weil and the Postsixties Promises of Food 133

CHAPTER 5
Natural Foods Conservatism 168
From Hippie Evangelism to Whole Foods

CONCLUSION
The Future of Countercultural Food Politics 196

NOTES 203

INDEX 233

PREFACE

In the early 1970s, Mollie Katzen, the author of what became the most widely read countercultural vegetarian cookbook—*Moosewood Cookbook* (1974)—was flipping lentil walnut burgers at Moosewood Restaurant in Ithaca, New York, for a small clique of hippie vegetarians. By the turn of the twenty-first century, "natural foods" had seized America's imagination and its shopping cart. The stunning success of this originally politically charged and initially unpalatable cuisine drove my interest in natural foods and in the counterculture from which it sprang. I wondered how and why these gastronomically challenged foods moved from the cultural and commercial fringes to the heart of new millennium epicureanism. Moreover, I was curious about the political consequences of using the essentially private acts of buying, cooking, and eating as tools for cultural revolution. *Food for Dissent* is the culmination of my research into these questions.

Many of the figures who first gave form to the natural foods movement did not play the leads in the defining dramas of the 1960s. They were not members of Students for a Democratic Society (SDS). They did not live in San Francisco's Haight district or Manhattan's East Village. They did not drop acid at Timothy Leary's Millbrook estate (although chapter four's main character, Andrew Weil, would have jumped at the chance). Indeed, if the counterculture applied only to such rarified locales and persons, it may have panned out as an ephemeral episode of little historical note. Instead, it is the idealistic reverberations and experimental activities, incubated in the hippie milieu but not directly connected to its famous happenings, which were most responsible for sustaining the countercultural imaginary in postsixties America. The natural foods movement—which gained traction in the early 1970s—qualifies as just such a countercultural force.

As a point of clarification, in this book, "natural foods movement" stands for an elastic consumer cultural trend—with political intonations—that persisted from the late 1960s–early 1970s through the twenty-first century. Not every natural foods patron and producer considered herself part of a movement, but many did. Health foods, organic foods, local foods, whole foods, "real" food, and the "food revolution" all fit under this admittedly imprecise title.

It seems that natural foods survived and thrived after the 1960s for several reasons, the first of which is that the revolt against the industrial foods system was, and is, a piece of a broadly felt discomfort with the unnerving pace and size of modern American life. In 1969, New Left student radical Gregory Calvert described this discord as his generation's "gut level alienation from America-the-Obscene-and-the-Dehumanized."[1] Over time, this estrangement seeped out of New Left circles, gaining cross-partisan currency. The natural foods movement offered dissenters a particular focus and a concrete solution: the creation of a meaning-filled, principled, and self-protective marketplace, outside the mainstream economy.

The second quality that sustained the natural foods movement was its consumer orientation. Disaffected from conventional politics and inspired by the do-it-yourself ethos of the civil rights and the New Left movements, many young dissidents decided that, rather than taking on the system, they would build the world they wanted. To this end, hippies constructed alternative community and commerce in head shops, secondhand clothing stores, food co-ops, and other businesses. This commercialism gave structure and momentum to the natural foods movement, expanding it beyond its original circle of dietary aesthetes and leftist utopians to a larger citizen-consumer contingent. A particularly potent strain of twentieth-century antistatism— which would attract both the Left and the Right—found a voice in the natural foods movement's politics of consumption. Thus contrary to the dominant historical narrative that ties the rise of entrepreneurial and market idealism to Reagan-era conservatism, the counterculture lost faith in government and adopted commercial solutions to civic problems much earlier on.

Finally, the continued potency of natural foods can be attributed to the fact that, since the 1960s, America's middle and upper classes have bet considerable economic and cultural capital on food and health. Natural foods proved a mutable platform from which they could register disdain for the powers that be, fears about bodily and earthly contamination, and contradictory desires to live morally but with pleasure and status intact. Their substantial authority as academics, journalists, moviemakers, organic farmers, craft food producers, and discerning consumers kept this originally antiestablishment campaign pulsing through mainstream media and merchandise into the new millennium.

The natural foods movement launched many citizens into activism for nutritional equity, food workers' rights, and sustainable agriculture. However, it would be myopic to describe these engagements as the movement's most pervasive effect on American culture and politics. *Food for Dissent* suggests another lens through which to view the natural foods countercultures. In framing shopping, cooking, and eating as important political acts, natural foods advocates contributed to the neoliberal redefinition of the marketplace as a force for social justice and self-fulfillment. Ultimately, the movement's pocketbook and personalist food politics refreshed and sustained the capitalist order.

ACKNOWLEDGMENTS

Many people supported this book's long journey. At Lehigh University, Roger Simon, Steve Cutcliffe, Ted Morgan, Gail Cooper, and Chava Weissler were instrumental to the improvement of this project in its earliest stages. Martin Sutton, John Petito, and Lynn Della Pietra, at Bucks County Community College, provided generous financial support and time away from classes so that I could attend conferences, go on sabbatical, and remain engaged in my field. When my energy and optimism flagged, my Bucks colleague, Max Probst, kept me afloat with his sardonic wit and openhearted encouragement.

The National Endowment for the Humanities "Food in the Public Square" grant team—Breena Holland, Ben Cohen, Dawn King, and Sandra Aguilar—clarified my thinking on public perceptions of natural foods and the character of the food revolution. Julie Guthman, who was the keynote speaker in our final public forum, heavily influenced the ideas developed in the conclusion. A special thanks must go to the grant leader, Kelly Allen, who included me in the project and who pushed me to think more deeply about the role of the intellectual in society.

In the midst of revising this book, I submitted an article on Bloodroot Restaurant and Collective to *Sixties* editor Jeremy Varon. His steady editorial hand was crucial to that article's success. Moreover, our exchanges deepened my understanding of the culture and politics of the 1960s. A big thank-you is also due David Farber, whose insightful and thorough review of the Bloodroot article and this book refined my thinking on the sixties counterculture.

I was lucky to have access to many of the natural foods actors and institutions covered in this book. The People's Food Co-op in Ann Arbor, Michigan, generously let me rifle through its records, before I even knew what I was looking for. Weavers Way gave me access to its files in the store's meeting room. Interviews and discussions with key co-op members and staff, including Ed McGann, Norman Weiss, and Dorothy Guy, provided important and personal insights on Weavers and New Wave co-ops. Selma Miriam, who created Bloodroot Restaurant and Collective, generously shared her experiences and offered incisive commentary on my analysis of her lesbian feminist collective.

The library staff at the University of Michigan's Bentley Library, Temple University's Special Collections, and Yale's Manuscript and Archives assisted me at different points along the way. A special thanks goes to Stephen Ross at Yale and Josue T. Hurtado at Temple for their patience and quick responses to my questions and requests.

It goes without saying that I am indebted to my editor, Matt Becker, at the University of Massachusetts Press. He enthusiastically supported my project and nudged and reassured me through every phase of the publishing process. Sally Nichols and Rachael DeShano deserve a resounding thank-you for their guidance through the book's production. Thanks to director Mary Dougherty for her words of encouragement and her friendship. I am also indebted to the two anonymous reviewers for their precise readings. Their advice was invaluable. Lastly, I am deeply grateful to copyeditor extraordinaire, Nancy Raynor, for her painstaking and thoughtful review of the entire manuscript.

There are two people who really made this book happen. The first, my husband, and all-around good person, Peter Ammirati, has listened to me talk (sometimes rant) about food, counterculture, and American politics for nearly two decades. His optimism for this project never wavered, and his editorial contributions to much of this book, over its many drafts, is substantial. He celebrated my successes and encouraged me during less confident moments. Thank-you hardly describes my appreciation.

Finally, with profound gratitude, this book is dedicated to my mentor and friend, John Pettegrew. John nurtured this project (and me) from the beginning. His voice is present throughout. Very sadly, he passed away, at far too young of an age, before the book's publication. My life is poorer without him. Thank you for everything, John.

FOOD FOR DISSENT

INTRODUCTION

THE GATHERING STORM
Baby Boomers and Their Discontent

In 1967, Carol Flinders attended an antiwar meeting in an apartment on Telegraph Avenue in Berkeley, California. As recounted in the introduction to the countercultural natural foods classic *Laurel's Kitchen: A Handbook for Vegetarian Cookery and Nutrition* (1976), after relocating to the Bay Area with her husband, Tim, and two-year-old daughter, Julia, Flinders was "increasingly oppressed by the war in Vietnam" and was looking to do something about it. Laurel Robertson, Flinders's future cookbook coauthor, hosted the gathering. Flinders did not know Robertson but had heard from friends about her arrest during the Berkeley Free Speech Movement's famous Sproul Hall occupation in 1964. Intimidated by her hostess's political chops, she hesitantly descended into what she expected to be a radical's hideaway. Instead, Flinders found a den of warm hippie domesticity with "potted plants [and] poster art" and a "sunny kitchen" where "four long, fat strips of dough" sat rising into loaves of French bread. Once baked, the bread was served with a "big pot of lentil soup," which "fueled" organizing and conversation into the evening.[1]

Despite the impression that Robertson and the antiwar organizers made on Flinders, this interlude with Bay Area activism did not mark her political ignition. In the next several years, she gave birth to her son Chris, dabbled in antiwar protest, encounter groups, potting, and the recorder. Like other cultural questioners of the era, Carol Flinders was looking for an answer to a problem she couldn't name. The nation seemed "without . . . centeredness," and she felt impotent and directionless. It was not until she and her husband attended a meditation lecture by a "man from India" that Flinders felt settled. Meditation made her realize the importance of "the old Quaker phrase 'living intentionally.'" Newly alert, she fixated on the most changeable part of her life, her family's health—in particular, on their eating and her cooking.[2]

Around this time Flinders reconnected with Laurel Robertson. Their relationship flowered as the more experienced Robertson instructed Flinders in vegetarian natural cooking; friend Bronwen Godfrey eventually joined them. Natural vegetarianism connected Godfrey, Robertson, and Flinders to a contingent of food-engaged Bay Area residents. Soon they were trading recipes with other natural foods devotees and participating in Berkeley's natural foods buying club, the Food Conspiracy. They found community and purpose along the way. As Flinders recalled, they traded the alienation of "Saturday mornings in supermarkets, shoving carts down glaring aisles where profiteering middlemen had placed thick (and costly) layers of cellophane between us and everything we were buying," for alternative foods intimacy in "one another's backyards and kitchens, weighing, bagging, laughing, and visiting as we divided our spoils." After years of searching she had a diagnosis. "Eating," she optimistically announced, "can become, most delightfully, just the beginning of a transformation of one's entire life . . . If the consumer refused to be manipulated and makes wise choices that are not based on advertising, he-she-*we!*—can save the planet."[3] Food was the problem, and food was the answer.

Thus, this young Berkeley mother became part of an alliance of natural foods mutineers who, by the late 1960s and early 1970s, had drifted from student activism and street protest to building principled careers and home lives. Favoring high-minded consumption and deliberative homemaking as her protest, Carol Flinders joined a web of food agents who rooted the burgeoning natural foods movement in a personalist rendering of politics.

In his best-selling book, *The Greening of America* (1970), Charles A. Reich championed the radical gestalt from which the natural foods movement sprang. The revolution, he explained, "will originate with the individual and with culture and it will change the political structure only as its final act."[4] This formula for liberated personhood was a central precept of the multipronged rebellion(s) that came to be known as the "sixties counterculture."[5] With their whole foods, vegetarian cuisine, the authors of *Laurel's Kitchen* affirmed this countercultural script. Declaring deliverance from unreflective postwar materialism through real eating, real cooking, and controlled consumerism, they lived their revolt.

The shapers of the natural foods movement, like other mutineers at the time, worried over the cost of the postwar order. America's social and political fragmentation, its industrial toxicity, and its nuclear militarism prompted many college-aged citizens to wonder what to do with the world they were inheriting. For this unique and large generation—the 76.4 million born between 1945 and 1960—who grew up in the paradoxical soup of carefree affluence and apocalyptic Cold War paranoia, these issues could not be more pressing.

Countercultural critics believed that processed foods displayed the denaturalization and commoditization of America. Factory production sapped the nutritional worth out of food, creating plastic imitations of natural originals. And commercialization corrupted food's ultimate purpose—to nourish the body and to create communion—by planting artificial desires for instant concoctions. As Carol Flinders judged, "Slapping together a sandwich from 'balloon' bread and pre-ribboned peanut butter and jelly spread," and calling that motherly care, proved that women had lost their way.[6]

Despite the certainty of food dissenters that convenience innovations of the 1950s had destroyed home cooking, food's modern march had begun much earlier. By the turn of the twentieth century, Jell-O desserts, Campbell's canned vegetables and soups, Underwood canned meats, and other ready-made products had hit the grocery store shelves, becoming commonplace in the American larder.[7] Frozen foods took hold during World War II, when metal shortages made canned goods too expensive. Chasing opportunity, wartime food companies invented iced versions of everything from bouillabaisse to baked beans.[8]

Of course, the postwar period stood out in the breadth of processed fabrications. Between the 1940s and the 1960s, a multiplicity of factory foods flooded America's kitchens, including instant potatoes (1954), aerosol whipped cream (1954), Cheese Whiz (1952), and Lipton's dried onion soup used in the "California Dip" (invented in 1954) eaten at backyard barbecues and suburban cocktail parties. Food companies, hoping to replicate Birdseye's fish stick success, resoundingly failed with copycat ham sticks, veal sticks, and dried lima been sticks.[9] Wild combinations—such as gelatinized "Ginger Ale Salad" or "Spaghetti Oven Dinner," which called for onions, grated American cheese, link sausages, and one can of spaghetti in tomato sauce, oven baked for twenty minutes—took their place in the pantheon of quick and kitschy fifties fare.[10] Most radically, it was the 1950s that moved supper from the dining room to the den with Swanson's TV dinner (1954) and made cake baking a cinch with Duncan Hines mixes (1951). Food company advertising and women's magazines consistently sold premade goods as the harried housewife's hero.[11]

Young people coming of age in the countercultural context determined that food marketers had bamboozled American women at great cost to the health of their family and the earth. As Carol Flinders worriedly reflected, there was "something terribly wrong with our whole culture's attitude towards food . . . the original important function of food—to nourish the body—was fast slipping into oblivion."[12] In the name of authenticity and self-rule, Flinders, alongside others in the fledgling food revolt, took a whole grain, homemade stand, passing on their nutritional ethos to other culinary renegades in cookbooks, magazines, co-ops, and other natural foods channels.

LOCATING THE MOVEMENT

Food for Dissent takes a case study approach to the history of the natural foods movement, following key sites of activity—food co-ops, vegetarian cookbooks, Rodale Press and its readership, and natural health celebrity Dr. Andrew Weil—from their countercultural fringe beginnings to their new-century "food revolution" ascendance. Chapter 5 scrutinizes the seeming contradiction of the presence of political and cultural conservatism in this movement with a hippie-leftist genealogy.

With the exception of Warren Belasco's keynote analysis of the late sixties/early seventies natural foods phenomenon, *Appetite for Change* (1989), food defectors and their consumer and entrepreneurial efforts have, until recently, been overlooked in chronicles of the counterculture and the 1960s.[13] Hippie superstars and New Left leaders are the planets around which sixties historiography has traditionally revolved.[14] Yet, away from these bright lights and infamous happenings, the dramatis personae of the natural foods movement were testing the cultural and commercial waters in quieter and more personal ways. They were integrating countercultural enthusiasms—authenticity, altered consciousness, self-expression—into their lives.

Andrew Weil, who later became a natural diet and health guru, was bucking the academy by convincing his Harvard professors to allow his group of "brash" science students to follow a course of self-directed study, exempting them from class attendance.[15] As early as 1963, those undergrads could buy LSD (for a dollar a dose, according to Allen Matusow), pot, and other drugs in college sites such as Harvard Square.[16] Weil took part in this mind-expansion subculture that stretched from his mainline Philadelphia home to Harvard, imbibing everything from nutmeg to acid. He was also starting to contemplate the interplay of consciousness and diet with health and healing.[17]

In her family home in Rochester, New York, Mollie Katzen, future *Moosewood Cookbook* author, tested self-expression through art, music, and fiction—and by studying the most exotic food in her life, her mother's carefully prepared Sabbath challah bread. Across the nation, in San Francisco, Edward Espe Brown, *Tassajara Cooking* author, began his lifelong Zen Buddhist practice at the Green Gulch Farm Zen Center in Marin County. Weil's, Katzen's, and Brown's countercultural activities are archived because they became famous as natural foods advocates and celebrities. But their biographies suggest a wide, and underdocumented, corps of folks "living the revolution," from the late 1960s forward, in apartments and restaurants, in kitchens, and in hippie stores.[18]

Countercultures are inherently protean and ephemeral. They intermingle with political movements and spawn subcultures, many of which dissipate quickly. Claims about the composition of such diffuse phenomenon are always incomplete. *Food for Dissent*, therefore, is a composite sketch of the ideas, people, and mechanisms that were formative in fashioning the character of the natural foods movement, not an encyclopedic accounting of all things natural. For instance, other radical food and farming projects, such as black nationalist agrarianism that arose alongside the natural foods critique, are not considered.[19] While pastoralism connected these two movements, there was little interaction between the largely white natural foods movement and Black Power agricultural self-sufficiency.[20] Moreover, African Americans' exclusion from American politics and economy ensured that black agrarianism did not seep into the mainstream the way the natural foods ethos did. The history of organic agriculture, while a significant part of the natural foods story, is also not comprehensively examined, and consumer advocacy organizations that supported small, antiestablishment food farming, such as Oregon Tilith or biodynamic certifier Demeter USA, are not covered.

Without the demand generated by hippie cookbooks and co-ops, by Rodale's *Organic Gardening* and *Prevention* magazines, and other natural foods broadcasters, alternative agriculture would not have developed as much as it did. Therefore, the tastemakers and institutions that became popular touchstones for natural foods reference and that wrote the most widely adopted ethical/healthy foods consumerism narrative are the foci of this story. These sites show how sixties countercultural conceptions and people shaped the natural foods discourse and influenced American culture at large. Stacked one on the other, they implanted natural foods in the turn-of-the-twenty-first-century cultural and commercial imaginary.

NATURAL FOODS AT THE INTERSECTION OF COUNTERCULTURE AND CONSUMER CULTURE

While some manifestations of sixties counterculture, such as communal childrearing and group acid trips, stayed on the outer edges or disappeared altogether, natural foods took on new dimensions in each decade after the 1960s, imbedding antiestablishment sensibilities in a broad, consuming populace. The constancy of the natural foods movement can be attributed to its consumerist design, its class constituency, and its content.

Consumerism was not invented in the 1950s–1960s, but the quality and the intensity of postwar mediatized commercialism surpassed earlier stages in American capitalism. In *Advertising the American Dream* (1985), cultural historian Roland Marchand revealed that in the twenties and thirties, commercialism "took on a new scope and maturity" which fundamentally altered the fabric of American life.[21] The postwar era marked the next major growth spurt in the country's consumerism.

Middle-class baby boomers, the first generation raised in a widely affluent and televisual society, assembled their identities in this sea of commodification.[22] In the fifties, discontented youth used fashion and pop culture—produced by record companies, pulp fiction publishers, cosmetics and clothing marketers—to register their disapproving distance from mass culture. In the 1960s and 1970s, this same class cohort, with naïve optimism, set out to challenge industrial agribusiness with selective consumption. They did so because, from their perch, the marketplace and the home seemed like the last open spaces for citizen influence. (By the new century, "crunchy" conservatives concluded the same.)

The sociocultural authority of food ensured the movement's durability. While food is an elemental part of life, the meanings we attach to it are quite complex and often surpass nutrition and nourishment. Food can be used for ritualistic or religious purposes. Diet can announce obedience to or rebellion from orthodoxy. Food choices can connote wealth or poverty, health or debility, indulgence or discipline, sympathy or selfishness; food is a broad canvas for symbolic representation.[23] The actors and businesses that hatched the natural foods movement introduced the counterculture's personalist politics into the most productive and influential commercial and cultural activities of the late twentieth and early twenty-first centuries: eating and cooking.

The countercultural emphasis on individual action and expressive consumption has often been interpreted as the Left's retreat into private affairs after the political frustrations of the 1960s.[24] But, in fact, cultural rebels hyperpoliticized the quotidian by saturating it with public heft. Hippie Raymond Mungo expressed this public-private synthesis when considering the meaning of his Vermont commune, Total Loss Farm: "We *are* saving the world," Mungo opined in 1970, "as the world for us extends to the boundaries of Total Loss Farm and the limits of our experience."[25] Life itself had become a political presentation. With their enlarged selfhood, from the 1960s on, progressive Americans aesthetically and ethically judged the mundane acts of eating, child care, and shoe shopping—everything.[26] And they constructed a parallel and calculatedly separate realm of healthful and ecological commerce.

Insisting on a national healthy food conversion and very vocally alienating themselves from the average American eater, natural foods champions reenacted a long-standing middle-class (and predominantly white) compulsion to discipline and change the nation through its diet—employing what food historian E. Melanie Dupuis calls "gastropolitics."[27] Charlotte Biltekoff, in *Eating Right in America* (2013), notes that at various junctures in America's history, dietary reformism has been used to "shape certain kinds of subjects and citizens." This nutritional activism, she explains, "[shores] up the identity and social boundaries" of the "ever threatened American middle class."[28]

Norman Mailer's 1960 *Esquire* article "Superman Comes to the Supermarket" conveyed this "shoring up," as he drew postwar consumerism as the Maginot Line between his alienated intellectual self and the materialist, obedient many. The "roots of American life," Mailer warned, were being drowned by "the spirit of the supermarket, that homogenous extension of stainless surfaces and psychoanalyzed people, packed commodities and ranch homes, interchangeable, geographically unrecognizable, that essence of a new postwar SuperAmerica."[29] In 1956, Beat poet Allen Ginsberg portended Mailer's disaffection, pondering the nation's fate in "A Supermarket in California." Strolling through an icon of fifties excess, Ginsberg wondered whether the "brilliant stack of cans" and "solitary fancy tasty artichokes" of the "neon fruit supermarket" could be replacing a "lost America of love."[30] Ginsberg and Mailer abhorred the commercial values that made Supermarket America. And they also disapproved of their fellow citizens' easy adjustment to that order. In concord with Mailer's and Ginsberg's opinions, the natural foods vanguard continually distinguished itself from supermarkets and "SuperAmerica."

Although countercultural critics fretted over the postwar ascendance of factory food and its threat to the family supper, in *Something from the Oven: Reinventing Dinner in 1950s America* (2004), Laura Shapiro reflects that surveys, taken in the 1950s, show that homemakers cooked with both instant and raw ingredients and considered the results of their labor "real food." In these polls, full-time homemakers and working women reported taking pride in cooking, ranking it as their favorite household chore.[31] Natural foods critics may have overwritten the processed invasion to warn about the changes in American cooking and culture. Indeed, the food recollections of the leading natural foods cookbook writers of the era actually show their fifties mothers and their young selves putting together perfectly respectable meals from whole meats, poultry, and fish with ready-made assists.

In her cookbook, Mollie Katzen recalled that as a child of the 1950s and 1960s, her family's diet revolved around "the miracle convenience foods of the era." At the same time, she lovingly remembered that every Friday her mother kneaded and baked homemade challah bread. Carol Flinders complained about magazine and cookbook convenience come-ons. Yet, before her countercultural conversion, she served her family a combination of from-scratch standards and convenience products. *The Vegetarian Epicure*'s Anna Thomas remembered an Eastern European immigrant childhood, where food was taken very seriously. The rest of America, she assumed, hadn't had such advantages—a deficit she repeatedly pointed out.[32]

Natural foodists' sorting of healthy and unhealthy eating and fake and real cooking was never done with malicious intent. Greedy food merchandisers, they judged, were really at fault, confusing and severing Americans from their culinary and farming heritage. The unconverted lacked nutritional education. Once reoriented, they would enthusiastically adopt the prescribed behaviors. Of course, the power to name good and bad food was always in the hands of the educators, not the educated. Who got to be a reformer and who required reform ratified existing sociocultural hierarchies.[33]

Beneath the natural foods movement's reformist pronouncements also lurked a distinctly bourgeois concern with high-quality food and with experiential exclusivity. Elite natural foods standard setters, such as Alice Waters, of Chez Panisse restaurant fame, employed the countercultural foods critique for gastronomic ends. As she confessed in her culinary memoir, *Coming to My Senses: The Making of a Countercultural Cook* (2017), "There was an aesthetic demarcation between the hippies and me. I thought their approach was absolutely uncivilized and unrefined... My friends and I valued a Eurocentric aesthetic that was at odds with the Summer of Love aesthetic."[34] Purchasing and cooking superior food, that is, organic/local/fresh, natural sponsors, like Waters, "shored up" both their gastropolitical and aesthetic distinction. In fact, by the twenty-first century, food naturalism became the epicenter of upper-class life, establishing a cultural-consumer orthodoxy that was energetically adopted by the broad middle class as well.

A segment of the seventies natural foods movement blanched at fellow campaigners' dietary elitism. For instance, many co-op creators saw themselves and their businesses as instruments of guerrilla food and social justice. "Food for People, Not for Profit" was their motto. Yet, even within these politically driven, sometimes anticapitalist, natural foods institutions, co-op members battled over whether their stores should be vehicles for revolution or nutritional evangelism. Both perspectives endured in the movement, with some activists and food pundits returning to the "Food for People" obligation in the new century. Nevertheless, the robust growth of the whole foods marketplace and the cultural conquest of the dietary health imperative indicates where movement creativity thrived.

Wagering their cultural and political capital on ethical healthful consumerism, from the 1970s forward, middle- and upper-class consumers and producers lifted natural foods to unprecedented commercial success. By the late

1990s, national supermarket chains carried organic produce, tofu, brown rice, and other hippie icons. And the "natural" label found its way onto everything from Clairol hair-coloring products to dog food. In the new millennium, the small natural foods company, community-supported agriculture (CSA), and the local organic dairy or vegetable farm became main attractions for natural foods followers.

TAKING STOCK

Looking from the twenty-first century backward, it is indisputable that countercultural mavericks transformed America. A growing body of literature concludes the same, adding that countercultural businesses and entrepreneurs reconceived American work and business—and for the good. Andrew Kirk, in *Counterculture Green* (2007), argues that the *Whole Earth Catalog*, its founder, Steward Brand, and other hip business pioneers invented the green economy and the socially conscious company model at Ben & Jerry's, Apple Computer, Smith and Hawken, Williams-Sonoma, and Patagonia. These corporations, according to Kirk, radically renovated American consumerism, business, and work styles along countercultural-democratic lines.[35]

Somewhat in accord with Kirk's conclusions, Joshua Clark Davis, in "Activist Businesses: The New Left's Surprising Critique of Postwar Consumer Culture," characterizes alternative businesses (including natural foods supermarkets, head shops, feminist credit unions, radical black bookstores, and others) as important points of mainstream-countercultural contact and as seedbeds for the new public-minded businessperson: the "activist entrepreneur." Clark Davis asserts that, although the political effects of counter-institution were limited and fleeting, radical sixties imaginativeness broke down barriers between business and politics.[36]

Indubitably, hippie engineers and entrepreneurs made a deep imprint on American commerce. But as Fred Turner importantly qualifies in *From Counterculture to Cyberculture* (2006), the hippie followers of the *Whole Earth Catalog*, who would later become Silicon Valley movers and shakers, were "well-educated, and white . . . a new elite [who] would turn away from questions of gender, race, and class towards a rhetoric of individual and small-group empowerment."[37] Indeed, as America deindustrialized and exported labor and postwar prosperity unwound, poorly paid service sector jobs became the status quo for the working and middle class. "Creative class" innovators at Apple and Patagonia soared to new heights of workplace virtuosity, while the working and precarious middle slid into career and economic stagnation.

The natural foods system also created meaning-filled, politically framed work and businesses that had previously not existed. In the 1970s and 1980s, jobs in co-ops and natural foods production and retail were not necessarily lucrative or high status, but they were qualitatively different from being a supermarket manager or a General Mills advertiser. In natural foods companies and co-ops, work relations were personal, hierarchy was muted. The products were made and sold with larger socioecological goals in the forefront. Attracting like-minded individuals, these operations were enclaves of progressive affiliation and activism.

For many Americans who had watched their postwar parents grind out lives in soul-deadening careers for the security and pride of middle-class living, the work world made by the counterculture was liberatory.[38] Mind-numbing white-collar conformity was swapped for the dressed-down authenticity of counterinstitutional participatory democracy and, later, dot-com and Whole Foods career cool. By the 1990s and 2000s, when healthy, green eating became a national preoccupation, food jobs, from farming to artisan food production to organic merchandising and advocacy, held all the prestige of conventional careers.

Thanks to countercultural iconoclasts who demanded a better quality and kind of food stream, the new economy's beneficiaries enjoyed tastier, healthier, and more interesting eating. On the flip side, since the 1970s, lower-income Americans found themselves more tightly tethered to processed and fast foods, leading to the twenty-first century's great national worry—the obesity "epidemic."[39] As Whole Foods soared nationally, urban dwellers watched grocery stores abandon working-class and poor city neighborhoods, creating the conditions for their nutritional and commercial isolation.[40] The natural foods movement transformed work, eating, shopping, and cooking for many, but clearly not for the majority.

It was able to do so because, on the whole, white, college-educated cultural mavericks made the movement. It goes without saying that counterculturalists' disquietude was far from universally felt. Their objection to conformity, dismissal of traditional authority, preoccupation with experiential freedom, and appetite to control and invent consumption were largely (but, of course, never exclusively) white and middle- and upper-class vexations and aspirations.[41] Hippies' class and racial standing gave them cultural and political suasion from the get-go, despite their antiestablishmentarianism, multicultural admirations, and voluntary downward mobility.

The farmers, producers, shop owners, and consumers who kept the natural foods movement alive and vital fit the description of a "hegemonic historical bloc," which, according to Jackson Lears, is a "loose coalition of groups cemented by cultural as well as political dominance." This bloc assumes the universal appeal of its critical analyses and the rightfulness of its social remedies. Historical blocs do not control culture and politics through manipulation. They do so through "legitimation."[42]

Legitimation is not automatic, nor is the historical bloc's cultural command. This was certainly true for the natural foods movement. From the late 1960s to the 1990s, food's corporate commercialization did not alarm the plurality as much as it did its detractors. A good percentage of Americans delightedly indulged in processed gewgaws and fast foods brought to them by supermarket chains and industrial processors. In the 1980s, the food industry (often supported by government agencies) used its advertising muscle to disqualify countercultural food critics as kooks and antiprogress reactionaries.[43] It took time to shake off those "granola" associations. In the meantime, rather than waste energy confronting the food establishment, natural foods actors built an alternative consumer system that (eventually) set eating ideals.

Under the tutelage of Ed Brown, Anna Thomas, Alice Waters (one of the founders of "New American" or "California" cuisine), and others, by the 1990s natural foodists added craft, worldliness, and aristocratic prestige to their eating ideology. Waters's later "delicious revolution" and "edible schoolyard" project—a curriculum development program which included schoolyard organic gardening and cafeteria conversions—loaded natural foods cuisine with layers of socioecological weightiness. When asked by a Sierra Club interviewer to explain her environmental-gourmet hybrid movement, Waters replied: "You set a table, and make it a beautiful experience that they don't forget. This is an environmental movement that's about pleasure on the table . . . Through beauty. It's not telling people what to do. It's bringing something to people that can change their lives, and that they can do easily. Pleasure is in our systems for a purpose. Why do we have to be denying ourselves? We don't. This isn't hard. This is delicious. That's why I call it a delicious revolution."[44] The success of this good foods revolution, celebrated by

Waters, never depended on rectifying farm labor mistreatment or addressing economic-racial structures that created nutritional inequality—sometimes quite the opposite. Indeed, globally, affluent consumers' desires for natural and specialized food stuffs (organic, free trade, cruelty free) instituted a politically and economically uneven world food nexus, with producing nations and workers placed in postcolonial subservience to tastes and shopping ethics of the industrialized West.[45]

In the decades when mainstream America dismissed natural foods as a hippie hangover, it would have been hard to imagine that by the turn of the twenty-first century these foods would impose global control or that they would sit at the center of debates over national health, the environment, agriculture, and other social issues. In those marginal days, the amalgamation of cookbooks, co-ops, and natural health and organic media gave food-concerned citizens an oppositional structure within which to live out moral communalism and consumption. Despite their optimism about their food agenda's rightness, in those dog days, natural food devotees could not have predicted that their critique of corporate capitalism would make an imprint on conventional business and consumer culture. Moreover, it would have been hard to see that someday organic, whole, and local food consumption would signal a shopper's aesthetic-ethical refinement.

Standing at the intersection of countercultural idealism and commercial materialism, the story of the natural foods movement reveals the paradoxical legacy of the sixties rebellion. Every stage of the natural foods movement contained creative capabilities and progressive intentions. Indeed, from the countercultural 1970s to the food revolution 2000s, a cohort of natural foods activists recognized the inequities in the natural foods marketplace and got to work on urban gardens, farmworkers' rights, environmental justice, and the like. That being said, in the main, the movement has tended to, and has been peopled by, a prosperous constituency. Its core food values of quality, naturalness, healthfulness, and authenticity, at any cost, created conceptual and material boundaries that limited entry. Its consumer orientation forced the movement to apply market solutions to social problems, with circumscribed results. While many natural foods initiates anticipated that a snowball effect of alternative production and consumption would compete with (and maybe overtake) conventional food production, it did not. The movement's nutritional idealism did win widespread regard, making health a national obsession worthy of presidential valorization in Michelle Obama's "Let's Move" campaign and the backing by the Obama administration's United States Department of Agriculture of organic business. But, from the 1960s forward, agribusiness, convenience food science, and fast food remained largely uninterrupted by the comparatively minor natural foods sector.

There is no assurance that a legislative or a traditionally "social movement" challenge would have hampered the unstoppable momentum of corporatized food and agriculture or that either methodology would have more directly tackled the nation's nutritional and socioeconomic hierarchy. But the marketplace faith and cultural separatism of the natural foods movement guaranteed that it would leave America's deep-seated inequalities largely unperturbed.

CHAPTER 1

"MORE THAN JUST CHEAP CHEESE"
Community, Class, and Consumerism in Countercultural Food Co-ops

The sixties counterculture, by many accounts, was rife with childlike indolence and hedonism. Sex, drugs, and rock 'n' roll were its vocation and avocation. While this sweeping characterization minimizes the breadth of hippie ingenuity in the 1960s, it completely falls short when considering countercultural activities in the 1970s. In fact, in the years following the well-publicized events of the 1960s, cultural nonconformists across the country decided that rather than waiting for America to wake up, they would create the markets, services, and societies that matched their dreams for a better world. In their often collective associations, insurgent doctors, lawyers, and concerned citizens funneled their skills into the pursuit of "right livelihood."[1]

Because of their open indulgence in nudity and drugs, of all collective experiments, rural communes received the most national notice in the 1960s and 1970s. But countercultural collectivity took many more sober forms. Radical feminists, such as the Bloodroot Collective discussed in chapter 2, would never self-describe as hippies, but they adopted communalism in their vegetarian restaurant and bookstore in Bridgeport, Connecticut, as did the coffeehouses, bars, record companies, magazines, and other lesbian spaces constructed in the 1970s and 1980s.[2] Nonprofit operations, such as free clinics, free schools, and free legal services, formed collectively to counteract the bureaucratic impersonality of mainstream institutions. As Anthony P. Sager explained in his 1979 profile of Boston legal collectives, radical legal organizations identified as "communes" or "collectives" to indicate their "difference from establishment law firms" and to communicate membership in a "nationwide movement for social change."[3] Food co-ops played prominently in this era's institutional experimentalism, growing from approximately five thousand to ten thousand between 1969 and 1979.[4]

Laura Wilson's route to food co-op membership typifies the seventies food collectivist's course. A "Swarthmore-educated" civil rights and antiwar activist, Students for a Democratic Society (SDS) community organizer, and radical teacher, in the early 1970s Wilson and her husband "gave up city life and politics" to move to a group-owned farm in Vermont. That arrangement quickly collapsed, but Laura continued her communal quest, eventually helping rehabilitate an ailing local co-op.[5] Brimming with utopian zeal, "New Wave" co-ops, like the one Wilson joined, believed that their original business structure, their healthful natural merchandise, and their commitment to community uplift offered a persuasive substitution to the profit-driven, suburban supermarket.

For food co-op founders, America's postwar supermarkets represented the unpleasant result of the nation's economic nationalization and corporate consolidation. Although chain grocery stores had made inroads in the 1920s and 1930s, overtaking many independent shops, Depression-era Americans still bought most of their food in small corner stores from a trusted local grocer, butcher, or baker.[6] In the 1950s, this all changed, with supermarket sales increasing from 35 percent of total U.S. food retail to 70 percent. By 1956, the corner grocer was, according to Harvey Levenstein, "a relic of the past."[7]

Built in the rambling openness of the new suburbs, supermarkets had distinct advantages over the retailers that they eventually drove out of business. With generous square footage, they could warehouse goods they bought in bulk, cutting consumer cost by 8–15 percent below the neighborhood food store. Abundant shelf space allowed supermarkets to take risks with the unprecedented variety of new processed foodstuff, making them a major purveyor of factory-made goods and marketing. By 1960, the average supermarket carried 5,600 different products.[8]

Supermarkets embodied modern convenience, offering one-stop shopping for meat, produce, dry goods, and nonfood products. Their large parking lots, necessary in the automobile-dependent suburbs, accommodated the river of families flowing out of America's cities in the 1950s. Supermarkets' wide aisles, shopping carts, bright fluorescent lighting, and self-service setup cut out the middleman, making food shopping a "one-on-one [interaction] . . . between the processor and the housewife."[9]

In the Cold War context, supermarkets were spun as proof positive of the greatness of democracy and the United States. In the legendary "kitchen table" debates between Vice President Nixon and Soviet Premier Nikita Khrushchev, Nixon preened over the supermarket cornucopia at American homemakers' fingertips.[10] For its critics, on the other hand, the supermarket signified consumer capitalism's unchecked excesses and civic irresponsibility. Disturbed that a necessity of life had been captured by a system that always put profit over people, nature, and quality, ambitious progressives established food collectives as a socially forward and healthful outlet from the industrial-food Goliath. Like natural foods cookbooks and other components of the nascent natural foods movement, seventies food co-ops were instrumental in spreading a critical nutritional mindset and creating alternatives to mainstream eating and shopping.

THE NEW WAVE MISSION(S)

New Wave co-ops (as opposed to Old Wave, Depression-era co-ops) shared a similar look and structure. Their bare-bones operations and dingy aisles, infested with fruit flies and pantry moths, announced aesthetic dissent from corporate grocery chain glitz. The member-ownership structure and obedience to the Rochdale Principles of cooperative business demonstrated their departure from conventional business arrangements. Beyond these common attributes, countercultural co-ops and cooperators accommodated many different progressive and practical aspirations.

The People's Food Co-op (PFC) in Ann Arbor marshaled University of Michigan graduates' and students' collective energy to "supply itself with an economical source of natural and organic foods." In the early 1970s, these specialized commodities were almost impossible to find in this midwestern college town.[11] Co-op member Allan Sirotkin recollected his first encounter with the PFC on "a typical frigid Michigan day in January 1971." Sirotkin, on a search for brown rice, "stumbled upon a small food stand" selling the elusive rice as well as bags of grain, seeds, and natural peanut butter. From that point forward, he was a devoted and active PFC member.[12]

In its 1968 statement of purpose, the Mifflin Street Community Co-op, in a student neighborhood in Madison, Wisconsin, envisioned a sweeping social aim of "embody[ing] a belief in community self-determination in opposition to the dominant trends in all communities in which control is increasingly concentrated outside the community and operated for profits which are not used for the betterment of the community." In the words of one of the early founders, Bill Winfield, Mifflin Co-op was to be, first, a "community center and political hub" and, second, a "corner store."[13]

On the East Coast in 1973, residents of Mount Airy, a middle-class, leftist, family neighborhood in Philadelphia created Weavers Way Co-op—named after a nineteenth-century food cooperative of British flannel weavers. Pragmatic from the start, Weavers stated charge was to increase "purchasing savings for a wide spectrum of members through cooperative buying." At an early 1970s co-op meeting, founder Jules Timerman expressed what he believed to be the ideological underpinnings of Weavers' simple mission statement: "An individual who works alone in our economy often experiences difficulty in obtaining a fair exchange for his or her efforts for the necessity of life." Instead, Timerman proposed, "real security comes from being part of a community."[14] In those early years, Timerman put endless hours and muscle into the formation of an enterprise that nurtured community affiliation and served his neighbors' needs.

Weavers Way distinguished itself from its cooperative brothers and sisters in its modest mission statement. The Mount Airy residents who built Weavers were not college students activated by New Left–counterculture currents. As slightly older leftists, they drew from the political well of the labor movement, New Deal liberalism, and civil rights activism. At the same time, as citizens committed to America's betterment, they quickly came under the influence of the sixties "movement" spirit. Their co-op acted as a magnet to younger Philadelphians, who brought with them the high expectations and political absolutism typical in other New Wave co-ops. Weavers' very existence attests to collectivity's widespread allure in the 1970s and also to the influence of countercultural concepts and institutions on Americans of all generations and types.

In the 1970s, two overarching and competing objectives began to vie for prominence in the New Wave cooperative movement. The first vision, shaped by New Left community organization practices, imagined co-ops as grassroots conduits of social justice delivering cheap food to America's needy, particularly minorities. Co-op members subscribing to this vision saw their establishments as revolutionary exemplars—directly rectifying economic inequities in black and brown city neighborhoods, while presenting an anti-profit retail challenge to the status quo economy. This faction's motto was "Food for People, Not for Profit."

Cooperators following this calling generally did not impose natural foods rules on their customers, although some did. In 1979 in Frederick, Maryland, Common Market Coop's business coordinator explained his store's uneasy reconciliation of some member's health food desires with the preferences of working-class shoppers: "Unhealthy products . . . must be carried both as a service to the neighborhood and to keep the coop alive economically."[15] Inexpensive, accessible goods were the Common Market's bottom line. Bill Coughlin, chair of Boston's Food Co-op, directly expressed his food justice commitments in an early seventies debate over whether only healthy foods should sit on his co-op's shelves. "Don't give me any of this purist shit," he scolded. "Feed the people."[16]

The second vision, informed by countercultural and environmental longings, imagined co-ops as centers for cultural interconnection and ecologically conscientious merchandise. Shoppers and producers derived moral sustenance and tangible belonging in co-op interactions and in the natural foods community at large. According to this model, the business upstart would undermine the corporate Goliath, pushing conventional agriculture and food processing to meet consumer want. Organic technique would replace America's chemical farming. Whole foods production would overtake processed production. And a decentralized, local economic system, fostering consumer-producer intimacy and control, would replace multinational corporate alienation. It would be a market revolution sparking social transformation.

Over time, the co-op and natural foods movements leaned more determinedly toward a principled consumer-producer network over socioeconomic intervention. This is not to say natural foods sponsors and co-op entrepreneurs forgot their obligation to the needy. But increasingly, as nutritional dogmatism and environmentalism became a foremost middle- and upper-class concern, natural foods participants' community involvement centered on solidifying local and healthful food consumption systems. Somehow—never altogether explained or practically theorized—these righteous systems would serve the less well-off. But just "feeding the people," if that meant satisfying their junk food habits, could not stand.

Critical commentators have argued that their interpretation of shopping and fellowship as activism signaled the retirement of the post-sixties Left into hip consumerism and lifestyle narcissism.[17] But rather than a retreat, the sixties movement and the seventies counterculture totalized the political. As a Minneapolis co-op member stated in 1974, "Everything is political—what you eat, what you wear, who you sleep with ... Limiting the word 'politics' to elector politics or to protest politics leaves out consumer politics and lifestyle/sexual/cultural politics which seem to be ultimately at least as crucial as the exercise of power as electoral or protest activity."[18] This wouldn't simply be one-issue consumer boycotting; it would be *consumption as persuasion, consumption as ethics, consumption as community.*

FROM OLD WAVE TO NEW: DEFINING THE POSTWAR COOPERATIVE

In general, all seventies co-ops classified themselves and their movement as dissimilar not only to supermarket America but also to Old Wave co-ops that came out of the New Deal 1930s. William Ronco explored the essential dissimilarities between New and Old Wave co-ops in his 1974 user's guide and propagandist monograph, *Food Co-ops: An Alternative to Shopping in Supermarkets.* According to Ronco, Old Wave co-ops—many of which were still around in the 1970s for New Wavers' examination—acted and looked like supermarkets. New Wave co-ops, he argued, could easily be distinguished from both supermarkets and the Old Wave. Self-financed, the New Wave rejected federal "start-up" funds on which Old Wave co-ops depended. Housed in unconventional buildings, modestly sized, with loose bookkeeping methods, "the tone of business [was] friendlier, warmer, looser," according to Ronco.[19] Most important, seventies cooperators believed that their stores provided sanctuary for unorthodox and revolutionary folks. As a member of Fields of Plenty in Washington, D.C., explained in the late 1970s, "Selling food isn't our goal. It's just a pretext for building living and breathing models of revolutionary change."[20] Not all seventies co-ops agreed with this sweeping proposition. Yet they would concede that co-ops "were not just about selling cheap cheese," as longtime Weavers Way member Vince Pieri was known to say about his co-op.[21] Despite the New Wave's anticapitalist and radical self-perception, the history of one of the largest Old Wave cooperatives, the Consumers Cooperative of Berkeley (CCB), suggests that from the 1930s onward, consumerism tied one wave to the other.

Rochdale to Berkeley: American Cooperation

Until the twentieth century, America's cooperative enterprises developed through two influential nineteenth-century associations—labor unions and agrarian clubs. The strategy of workers' collectivity began in England and spread throughout Europe in the early nineteenth century as class defense against industrial de-skilling and company store price gouging. A group of striking flannel weavers in Rochdale who pooled their waning resources to set up a cooperative grocery store in 1844 became the most famous developers of Great Britain's worker collectivity. Their co-op lasted sixty years and their alliance, the Equitable Pioneers of Rochdale, England, established what came to be known as the Rochdale Principles. The Rochdale Principles—democratic control, open and voluntary membership, limited interest on shares, return of surplus to members—became the cooperative movement's foundation on both sides of the Atlantic.[22]

Through two waves of nineteenth-century emigration, European migrants introduced the Rochdale system into American culture and politics via urban labor unions and New England and Midwest agrarian collectives such as the Grange (in the 1860s and 1870s) and the Farmers Alliance (in the 1880s and 1890s). Although cooperatives always held a more prominent place in Europe than in the United States, American collective institutions surged in the nineteenth century. By the end of the century, a mix of structural transformations—challenges to working-class cohesion, the rise of the credit system, and consumer protection regulations—undercut a tentatively rooted cooperative movement.[23]

Kathleen Donahue argues that while many turn-of-the-twentieth-century U.S. cooperatives championed the radical communalism and class consciousness which defined European cooperation, at least as many portrayed their consumer collectives as an American "middle road" between socialist revolt and monopoly capitalism.[24] This middle road approach made sense in the 1930s when Depression-era "Old Wave" collectives revived consumer cooperatives from dormancy in the "Red Scare" twenties.[25]

A consumerist perspective, while always present to some degree in American collectivity, matured in co-ops emerging in the Keynesian economic environment of the Roosevelt administration. New Deal programs, such as the Federal Emergency Relief Administration, facilitated cooperative growth in the 1930s through cash outlay and through rhetoric that established consumers as influential civic stakeholders.[26] Franklin Roosevelt coupled consumption and citizen rights in his 1936 acceptance speech for presidential renomination: "If the average citizen is guaranteed equal opportunity in the polling place, he must have equal opportunity in the market place."[27] Co-op membership increased 40 percent between 1929 and 1934 because of federal advocacy of consumer democracy. By April 1935, 6,600 co-ops with $30 million in surplus savings served 1,800,000 members, a decided leap from the 78,000 national-member tally in 1929.[28]

The Consumers Cooperative of Berkeley (CCB) represents the typical New Deal co-op. Influenced by Upton Sinclair's End Poverty in California (EPIC) governor's campaign and the exigencies of the Depression, in January 1936 a group of Berkeley families pooled their cash and energies to start a "buying club." By 1937, they had grown enough to open their first storefront, with Robert Neptune as "manager and man-of-all-work." Except for a short period of crisis during World War II, the CCB experienced fiscal success and expansion. By 1979, the CCB oversaw thirteen stores in northern California with 86,000 members.[29]

Despite the New Wave's disdain for the Old Wave, Berkeley's cooperative routinely involved itself in national and local progressive causes, particularly those related to consumer advocacy. Before formally incorporating, it rallied its membership to campaign for a revised Food and Drug Act. It also joined the Northern California Cooperative Council to condemn FDR's administration for destroying California oranges to induce demand. The Consumers Cooperative of Berkeley used its clout to support labor, as well as consumer protection.

In 1955, when membership grew to six thousand but member participation precipitously declined, the February issue of the CCB's newsletter, *Berkeley Co-op News*, raised a concern that would preoccupy New Wave co-ops: "How do we keep democratic control and participation while we continue to expand?"[30] As the second largest postwar cooperative, with numerous branch stores, the CCB's answer to this question reverberated throughout the cooperative society. After much discussion, in 1958, Berkeley's cooperative instituted an experimental parliament with sixty delegates. As its first act as a representative governing body, the parliament addressed a proposal to send all members a letter encouraging them to join a ban on nuclear weapons testing. Half of the parliament believed that Rochdale Principles forbade using the members list for political appeals, whereas the other half argued that political neutrality applied only to partisan issues.[31]

This debate underscores a unique attribute of twentieth-century consumer cooperatives. Unlike their nineteenth-century ancestors that were bound to the working class, Old Wave collective grocery stores had no unifying political commitments. The consumerist standpoint, instituted during the Depression and standardized in the postwar period, left collectives with two distinct obligations—protecting members' health and well-being and safekeeping their financial investment. Given these constraints, in the 1950s, the CCB's board and voting membership, like many co-ops thereafter, took a conservative institutional stance on nuclear weaponry, opting for a co-op–sponsored symposium on bomb testing. To assuage member's anxiety about uranium-contaminated foods, the CCB instituted regular inspections of co-op milk for traces of strontium 90 and of all foods for radiation.[32]

To New Wave cooperators, the Old Wave looked like, in the words of the Co-op Handbook Collective, a bureaucratic "perversion of cooperativism."[33] New Deal–era cooperators were undeniably more conservative than their countercultural offspring. As survivors of the Great Depression, Old Wavers embraced postwar material abundance and modernization. For CCB members, many of whom joined in the 1930s and remained until the co-op's closure in the late 1980s, expansion indicated the proliferation of a civilized business archetype.[34] For countercultural critics, the crucial question was not how to contribute to America's economic growth but how to, in Arthur Miller's words, "escape being overwhelmed by a mindless, goalless flood, which marooned each individual on his little island of commodities."[35] Nonetheless, consumerism connected both waves. Depression-era co-op members united to invigorate America's flagging economy and to announce their consumer rights. Seventies cooperators united to support goods and institutions that aligned with their natural aesthetics and outsider principles.

To remain viable, New Wave collectives had to provide a consumer experience that confirmed members' sundry political, cultural, and dietary identities and standards. Trying to live up to such demanding and multifold agendas, many seventies co-ops burned out. Others, such as Weavers Way, survived but not without ongoing conflict. Like every other seventies counterinstitution, Weavers had to come to terms with running a communally owned and collectively run food business in the midst of a free-market economy. It had to balance member's countercultural utopianism with the staff's and board's business realism. It had to regularly debate the political correctness and the healthfulness of co-op merchandise. And it had to assert the co-op's duty to the greater Philadelphia community. Weavers Way took up these debates, formed committees, and enacted programs in the name of social justice and food politics, but always with an eye to conserving its beloved co-op community.

WEAVERS WAY: A CASE STUDY IN URBAN COOPERATION

On January 19, 1973, Weavers Way Cooperative Association, founded by Jules Timerman, opened a grocery store on 555 and 557 Carpenter Lane in West Mount Airy, Pennsylvania. Four buying clubs already existed in the neighborhood; Weavers was the first storefront. An organizer of the earlier People's Food Co-op of Mount Airy, Timerman invited other local clubs to create a grocery store, but they declined. Set on the idea, he leafleted homeowners, found a store location, raised members and funds to begin the co-op, and used area papers to bring the enterprise to Philadelphia's attention.[36]

Weavers' initial operations were pretty bare bones. Members would stop into 555 Carpenter Lane to pick up an order card and walk over to 557, a space that could hold only eight members at a time. There, Jules Timerman would serve up whatever cheese, deli meats, breads, or produce that he had procured that week. With baskets filled, shoppers would then walk back to 555 to pay. Members volunteered their time working the cash register, in return for monthly grocery rebates. Recollecting the store's jury-rigged first year, longtime member Dorothy Guy marveled: "It was a total honor system.

FIGURE 1. Weavers Way Store Front, late 1970s–early 1980s. *Courtesy of the Special Collections Research Center, Temple University Libraries, Philadelphia, PA.*

Once you walked out of the store Jules didn't know whether you went up and paid. But I would find it hard to believe that anybody cheated."[37] She was probably correct; the Mount Airy section of Philadelphia had a history of community cohesion and civic involvement.

Until the 1950s, Mount Airy, which consists of two sections, East and West Mount Airy, existed as a bedroom community for white, middle- and upper-class families. Like many other urban neighborhoods in the postwar period, Mount Airy experienced its first taste of racial integration in 1951 when a black family moved into the borough. By 1956, forty-six African American families made Mount Airy their home. This trend continued: by 1970, 33.4 percent of West Mount Airy—the locale of the first Weavers co-op—residents were nonwhite.[38] Rather than responding defensively, West Mount Airy residents organized to prevent racial hysteria from taking root.

In February 1959, a West Mount Airy organization, the Sedgwick Neighbors Association, met and drafted a six-point code of real estate ethics to ward off, in the words of the association's chairman, "unscrupulous real estate men who have tried to panic white residents into selling and getting out while they could." The association enforced their ethics by carrot, not stick, funneling sellers to real estate agencies that followed their antibias code. The code stipulated that agents "help promote 'democratic living,' to show houses for sale in the area to all groups, but to refrain from commenting on the racial structure of the neighborhood unless asked."[39]

Mount Airy residents held true to their principles through the first flush of integration in the 1950s and into the 1960s, when African American migration reached East Mount Airy and the Oak Lane sections. To subvert "panic selling," the West Oak Lane and East Mount Airy associations joined together in 1966, inducting a new "antibias code" for real estate agencies seeking business in their neighborhoods.[40] Mount Airy residents also created civic leagues (the West and East Mount Airy Associations) and a cultural center (Allens Lane Art Center) to connect older white residents to newer African American families. The East Mount Airy Association arranged its neighborhood into fifty "together blocks" that held regular meetings to talk about combating Philadelphia's rising crime rate. The West Mount Airy Association met for less serious reasons in "walk and talk" block parties that helped residents get to know one another—a community-building stratagem that Weavers Way employed in the early 1990s to address declining member participation.[41]

This socially alert community was primed to respond to the stream of food cooperation rippling through liberal-left circles in the late 1960s and 1970s. In West Mount Airy, strong and articulate personalities, such as Jules Timerman, quickly became leaders. Described by co-op members as everything from "a good talker" to "the king" to "irascible," if nothing else Timerman was the brain and brawn behind the making of Weavers Way.[42] Accordingly, Weavers Way's initial philosophy and form reflected Timerman's collectivist aims and bottom-line practicalities.

In the inflationary 1970s, Timerman's ability to obtain merchandise at rock-bottom prices unquestionably helped member growth. Yet within the co-op's ranks, his cost-cutting mentality competed with the dietary needs and social values found in this middle-class, diverse (about 60 percent white, 40 percent people of color), college-educated, substantially Jewish, and increasingly gay urban neighborhood in the 1970s. Weavers Way never fully discarded its original mission of empowering consumer-members through collective purchasing, but over time, as the co-op became members' primary political outlet, the collective store wrestled to balance participants' social, political, nutritional, and cultural requirements.

Weavers Way's multidimensionality, as well as its growth from eight hundred members in 1974 to five thousand members in 2011, while remaining a working members' co-op until 2010, makes this urban cooperative an informative case study in New Wave collectivity and natural foods consumerism. While part of a broad social-cultural movement, Weavers possessed its own inimitable history. That being said, co-op governance and management, product choices, food politics, community service, and expansion preoccupied all co-ops as they strove to balance daily grocery store business with the increasingly precise food moralities of their constituencies. For Weavers Way, the very first hurdle—the implementation of a managerial and governance structure—proved a serious test of its cooperative mettle.

Cooperation and Governance at Weavers Way

After getting by in the first month of operation by the seat of their pants, with a split store system and one man in charge, Weavers Way's members and manager recognized that they needed a traditional business configuration. At the first general members meeting in April 1973, Jules Timerman presented his "manager's report," arguing for an assistant manager to relieve him of his average eighty-hour workweek. At the co-op's first general meeting, members resolved to lighten Timerman's load by hiring an assistant, electing a board of directors, and creating a set of bylaws. After less than a year of business, Weavers Way was on its way to a governance framework that, predictably, roused member resistance.

Member Greg Moore's 1974 editorial on the issue of leadership, for the newly named co-op newspaper, the *Shuttle*, exemplifies the antistructuralist factionalism brewing at Weavers Way.[43] Entitled "Feast or Famine," Moore's article warned members to seriously ponder the repercussions of a board-led co-op: "We have operated successfully for a year behind the sweat, dedication and foresight of one man, Jules Timerman." Why rock the boat, especially since the current leadership had "evolved naturally (to those willing to do the work) in the co-op," he wrote.[44] New Wave cooperators across the nation shared Moore's conviction that power and leadership should arise from experience and desire. Why impose formulaic control over the impromptu structure which emerged from the "sweat and dedication" of committed individuals?

The New Wave movement's cooperative primer, *The Food Co-op Handbook*, while not entirely opposed to boards of directors, argued that participatory democracy thrived when leaders rose naturally. "If things become so overstructured that people don't feel free to be innovative and contribute more than is expected of them," this guide argued, "the co-op can become cold, formal." As the authors of the *Co-op Handbook* surmised, "The closeness of the collective means that members can deal with interpersonal problems and conflicts ... unnecessary structures can block the natural flow of people's energies and thwart their free participation."[45] Setting themselves against both hierarchical capitalist businesses and Old Wave co-ops, many New Wave cooperators wanted to sustain their collectives through, what they believed to be, the cohesive vigor of personalism.

Weavers Way member Greg Moore, like the *Co-op Handbook*'s collective authors, announced discomfort with the future thinking and planning common in the present-oriented counterculture. As illustrated in the popularity of spiritual guru Baba Ram Dass's treatise *Be Here Now* (1971) and seventies "be-ins," cultural rebels and political dissidents of the 1960s and 1970s perceived alertness to the rhythms of daily existence to be a more honest life strategy than preparing for an unknowable future. Planning, structure, and order were the anxious "head trips" of mainstream businesses, all of which repressed individuality.[46] Counterinstitutions needed to invent

FIGURE 2. The personalism of Weavers Way's early do-it-yourself checkout counter. *Courtesy of the Special Collections Research Center, Temple University Libraries, Philadelphia, PA.*

nontraditional means of associating and selling to break free from the mass food system's competitive compulsions, many New Wave cooperators suggested.

This go-with-the-flow counterstrategy did not appeal to all Weavers' members. In response to Greg Moore's editorial, member and first board vice president, Lyn Davis, voiced her objections to leaving Timerman with "the mammoth burden of operating an entire coop structure himself and having our existence as a viable business depend on his physical and emotional energy." A board, in Davis's opinion, would ultimately enlarge democracy and "achieve a working, member involved food coop."[47] Davis's ambitions represented the majority; in January 1974, Weavers elected its first board of directors. Thus began what member Maggie Heineman described as the board's fifteen-month "struggle to establish its authority"—a battle that every New Wave co-op eventually confronted.[48]

To democratize business operations, countercultural cooperators invented nonhierarchical organizations. In theory, with member work requirements, a store's daily operations—including ordering, accounting, work schedules—would fall out naturally to members on duty. Any larger changes would be decided at regular co-op meetings by member consensus. Too often this lack of structure created chaos with one overworked co-op ideologue carrying the store on his/her shoulders. Despite these inefficiencies, many New Wave cooperators balked at any chain of command, especially member-workers most involved in the co-op's daily operations. This was the case at Weavers Way.

In February 1974, when the first board asserted its authority by freezing its over-capacity membership, manager Jules Timerman found a loophole and continued to admit groups of neighbors assembled as "mini-co-ops." The conflict between the board and Timerman worsened when Weavers' rogue manager purchased a new and larger storefront space at a bartered-down settlement of $5,000 from the $14,000 asking price. Although the funds for the purchase came from member cash investments, Timerman's name appeared on the deed. With a new building and much needed to bring it up to speed, the co-op established a building renovation committee which put a security system at the top of its to-do list. Timerman interpreted this proposal as contrary to neighborly openness. "Real security," he protested at a membership meeting, "comes from being part of a community. We do not want to move toward physical security measures which would wall off or shut out the community from the co-op."[49]

In the same period, Timerman found himself pitted against another board policy as newly elected treasurer, LeRoy Snyder, tried to tighten the reins on the store's haphazardly controlled monies. One night after she tallied the day's intake and brought it home for safekeeping, member Dorothy Guy recalled Timerman at her front door demanding that she hand over the money. Startled, Guy responded that she could not give him the money because "the board is trying to regulate things." Unsatisfied, Timerman shouted, "I'm out of money; I've gotta have that money. I need to buy something. We can't run this damn store this way." Frightened, she handed him some cash and thankfully watched Timerman stomp off her porch. "I just remember the anger at the door and that I was scared. It just went downhill from there," Guy recounted.[50] After repeating Guy's account of this interaction to Weavers' purchasing manager, Norman Weiss, in 2003, Weiss (who had worked alongside Timerman in the early 1970s) described Timerman as a very good buyer who "needed ready access to cash to make his deals. He wasn't interested in going through the formal steps in order to buy. Procedures would have been in his way."[51]

Procedures did get in his way, so much so that Timerman resigned in September 1974. In his letter of explanation, he insisted that with the constant manager-board conflict, the co-op could "deteriorate and eventually fail unless [issues were] resolved." His list of complaints, followed by illustrative questions, included: "Lack of a sense of membership, 'Why do so many members behave like customers?'—Unwillingness to Invest Effort and/or Money, 'People who cannot learn that give and take are two sides of the same coin should be dropped from the membership.'—Overconcern for the Political Aspects, 'We are supposed to be realistic about money, yet we lose sight of how our money should work for us and worry more about who can make decisions, about what.'"[52]

For many Weavers cooperators, decision making was a loaded issue. From the Clearness Process for conflict resolution, adopted by the People's Food Co-op of Ann Arbor in 1976, to the consensus model, implemented by Weavers Way's first woman president, Dorothy Guy, New Wave food collectives eagerly experimented with paradigms that eliminated conventional decision processes. For members of Weavers Way who witnessed their manager's endless enthusiasm for the grocery store and collectivity devolve into bitter civil war, this difficult first year made the need for deliberate administration incontrovertible.

Clashing personalities do not fully explain Weavers' rocky beginning. New Wavers brought countercultural ethics—such as informality, egalitarianism, self-realization, and personal freedom—into their enterprises, which were not conducive to running orderly and fiscally healthy stores. Meant to be realized through action, these counternormative principles opened up every working day to critical evaluation. Because they wanted to succeed, seventies cooperators took their co-ops very seriously. They expected their food stores, in product, structure, and style, to dismantle routine grocery store practices. The most ardent co-op workers and members believed that a food and community revolution was at stake. For some co-ops, balancing countercultural idealism with business realism proved impossible; at the same time other co-ops staggered from one minicrisis to another.

In case after case, New Wave cooperatives started out strong and then fizzled into a small coterie of zealous workers who surrendered their lives keeping their collective stores afloat. If the membership and staff did not elect or appoint a decision-making body and implement managerial plans, co-ops, in general, fell apart. Weavers successfully avoided implosion in its first year.

Other more purist cooperatives avoided formalization as long as possible. Yet, inevitably, all collective grocery stores that made it out of the 1970s intact settled on administrative and governance mechanisms that balanced their membership's nonconformity with more orthodox business methods.

RELUCTANT REGULATION AT THE PEOPLE'S FOOD CO-OP

In the same period that Jules Timerman and others created Weavers Way in Philadelphia, a few committed communalists built the People's Food Co-op (PFC) of Ann Arbor, Michigan. The PFC less readily abandoned collective worker control of its several enterprises to a board of directors and a paid general manager. Nevertheless, as member Karen Zimbelman succinctly surmised, like most New Wave co-ops, the PFC began to seriously consider systematic management and governance after watching its Packard Avenue store (established in 1972) hemorrhage revenues year after year.[53] Before the PFC resigned itself to the necessity of an elected board of directors and a general manager, members and paid coordinators attempted to solve Packard Avenue's problems through hippie ingenuity.

Paid coordinators and member volunteers stabilized the PFC's first grocery store. In theory, every issue—from the politics of product choices to new storefront locations—was collectively decided at membership meetings convened by elected corporate officers. Yet, without a general manager or approved bylaws, the workers collective on duty resolved issues on the fly. By 1976, a group of members deemed this antiorganization insufficient. Presenting themselves to the general meeting as the "consensus committee," they criticized the existing arrangement as "a bit of a non-model," with decisions being made in "a fairly loose quasi-consensus form."[54] From their perspective, without a formulated and enforced institutional methodology, the PFC stumbled along with antidemocratic decision-making. To reverse this trend, they proposed consistent member input to improve engagement.

Wary that a governing system might result in a pecking order, while simultaneously plagued with the New Wave paradox of participatory democratic idealism in an institution with declining member involvement, the PFC proceeded in a stopgap manner throughout the 1970s. Problems were addressed through co-op coordinator initiative, ad hoc committees, and open meetings.

The PFC's pre-board years were not simply a muddled failure. With young, passionate volunteers and paid coordinators at the helm, it survived its first eight years, 1971–79, with noticeable successes. It started a newsletter, opened three storefronts—Packard Avenue, 4th Avenue (established 1975), and Herb and Spice Co-ops (established 1978). The PFC also supported or assisted the creation of other cooperatives in Ann Arbor, such as the Wildflour Bakery, the Ann Arbor Tofu Collective, and a cooperative warehouse, People's Wherehouse. In this growth period, the co-op implemented policies on membership and hiring practices, administered various surveys, and sponsored petition drives and boycotts on such hot, progressive causes as nuclear power and nonunion produce. By 1979 its three stores had gross annual sales of $782,573.[55] At the same time, as the PFC expanded its cooperative impact on Ann Arbor, worker disgruntlement, fiscal instability, and member and store factionalism roiled beneath the surface.

The Packard Avenue store's irreversible financial losses augured the PFC's unstable condition. Such PFC members as Reuben Chapman perceived early on that the co-op's lack of a system would lead to crisis. He optimistically joined the Packard Avenue co-op in the early 1970s because "there was certainly a feeling that this was a counter movement to the way our economy worked at the time. And there was the feeling that this was a way the whole economy could run if people found it practical." Yet Chapman quickly realized that without some kind of power distribution, the hopeful alternative would eventually burn out and doom the New Wave movement to obsolescence. "I was conservative in the sense that I thought we should be more business-like if we were going to be a successful business," he reflected. "But some members said, 'that's capitalism, not a co-op.'"[56]

Not all Ann Arbor cooperators agreed with Chapman's pragmatic approach. The most radical enterprise associated with the PFC, People's Produce Co-op (which had a lounge for political discussions and a reading room) believed so fervently in subverting the money system that it refused to hire paid labor, wondering "what are the tradeoffs on the cooperative concept when you pay a person? Is it a co-op movement function to provide employment?" Many of the young, highly educated, and politically earnest cooperators in this Midwest college town certainly shared the absolutism of the People's Produce Co-op. At the same time, considerable support for stabilization via a conventional hierarchy could be found in the PFC's group of active members who, like Reuben Chapman, worried that if the co-op did not begin "making more money than it spends, it won't exist to serve anyone or meet their needs."[57]

Many counterculturalists expected their co-op not just to sell healthful unprocessed foods but also to be an enactment of anticapitalist mutiny. Over time, they settled for celebrating the fact that, while it had not disestablished capitalism, the New Wave had created nourishing progressive reserves where folks could put their money into righteous producers selling righteous foods. If regular business plans could save these bohemian outposts, so be it.

For PFC member Diana Slaughter, the Packard store's knee-jerk denunciation of standard business modes exemplified hippie anarchy, not enlightenment. Recollecting the dangers of Packard's lackadaisical cash accounting, Slaughter said, "I always weighed my stuff out as best I could on the old rolling butcher scale we had at Packard, but other people would sort of estimate." As far as totaling one's purchases, she remembered, "You would ring up your own order on this ancient cash register that would take entries only up to $9.99. Self-cashiering was scrapped after the cash box got ripped off . . . I was one of the first members to push for the election of a board to give some stability and continuity to the PFC."[58] Eventually, the PFC followed Slaughter's lead. After nearly two years of discussions, committees, and false starts toward formal governance, the PFC elected its first board of directors in April 1980.[59] In 1981, Packard Avenue hired its first store manager in PFC history, while the 4th Avenue Co-op worked without a paid manager until 1983.[60]

Interestingly, like Weavers Way in Philadelphia, for Ann Arbor's People's Food Co-op to achieve regular participation among all member-owners, the most devoted collectivist's vision had to be supplanted by a conformist but inclusive framework. A board and a set of bylaws, which countercultural cooperators originally believed would weaken member control, made the co-op less beholden to the default influence of a tireless but insular group of workers and supervolunteers, who would willingly watch the co-op go under if it wavered from their communal totalism.

When New Wave cooperatives jumped this initial hurdle and transformed themselves from trials in utopian collectivity to communally owned but professionally operated businesses, they did not suddenly devolve into cutthroat corporations, as many had feared. Members revamped their expectations of cooperation to buoy their grocery stores. Yet this constituency still believed in their generation's charge to disrupt American consciousness and culture. After the anticapitalist bloom fell off New Wave cooperatives, member-owners at the People's Food Co-op and other food collectives vigilantly monitored their stores, making sure that the food within coincided with their ecological and health criteria. They continued to expect their cooperative community to advance social goods beyond satisfying the natural food aesthetics of their predominantly well-off memberships. This last goal became trickier as the "opulent hipness" of natural/local/organic foods firmly rooted in the middle- and upper-class cultural-consumer imaginary at the turn of the twenty-first century.[61]

BOYCOTTS, BEAN SPROUTS, AND BALONEY: THE POLITICS OF FOOD

In the early years of Weavers Way, manager Jules Timerman's scouting and bartering determined the co-op's weekly offerings. Cheese, deli meats, and produce, all easily found in Philadelphia, regularly filled the co-op's shelves. At discounted prices, Weavers' member families—such as Dorothy Guy's brood of eight, who squeaked by on "a very modest income"—eagerly awaited the arrival of these staples.[62] Unlike many other New Wave collectivists, West Mount Airy residents did not have inaccessible health foods in mind when they developed their collective business. However, the natural foods revolution spoke to Weavers Way's middle-class constituency.

A review of Weavers' history shows a de facto policy to expand natural foods products. In the first issue of the co-op's newsletter in October 1974, the ten members up for board election named collective savings and neighborly camaraderie as the co-op's two outstanding merits. Candidate Martha Popp also congratulated Weavers for providing "unrefined foods and prime products." Board hopeful Chester Jones appreciated Weavers as an "extremely good alternative to the limited options people have in dealing with the retail food industry."[63] Thus, while the first board aspirants named civic accomplishment and social solidity as the co-op's overriding assets, some members admired Weavers for its noncorporate, unprocessed merchandise.

Norman Weiss, the first board-hired general manager, was instrumental in nurturing natural foods taste in the membership. Weiss, then twenty-one, remembers that he was "full of ideas and energy" when he replaced Timerman.[64] "We were in an area where the education level is high; these were the people who first gravitated toward natural food," Weiss explained.[65] That said, Weavers' only official policy—"to be owned by the members and to serve the community"—differed from other New Wave projects such as a neighboring co-op, Germantown Ecology, which refused to sell "products with white flour, white sugar, etc."[66] While Weavers' buyers hunted down the unconventional bean curd and brown rice for health foodists, it also carried crackers, cookies, and fresh meats for the unconverted.

Germantown Ecology's food regulations were common in the New Wave. Unequivocal about co-ops' nutritional duties, *The Food Co-op Handbook* cautioned that "co-ops should accept their responsibility to safeguard their members' health by not carrying junk food, and to educate them about nutrition by carrying whole unprocessed foods and by posting recipes, articles and nutrient charts on co-op walls, and in newsletters." If the faithless continued to request "air-filled white bread, TV dinners, and tortilla chips, it's the responsibility of the minority to try to educate them and try to change the policy," the Handbook Collective unapologetically resolved.[67]

Natural foods currents streamed through Weavers Way, even during Jules Timerman's bottom-dollar jurisdiction. In 1977, the board, staff, and merchandising committee asked members to consider whether the store should steer "toward more health food items, since the suggestion book is loaded with requests for unusual products" or "toward one-stop shopping and a more complete product line, adding paper products, cold cereal and salad dressings."[68] Beholden to Weavers' charter to serve its multiracial and economically uneven neighborhood, when devising its product selection criteria in 1977–78, the merchandising committee left room for both and for any other food proposals that might arise.[69]

Guidelines made Weavers' product line predictable. Nonetheless, food disagreement continued. Indeed, cheap merchandise could never be the long-range goal for most New Wave co-ops, especially as the natural/organic food ethos infiltrated middle- and upper-class consumer consciousness. New Wave co-ops, particularly those that opened as natural foods cooperatives, regularly reviewed merchandise content and quality and the relevance of both to individual members, the surrounding community, the nation, and the world.

Meat, a food problematized first by Frances Moore Lappé's *Diet for a Small Planet* jeremiad, provoked considerable controversy in New Wave co-ops. Most forbade animal flesh, in respect for vegetarian members. But some eventually considered adding a meat line. People's Food Co-op faced earthquake-like rumblings in the early 1980s when its Packard Avenue store's general manager, Peter Hiers, dumped slow-moving merchandise and added such "verboten" items as chocolate chips and canned tuna. By 1985, the Packard Avenue Co-op expanded its meat line to include fresh seafood and poultry. Hiers avoided battles with "militant vegetarians," by selling the tinned tuna out of the back room, in the first years of transition.[70]

In 1985, the Food Co-op of Brattleboro, Vermont, confronted a more protracted struggle when the management collective decided to place local lamb and pork in its new, larger facility. After a three-year dialogue, the board called the question at a membership meeting. Appearing with a thoroughly researched plan, the board, finding no opposition in attendance, passed the motion. Out of respect for members disturbed by butchering, the co-op situated the cutting equipment out of sight. According to general manager Alex Gyori, despite these dispensations the "anti-meat lobby finally read their newsletters, and began a heated but short-lived campaign to scuttle the new decision."[71] With over half the membership favoring the change, the management and board opened the new store, meat and all. On the first day of business in the co-op's new digs, the husband and wife who led the antimeat protest picketed the store and handed in their membership.

Ruminating on his co-op's meat controversy, Alex Gyori argued, "It has never been our intention to alienate anyone over any issue such as this. But our experience over the 17 years of the co-op's existence is that every major decision that has been made carries with it the certainty that some people will not like and a few will even quit the co-op as a result." As the general manager, invested both in the collective's survival and its progression to greater effectiveness and outreach, Gyori saw change as inevitable and necessary.[72] For others, like the couple whose animal rights principles outweighed the nutritional, communal, and economic virtues of cooperation, change represented their co-op's commercial slide into amorality.

Co-op members did not necessarily look on the heated member meetings, editorial interchange over food, or the division between everyday business practicality and member's ethics as a nuisance. Rather, as Weaver Way member and employee Norman Weiss explained, it was "democracy follow[ing] its course."[73] As the bearers of the rebellious sixties legacy, dissent and critical controversy became a defining character trait of this cohort—a character sustained through constant announcement and performance.

Co-ops' democracy-in-action debates over meat, health food, and canned goods, although boisterous, did not do in cooperative institutions. Yet, in a few cases the decision to "to boycott or not to boycott" caused irreparable damage. For some philosophically intractable counterinstitutionalists, a co-op proved its progressive resolve by embargoing any merchandise tainted by questionable labor or production practices. Finding a balance between advocacy chaos and political indifference tried all New Wave cooperatives. As far back as 1974, Weavers Way members insisted that Timerman secure substitutes for nonunion lettuce and grapes. Additional boycott proposals—some adopted, some discarded—included canned tuna, Ugandan coffee, Chilean produce, California grapes, and Icelandic fish cakes. In 1976, Weavers Way's board established a policy on politics allowing the co-op to act "on public issues of concern to consumers," but not on partisan issues. Product protocols were set by 1978. Nevertheless, each time they contemplated a boycott, the membership of Weavers Way split into warring sides.[74]

New Wave cooperators remained satisfied with their collectives as long as they responded to members' demand for boycotts or political petitions, supplied healthy food alternatives, sustained member control, provided a friendly forum for leftist discussion and activism, and furnished a staging ground for some cross-race and cross-class community cohesion. The first four goals—boycotts, health foods, member control, and political interaction—were often actualized in countercultural co-ops, even as they professionalized. The fifth, community building, remained elusive. At Weavers Way, the co-op sustained unity among its voluntarist, white membership but less successfully reached beyond the class and race divides within its neighborhood. This failure was a source of continual self-reflection and hand-wringing. In 1987, when Weavers debated a Chilean fruit boycott to protest Augusto Pinochet's dictatorship, member Joe Restifo protested, "We already have too much of an image as a white liberal activist group. We would do better to be simply a neighborhood group selling good food at cheap prices."[75] What kind of alternative community were they assembling, many cooperators wondered, when they looked around the co-op and saw only white (generally), well-off faces?

LONGING FOR BELOVED COMMUNITY AFTER THE 1960S

When Stokely Carmichael became chair of the Student Nonviolent Coordinating Committee (SNCC) in 1966, this significant civil rights institution began purging white liberals from its ranks. In the place of liberal, interracial, and integrationist organizations—like Martin Luther King Jr.'s Southern Christian Leadership Conference—rose the challenges of separatism and cultural revivalism in the Black Power and black pride movements led by SNCC, the Nation of Islam, the Black Panthers, and others. This shift toward black "identity" politics echoed throughout the late sixties Left, eventually stirring other social movements such as the women's liberation movement, gay rights, the American Indian movement, and La Raza. While black nationalism reinvigorated the African American struggle and opened the stage to nontraditional political players, it profoundly unsettled the white Left.

The sixties Left had an ill-defined political or notional center, well before the identity politics revolution scattered progressives into separate realms of civic activism.[76] Students for a Democratic Society and other postwar progressives had purposefully disjoined from the Left's historical anchor: the old labor movement's working-class politics. From the perspective of the *Port Huron Statement*, fifties industrial unions had "succumbed to institutionalization" with "[their] social idealism waning under the tendencies of bureaucracy, materialism, business ethics."[77] Wanting more direct influence on national issues, in the 1950s and early 1960s, liberal youth gravitated to civil rights. In this movement, white progressives discovered the authentic and purposeful community they found wanting in the liberal old guard and the labor Left.[78]

After cutting their teeth on race rights work, white activists Tom Hayden and his future wife, Casey, took grassroots direct action north into Students for a Democratic Society. Early SDS projects, such as the Economic Research and Action Project (ERAP), planned to bring white youth into northern black ghettos to construct an "interracial movement of the poor," to "let the people create their own plans for housing, schools, parks."[79] Bold in strategy and philosophy, SDS saw itself as a radical antidote to the dehumanization that, members felt, pervaded postwar society. The unification of liberal students in the New Left in the early 1960s positioned SDS as a leader of the college-based antiwar movement. With an urgent cause and a preestablished organizational fabric across U.S. college campuses, liberal and radical sixties youth felt part of a relevant, if not necessarily multiracial, grassroots web.[80]

In the late 1960s, when Left energy flowed into what Van Gosse describes as a "pluralist 'movement of movements,'" the realization of interracial progressive alliances, in the vein of Martin Luther King Jr.'s anticipated "beloved community," became less practical for both black and white Americans to imagine and endorse.[81] Without a definitive leftist fulcrum or a grand narrative, those progressives not involved in rights campaigns began to redefine politics in communes, co-ops, underground newspapers and magazines, and other exploits of the early 1970s. These utopian communal inventions reveal participant's longing to keep alive the tight-knit, sincere fellowships many had discovered in the civil rights and antiwar movements.[82]

Co-ops seemed a natural intermediary for interracial and cross-class partnerships. At the same time, socially conscious white cooperators had an acute awareness of the parasitism of some white activism in the 1960s—epitomized in Tom Hayden's comment, "Students and poor people make each other feel real."[83] Sensitive white progressives felt uncertain about how to respectfully build an interracial "beloved community." Still, filled with humanist idealism, and unable to fully discard what Todd Gitlin described as the sixties "divine premise that everything was possible," many co-ops believed that despite the land mines around cross-class and race bonding, they should breach segregation in their neighborhoods.[84] By constructing inviting spaces for interaction and supplying neighbors with an affordable food source, they believed they could prove the feasibility of interracial cooperation. By the late 1970s, the failure of Weavers Way (and other co-ops) to attract African American and Latino neighbors to their stores brought their professed community-building goals and the potential for countrywide interracial interaction into serious doubt.

The inconsistency between multicultural aspirations and in-store demographics came to a head at Weavers in the winter of 1977 as the co-op contemplated relocation. After attending a meeting on a new store site, Weavers' member Mrs. Johnson submitted a letter to the co-op newsletter asking fellow cooperators to check their resistance: "Could a shift in locale to a non-residential area, such as Germantown Ave, be a cause of concern, because it is a high percentage Black shopping center and could consequently increase Black membership," she wondered. "Perhaps most would have wished I had not cracked Pandora's Box, but this is one avenue that we need to honestly explore."[85] Several lengthy, introspective responses filled the next month's *Shuttle*. Member and board officer Bud Cook implored, "We could do with a lot less self-congratulations about what a racial utopia our 'liberal' Mount Airy is. Most institutions in Mount Airy are either predominantly black or predominantly white. Sad but true." To prove his point, Cook then listed the dimensions of Weavers' structural racism: The staff "is almost 100 percent white; Our product line is coming to reflect the lifestyle of 'well-to-do,' white, college-educated and health-food freaks (vociferous elements of our membership); There have never been more than two blacks on the board of directors at any one time."[86] As a standard-bearer of local uplift, Weavers

Way needed to confront its own racial, cultural, and class exclusivity head on, he concluded.[87]

How to do this? Cook's list was long. The board, he wrote, must "aggressively and systematically encourage co-op members from all class and racial backgrounds to get involved in leading the co-op." On Weavers' product line, an issue that Cook believed "goes to the heart of 'who the co-op is for,'" this reflective member suggested transforming Weavers' pricing and products to "respect the traditions and eating patterns of black and white people of low or moderate income." Anticipating the possible backlash against his and Mrs. Johnson's sweeping indictment, Cook lectured, "Instead of reacting defensively or denying that the problems exist, we should recognize that Weavers Way is not a 'well-integrated' organization and take affirmative action to improve the situation."[88] In their letter to the editor, members Jack and Anne Zucker corroborated Cook's critique, imploring members to "visualize the feeling of being black in a sea of white faces, white cashiers, white personnel. A friendly smile from a cashier (and they are friendly) does not answer the serious questions raised by Mrs. Johnson."[89] Despite these heartfelt pleas, Weavers' history disclosed a deep resistance to expansion and relocation that, consequently, prevented integration.

In the 1970s and early 1980s, Weavers Way, like other New Wave cooperatives, saw itself as one spoke in a national collectivist wheel. Weavers' members imagined their small co-op's success as inextricably linked to collectivism's national and regional destiny. Weavers created a Co-op Development Committee, met with neighbors in East Mount Airy and Germantown, and joined the Philadelphia Federation of Co-ops and the Delaware Valley Cooperative Association to forward collectivity. Members also believed, at the time, that these regional associations could promote interracial communication and connection. But, by voting to remain at their corner location, they privileged their "beloved community" at the possible expense of a multiracial cooperative movement in greater Philadelphia.

In response to Mrs. Johnson's and Bud Cook's critical call in 1977, Weavers Way founded an Affirmative Action Committee, which would later become the Diversity and Outreach Committee. These teams implemented various programs to breach the divides in postsixties America. But as manager Weiss stated in 2003, to attract members with different food cultures and economic means, the co-op would have needed to implement "target marketing" and renovate its product line. Moreover, to bear those alterations, Weavers would have had to move from its residential corner to a larger, more commercial spot. Yet, proposals for expansion threatened the quaint familiarity and quirkiness of the overcrowded alternative shop. Progressives' voluntary estrangement from partisan politics and mainstream culture, as well as their ongoing departure from institutional religion, fraternal organizations, and traditional civic clubs, made mutuality of any kind very dear. With strong emotional and social investments in their collective clan, many members seemed willing to nudge one goal—racial and class integration—slightly off center for the more readily achievable and equally laudable aim of sustaining a constant society of health food–fixated and environmentally activist stalwarts in their limited, inefficient, and cramped co-op.

Despite members' fealty to their "beloved community," from the 1970s through the 1990s, Weavers' board and staff consistently planned expansion to relieve customer and product crowding and to broaden the co-op's availability. Committees were formed, real estate brokers contacted, and properties assessed. Yet, time and again, membership meeting and board minutes record hostility to relocation. Despite a vote by the general membership in June 1977 "supporting the growth concept so that Weavers Way can serve more families and build the cooperative movement," President Dorothy Guy later noted the membership sustained "a deep concern . . . that through bigness something close and personal—intimate is a word that has been widely reiterated—may be lost."[90] Even in the 1980s, in one of the more concentrated search periods, when three successive presidents described the current co-op location as "economic suicide," when irritated neighbors organized to oust the co-op from its residential corner, member surveys showed slight agreement with the necessity for change, but no stomach for movement.

Member Linda Schatz reflected on her co-op's amiable solidarity: "The store provides a dynamic focal point of activity and energy of people working together, as well as the convenience of a local grocery store filled with unusual goodies of all kinds."[91] Members had met the contest of postwar social fragmentation by freezing their co-op's size and setting. For the time being, Mount Airy's food co-op was simply not willing to jeopardize the deeply satisfying bonds of small-scale collectivity. Other cooperatives met space limitations and expansion initiatives with the same obstructionist conservatism but with different conclusions.

THE CHALLENGE OF EXPANSION

When eighties neoconservatism, neomaterialism, and post-Vietnam neopatriotism seemed to overshadow the sixties contraposition, many cooperators blocked any co-op alteration, fearing that these important, friable artifacts of "movement" radicalism would be broken. In many instances, co-op enlargement disasters verified preservationists' trepidation. The downfall of one of the oldest food cooperatives in America, the Consumers Cooperative of Berkeley, in 1988, after its impressive increase from four to thirteen stores between 1962 and 1975, was a case in point. The Berkeley co-op had gone from being one of the biggest co-ops in America to a floundering giant, selling off failing storefronts and attempting stopgap measures through the 1980s, such as forbidding bans on controversial products and converting some CCB stores to worker/member ownership (an interestingly "retro" move). In the end, the CCB broke apart under the weight of its own ill-managed development, yet cooperatives of varying sizes—such as the People's Food Co-op of Ann Arbor (medium to large, with 7,500 members as of 2012), the Brattleboro Food Co-op (medium, with 6,700 members as of as 2014), and the Park Slope Food Coop (large, 16,000 members as of 2013)—quarreled passionately over expansion but remained intact after members conceded to advancement.

When the People's Food Co-op's board proposed expansion in 1986, a member block, the Committee for Fiscal and Social Responsibility (CFSR), formed to protest the co-op's "increasingly businesslike methods" and consolidation of its three storefronts. Committee-aligned board member Chuck Barbieri argued: "Most of us feel that economic growth for growth's sake is not a substitute for enhancing and increasing quality . . . as an alternative institution."[92] Well-organized and politically savvy, the CFSR tapped into member protectionist angst so precisely that four of its five candidates won board seats in 1986.

Similarly, contentiousness ensued in 1997 when the Park Slope Food Coop considered acquiring a neighboring building to double its size. Membership meetings became so charged that Paul Sheridan, a board member opposing the relocation, "worried about whether someone's going to [bring] a gun." Questioning the co-op staff's exclusionary deliberation process that led to the expansion proposal, three board members stood in the way of enlargement. Yet, when put to a vote, Park Slope cooperators greenlighted the move.[93]

Brattleboro's Food Cooperative met little member resistance to doubling its size in 1988 and again in 2012, when it acquired a 32,000-square-foot building. Besides the focused protest against meat products in the new store in the 1980s and some grumbling at membership meetings, voting members generally backed the plans. As former board president Donald Freeman thoughtfully reflected on the defiant undercurrents in his co-op, "There is always a certain mourning in losing old things."[94] Despite members' fretful anticipation, Brattleboro, Park Slope, and the People's Food Co-op all survived growth and were able to uphold what Richard A. Kaye of the *New York Times* described as the "unfragmented communal experience" sought by those who filled postsixties food cooperatives.[95]

For most of its history, Weavers Way members could not square largeness with familiarity. Despite every general manager's urgent pleas and successive board initiatives to acquire greater square footage for an operation that grew from 800 active members in 1976 to close to 3,000 by 2000, the membership steadily refused relocation and reconstruction. Consequently, Weavers' residential site, its constrained quarters, and its members-only shopping policy confined the co-op's municipal influence.

When asked why she thought that Weavers Way never stretched beyond its original location, cooperator Dorothy Guy remarked that it was a "mystical, mythical thing," a phenomenon that could not be explained simply by economics or demography. In her younger years, as a significant figure on the cooperative board and staff, Guy supported expansion and relocation because it made business sense. But when interviewed in 2003, in her eighth decade with her children gone and her husband deceased, the "convenience, ease, and familiar faces" at the co-op gave her a feeling of "safety and support and help." For this member of over thirty years, involved until her 2015 death, who could see the store from her front porch, the loss of this neighborhood hub would have been "devastating." Each time she entered the store she noticed "two or three people in earnest conversation." This vibrant atmosphere filled with "socially active people conversing" demonstrated why the membership blocked any enlargement that might destroy the one-of-a-kind "intimacy" of its co-op.[96] In a period when sprawling suburbs replaced small towns and depleted city neighborhoods across America, New Wave cooperatives reconstructed community out of the thin air of their shared progressivism and natural foods affinities. For several decades, Weavers' member community was the end itself.

JUST SURVIVING, THEN THRIVING
IN THE NEW CENTURY FOOD REVOLUTION

Weavers Way marched on, decade after decade, undeterred by shifts in staff and board direction, declining membership participation, the national co-op movement's diminishment, conflicts with neighbors, and the passing of esteemed co-op members and its founder, Jules Timerman. Then in November 2002, the co-op faced a crisis. It was their own "World Trade Center event," in the words of then manager Ed McGann.[97]

On November 20, 2002, McGann discovered that the co-op's bank account could not cover a $152,000 check he wrote for a loan related to the new co-op cafe. Weavers' bookkeeper of thirteen years, Andrea (Andi) Sheaffer, had assured him otherwise, but in his phone conversation with the bank, McGann discovered a deficiency of $61,000 in the co-op's escrow. After further inquiry, McGann found that of Weavers' two bank accounts used for operating expenses, one was overdrawn and the other held only a few thousand dollars. After sifting through the bookkeeper's work desk, McGann unearthed a pile of never sent signed checks for vendors. These facts, along with Sheaffer's disappearance, set off an alarm that led to the creation of an accountability committee and the co-op's first formal audit by an outside firm. The auditors learned that $618,000 of $678,958 member equity was gone, not due to embezzlement but to what they described as "gross financial mismanagement."[98]

The Accountability Committee's extensive investigation showed that for at least a decade, Sheaffer had been lying about the co-op's fiscal health. Her financial reports overstated the co-op's cash intake, understated the bills and costs of goods, and, for several years, had hidden mounting bank fees for 4,500 overdrafts worth $140,000. According to the audit, the co-op owed suppliers $336,000, which Sheaffer had kept secret by playing interference with irate suppliers. Weavers Way was on the brink of collapse, and everyone wanted to know why.

Petty thievery had always plagued New Wave cooperatives, especially in their early, unstructured years. Transient member-worker staffs, anticapitalist radicals who skewed communalism to mean the right to take things, and haphazard inventory and accounting predisposed seventies co-ops to pilfering. Yet, most New Wave cooperators believed that the closeness and moral rationale of their communal enterprises prevented the financial scandals of conventional businesses. Embezzlement and accounting malfeasance resulted from modern workers' debasement and alienation, or so New Wave cooperators supposed.

Crestfallen over the betrayal of Weavers' precious net of trust, in the January 2003 issue of the *Shuttle*, manager McGann emotively implored the membership to stay the course: "No one knows or even comprehends the agony, anger, sadness and disappointment I felt for the past six weeks. We all have put a lot into this organization: the days, weeks, months and years of our life. For me, it is fifteen years of my life that includes meetings upon meetings, working at home and on my vacations. We cannot let this organization die. Mark my words: United we stand, divided we fall."[99] To stay united, Weavers installed managerial and fiscal controls, as well as employee supervision, which for some members smacked of authoritarianism. Unmoved by what they saw as members' unthinking antistructuralism, McGann and the board began to restore a working co-op. Although some of the over 300 members who attended a special "crisis" meeting on December 8, 2003, expressed both anger and indignation at the staff and board for allowing such a catastrophe to occur, many others stood up to state their support of the co-op and their "willingness to help."[100] And help they did at the cash register, paying a 5 percent "recovery" surcharge from January to March 2003, with donations to the "Save Weavers Way" Fundraising Campaign, and with employee-members voluntary cut in health benefits.

To reassure its membership, the board convened an emergency meeting in February 2003. After much discussion about the nature of the crisis, President Bob Noble suggested that because the co-op had generally worked from a "culture of trust," derived from the early seventies spirit of humanism, the board never questioned Sheaffer's accounting representations. For Noble, Weavers' days of personalism needed to come to an end. Conventional financial and personnel management would be introduced.[101]

At the end of this "crisis" conference, the board asked Weavers' members to vote for or against the existing board. Overwhelmingly, Weavers Way cooperators raised their hands in a vote of confidence, after which a participant, identifying as member number fifteen, rose to express her concerns. Echoing seventies antiestablishmentarianism, she emotionally ruminated, "What I heard today is more like a corporation than a co-op. My challenge is, how do we get back to a deeper sense of cooperation? A co-op is . . . a necessarily interactive place. It's not neat and clean. I want us to get back to our soul."[102] For this woman, for-profit food stores relied on strict supervision because they assumed the worst of their employees. It seemed, she implied, that Weavers was drifting toward the same paranoia and recrimination.

As per its history, Weavers' leaders would have to tighten the business to defend the web of sociality this member worried would be lost. They searched for a new manager with executive leadership qualifications and found Glenn Bergman, a career chef with corporate food service experience. Bergman not only saved the co-op, he broke through Weavers' expansion barrier in a big way, turning the co-op into an influential commercial and civic stakeholder in Philadelphia. Bergman could do so because the co-op was primed for an overhaul. Moreover, at the beginning of the twenty-first century, organic foods, urban food activism, localism, and sustainability achieved a level of recognition unseen in the history of the natural foods movement.

Michael Pollan's *Omnivore's Dilemma* (2006) stirred new-century natural foods consumerism and awareness. *Omnivore's* narrative became the script for those devoted to natural, whole, local, and sustainable foods. Pollan did not tell a new story. Sixties natural foodists had blamed the agribusiness–food industry–government regulatory triad for alienating Americans from food and farming, for causing the nation's diet-based diseases, and for sullying the environment decades before the *New York Times* named *The Omnivore's Dilemma* one of the top ten books of 2006. They were going local and eating by their ethics aeons before *The Omnivore's Dilemma* made "community-supported agriculture (CSA)," "organic," "free-range," and "food justice" de rigueur nomenclature in twenty-first-century elite circles. A combination of reasons, including a looming climate crisis, bipartisan contempt for government, global vulnerability in the neoliberal age, and social media's rise, firmly stationed Pollan's anticorporate—but by no means anticapitalist—pastoral food idyll into the American psyche. Michelle Obama's organic garden on the White House lawn and her 2010 national dietary health program, Let's Move, coupled with the president's Task Force on Childhood Obesity and a series of Pollan-philic films and books, mainlined *Omnivore's* negative evaluation of the processed food system into the cultural bloodstream.

With established networks of small-scale commerce and institutional commitments to nutritional uplift, food co-ops delightedly came out of aging-hippie obscurity to become "good food" revolution leaders. In the late 1990s, middle-aged and older Mount Airy residents peopled Weavers Way's co-op. This fact concerned members as their co-op looked to a graying, diminished future, especially after its financial catastrophe. Yet, after 2000, young Philadelphians suddenly wanted to join. They also wanted to start urban farms, create organic and local food lines, and become co-op employees. Weavers' new manager, Glenn Bergman, seized this energy to revamp the co-op.

Between 2004 and 2015, Bergman ambitiously pursued the two competing motives of New Wave cooperatives since their countercultural inception: co-ops as catalysts of radical justice, and co-ops as enclaves of progressive consumer confirmation. The co-op's renovated mission statement, "to provide high-quality, fairly priced foods and a broader understanding of their importance to our members and community," indicated Weavers' self-perception as good foods educators.[103] Weavers' community projects—its two urban gardens, its CSA, its healthy school snack program—emphasized expanding merchandise channels for whole food and right farming. They also instructed students and adults in *correct* relationships with farming and food.

Natural foods edification and the sixties movement mandate to "feed the people" collided when Bergman boldly endeavored to take on Weavers' historical bugaboo—expansion. A student of the co-op's history, Bergman knew that relocating the still cramped original market was a nonstarter. Instead, he focused on new stores. Fortuitously, in 2008 a civic organization, the Ogontz Avenue Revitalization Corporation (OARC), contacted the co-op about opening and managing a corner produce store in the West Oak Lane neighborhood, just northeast of Weavers Way. West Oak Lane is a majority African American, middle- to low-income precinct. The U.S. Department of Agriculture (USDA) food access map shaded the West Oak Lane region as a food desert. Food deserts, an issue gaining considerable media, governmental, and citizen notice in the early 2000s, were defined as low-income neighborhoods without ready access to whole, fresh foods. These conditions, according to the USDA, contributed to poor diet and "higher levels of obesity and other diet-related diseases."[104] Weavers and the OARC presumed that a small produce store would be a perfect fit for West Oak Lane.

This project took Weavers in a direction it had shied away from—the lack of food access in the Northwest Philadelphia neighborhoods bordering the co-op. Co-op debates had circled around this prickly problem. But in the end, owing to the store's tight margins, fiscal wobbliness, and attachment to the storefront at the corner of Carpenter Lane and Greene Street in Mount Airy, members dismissed sacrificing their gathering place for the betterment of another neighborhood. But now, with obesity and food deserts on a repeat news cycle and with Philadelphia food activists putting money and time into solving the "national crisis," Weavers Way followed suit. Tapping into nonprofit and governmental grant monies, Bergman's team began preparing Weavers' second food store.

In July 2008, the West Oak Lane Weavers Way opened. Three short years later, Weavers pulled out, leaving the market under OARC control. The experiment had resoundingly failed. Despite various efforts—hiring and firing four managers, a store "reset" in 2010—the West Oak Lane grocery bled revenue every year of its existence. Bergman and other co-op leaders seemed perplexed and disappointed that the store never took off. "The Ogontz store is still a mystery as to why sales are flat still after a year. Either we find a new product line or message or we close or transfer the store to new ownership," Glenn Bergman reported.[105]

Hints of the source of the store's sluggishness ran through Bergman's later ruminations. "We could have done a large grocery store with conventional products," he said, "but larger selection, conventional products, milk, etc., goes against healthful and sustainable."[106] Weavers' communication director, Jon McGoran pondered the demise of the West Oak Lane venture in 2011: "We'd repeatedly tweaked the product line to find the proper mix of local and organic products while keeping an eye on the bottom line: the price points. Part of the thing that's tricky is trying to make it as affordable as possible while keeping to the values and principles we think are important."[107] And there was the rub: Weavers Way opened a miniature version of its Mount Airy store carrying its organic, local, and sustainable commission—with the premium costs—into West Oak Lane. It hoped that the new store's customers would make the right economic choices to afford those food and agricultural values: Mount Airy's co-op shoppers did. Under similar assumptions, in *The Omnivore's Dilemma*, Michael Pollan harrumphed: "It isn't only the elite who in recent years have found an extra fifty or one hundred dollars each month to spend on cell phones . . . or televisions . . . Is the unwillingness to pay more for food really a matter of affordability or priority?"[108] Weavers had also opened the store speculating that the emotive and ethical facets of countercultural collectivity had universal currency. Both ideas—good food and collective consumer control—had strong appeal for some West Oak Lane residents, but not enough to keep the business afloat.

Prior to shutting its Ogontz co-op, Weavers' letters to the editor in the *Shuttle* indicated membership infighting that echoed well-worn New Wave and Weavers factionalism over class privilege, the business bottom line, and community outreach. In a letter titled "Ogontz Store Should Go," member Lawrence Geller recounted his in-store observations of weak management, "poor oversight" of food, and "prices significantly higher than the exact same products at the local Shoprite."[109] The co-op's experiment in servicing a local food desert, "notwithstanding some idealistic intentions" he concluded, "has been and continues to be a financial and public relations disaster."[110] Indignant retorts from the Ogontz store's staff and shoppers filled the next month's newsletter. "I am shocked that so many people involved in this organization feel so negatively about it. I honestly think the West Oak Lane store is the best thing Weavers Way has going for it right now. Philadelphia does not need any more exclusive feeling co-op clones that many people don't feel comfortable or welcome in," assistant manager Michael Conley sharply replied.[111]

While Weavers' leaders and members wrestled over how to have a positive impact on Philadelphia's food deserts, it took a second stab at expansion. In 2009, Weavers bought a 6,700-square-foot building in moneyed and traditionally Republican Chestnut Hill. This space became its third co-op, opening in May 2010. With its upscale Chestnut Hill neighbors abiding by what food scholars Josee Johnston, Michelle Szabo, and Alexandra Rodney describe as the "dominant ethical eating repertoire," the store was a sure thing.[112] Some Chestnut Hill shoppers became members, buying into communalism. Others simply avoided the hassle, using the new co-op like a specialty market and paying a nonmember markup for the quality natural goods they sought. Weavers' Chestnut Hill branch took some pressure off the refurbished, but still bursting at the seams, Mount Airy operation; it gave Weavers a larger commercial and civic footprint in Northwest Philadelphia; and it washed the organization of much of its residual hippie reputation.

Weavers' choice to expand into well-heeled Chestnut Hill, along with the retirement of its member work requirement in 2010, heralded a significant turning point in this New Wave co-op's history and the natural foods movement trajectory since the 1960s. Member-workers had been the cornerstone of early seventies co-ops' anticonventionalism and participatory democracy. The buzz of individuals, from stockbrokers to stoners, sweeping floors and filling shelves with healthful products, supporting one another in satisfying a primary human need, was the New Wave's contribution to tearing down the depersonalizing "system." In practice, working membership did not pan out so triumphantly. Cooperators across the country avoided work duty in myriad ways—paying other members to do their hours, begging forgiveness, or just ignoring the requirement and finally quitting the co-op. New Wave co-op leaders had punished errant cooperators with fines, lost privileges, and strong rebukes.[113]

In the new century's go-go natural foods marketplace, it seemed that organic capitalism and local entrepreneurship, not communalism or worker-operated businesses, were meant to bring on the revolution. In Philadelphia's middle- and upper-class locales, consumers saw a deluge of stores, farms, restaurants, and food products that validated their environmental and health commands. In these enclaves, it appeared that natural foods purchasing had undermined factory farms and supermarket orthodoxy—a selective interpretation, since natural foods adherents' social and commercial world was generally detached from that of the average American. As Richard Reeves confirms, since the 1970s, high-income families (and the creative and intellectual elite) have "self-segregated" from the rest of America, not just materially but also in "family structure, education, lifestyle, and geography."[114]

Under these new sociocultural conditions, the burden of member work felt anachronistic, like a faded tie-dyed shirt stretched too tightly over an aging hippie belly. In 2010, as one of just a handful of New Wave co-ops still enforcing the working member requirement, Weavers' leaders simply could not find a reason to continue a practice that had bedeviled co-ops from the start. Formulating a recipe for the co-op's involvement in the city's and the nation's battle against racial and class-based food inequality had also beset Weavers, and the New Wave in general, from its inception. By the twenty-first century, the co-op hadn't solved that riddle either.

"A LESS PURE CO-OP"

In 1970, after a few years in business, Bill Winfield, a founding member of the Madison, Wisconsin, People's Grocery Food Cooperative (later the Mifflin Street Co-op) laid out his design for cooperatives as the tip of a grassroots entrepreneurial iceberg: "If a number of small, decentralized community co-op stores (forget big projects like the Berkeley or Hyde Park co-ops) could be started near a number of campuses, a sizeable amount of capital could be generated and used to help low income black and working-class co-ops get started. If people could get themselves together and build their own community stores, in other words, they could both save themselves money and generate capital to aid other communities with less income and less privileged backgrounds. And that could be the beginning of an intercommunity support system set up to do away with the government and foundation grants that buy off low income projects."[115] Vibrating with sixties "movement" can-do optimism, New Wave cooperators believed in this "beloved" communal future.

Compared with other co-ops, Weavers was not an exception in unsuccessfully answering this call. As a food store, it is hardly surprising that the foremost goal and the topic of interest to Weavers' members was (and is) the type and quality of food in their mutually owned markets. Despite members' competing visions of the co-op's meaning and duties, the base function of Weavers Way, as a supermarket substitution, has shone through as the most instantly rewarding and practicable target. The return of natural foods insurgency in the more current "buy fresh–buy local" milieu seemed to substantiate the New Wave's choice, as though in the eighties and nineties co-op doldrums, cooperators clairvoyantly predicted a politically inflected food renaissance and place-held their alternative infrastructures for this future. To a certain extent, co-ops *did* act as placeholders and protectors of a version of oppositionality, even if that oppositionality did not actualize "intercommunity support" but rather safeguarded the natural food and health market.

For Weavers Way, over its almost half-century history, serving member-owners has meant responding to increasingly stringent food requirements. In the 1970s and early 1980s, with no other natural foods source available, New Wave co-op members gratefully put damaged and wilted organic lettuce and stale whole wheat flour into their baskets, unconcerned about the food's source. By the turn of the twenty-first century, as the creative class made "local" and "farm-fresh" requirements of consumer and culinary acumen, the standard co-op member couldn't abide subpar natural products or even better-quality mainstream foodstuffs. Free-range and antibiotic-free chickens, fresh soybeans, frozen soy ravioli, as well gourmet treats—such as fresh Le Bus bakery fare brought in daily from center city Philadelphia and kosher whole grain hamburger buns—became regular co-op wares.

Serving Weavers' existing membership also meant keeping up with environmental mindfulness. Unlike women's, American Indian, and other postsixties identity politics which segmented the Left, the environmental movement proposed a macrosolution to the world's ecological problems: a unifying schema that in the eyes of participants could potentially generate a global and diverse network of earth-loving activist-consumers. In 1991 Weavers formalized its dedication to ecology by creating the Environmental Committee with board standing. Members informally reinforced the committee's surveillance of the co-op by stuffing the suggestion book with requests for biodegradable packing, bulk bins, and glass containers rather than nonrecyclable plastics. For cooperative food stores, environmentalism supplied members with direct legislation of their ecological doctrines and consumer agency.

New Wave co-ops that remained viable from the 1970s to the new millennium had to be fluid and flexible, perpetually open to self-interrogation and members' shifting philosophical and political penchants. And they had to fight constantly against the propensity of the powerful consumer culture, in which they were implicated and at the same time self-consciously divided from, to swallow up all things oppositional. They had to nourish their "beloved (alternative) communities" while sitting in the belly of the hyperconsumptive beast.

For Norman Weiss, involved in Weavers Way since founder Jules Timerman's dramatic exit in 1975, the co-op's new millennium makeover—its chichi Chestnut Hill digs, its glossy Mount Airy remodel, and the removal of member work contracts—was cause for weary resignation. Its financials were in order; its future was bright. But, as Weiss reflected, "We created kind of a less pure co-op experience. It's available to more people, but it's not as deep an experience."[116] Weavers Way was still wedded to a version of New Wave communalism. Yet, maybe, for this lifelong co-op defender, collectivity without member commitment and sacrifice, and in the service of nutritional correctness and foodie distinction, seemed to fortify, rather than challenge, the prevailing commercial food and social order.

CHAPTER 2

RECIPES FOR A NEW WORLD
Vegetarian Opposition in Seventies Natural Foods Cookbooks

In 1971, Frances Moore Lappé published *Diet for a Small Planet*, a groundbreaking work on the world food order. Presenting an exposé of the global repercussions of America's meat-centric diet, Lappé supplied instructions on how to reverse the conditions of starvation and environmental decimation resulting from the nation's carnivorousness. Her manual, with its prescription of protein complementarity (grains that when combined with legumes, dairy, vegetables and seeds yield high protein returns), granted readers a design for health and a plan to affect change.

Considering her metamorphoses from a conflicted shopper to informed dietary advocate, Lappé reflected, "I felt at the mercy of our advertising culture. My tastes were manipulated. And food, instead of being my most direct link with the nurturing earth, had become mere merchandise by which I fulfilled my role as a good consumer."[1] After carefully studying the earth's nutritional economy, Lappé noted: "I found that I *was* making choices, choices based on real knowledge about food and about the effect on the earth of different types of food production ... shopping became a real adventure."[2] For Frances Moore Lappé, those following her "diet for a small planet" could correct the maldistribution of nature's bounty and regain self-determination in, what seemed like, a food culture captured by slick advertisers and multinational monopolies.

Diet for a Small Planet is significant because it added a global political dimension to the natural foods movement's censorship of the American diet.

It proposed that choices made in one's kitchen, conventionally understood as a nonpolitical female arena, could turn the ecological tide. Women (and men if they chose to) could reverse world hunger, environmental contamination, and economic disparity through individual eating and cooking. The book's inside cover described this correlation between self and society through diet: "For the first time it is possible to implement an end to the gross waste of literally millions of tons of high-grade protein, to release men from the confines of a largely meat diet, to enjoy nutritionally sound protein from the richer and far more abundant sources that the earth provides. Here, step by step, is how you, the individual, can improve your own style-of-life—and at the same time help your very small planet."[3] Lappé's proposition replicated the New Left's and, more explicitly, second wave feminism's fusing of the private realm and the public political domain. For feminists, patriarchy enforced women's inequality in the home, at the job, in the courts: everywhere. Liberation, therefore, necessitated confronting all arenas. More generally, many young Americans argued that striving for self-fulfillment was as pointedly rebellious as marching in an antiwar protest. For natural foods evangelists, seditious self-actualization would be enacted in whole foods entrepreneurship, consumption, and cooking.

Lappé's *Diet for a Small Planet*, along with Mollie Katzen's *Moosewood Cookbook* (1974 self-published edition, 1977 Ten Speed Press edition), Edward Espe Brown's *Tassajara Bread Book* (1970) and *Tassajara Cooking* (1973), Anna Thomas's *Vegetarian Epicure* (1972), Laurel Robertson, Carol Flinders, and Bronwen Godfrey's *Laurel's Kitchen* (1976), and the Bloodroot Collective's *Political Palate* (1981) translated the sixties movement outlook into vegetarian dissent. With *Diet* hitting one million in sales by its second edition in 1975, clearly a growing audience eagerly received this socioculinary point of view.[4]

These were not the only natural/health foods cookbooks published in the period. Michio and Aveline Kushi spread the macrobiotic (vegetarian) word in their *East/West Journal* and in *The Macrobiotic Way to Natural Healing* (1978). Anne Marie Colbin, New York Natural Gourmet Cookery School founder, touted the health and spiritual benefits of seasonal and local vegetables in *The Book of Whole Foods* (1979). With even more far-reaching effect, Jean Hewitt dedicated her not purely vegetarian, *The New York Times Natural Foods Cookbook* (1971) to "the thousands of people across the country who believe in, and practice, the natural way of eating for good health."[5]

This list does not even take into account the many recipes and cookbooks of the countercultural food underground, such as Ester Dickey's *Passport to Survival* (1974), the True Light Beavers commune's *Eat, Fast, Feast: A Tribal Cookbook* (1972), or Lois Wickstrom's *The Food Conspiracy Cookbook* (1974), nor does it name the health food books of Adelle Davis and forager Euell Gibbons, which did not popularize the natural foods cookbook genre in the way that *Moosewood Cookbook* or *Laurel's Kitchen* did.

Countercultural perceptions shaped *The Vegetarian Epicure* and the others, but these books somehow transcended the "movement." *Diet for a Small Planet* set the dietary standards for many health food writers, but its influence faded when protein complementarity went out of fashion. Lappé's recipes were just not inventive or fine enough to stand on their own as flavorsome vegetarian food. The aforementioned natural food cookbooks possessed both ideological earnestness and culinary pizzazz, a magnetic combination for the college-educated, middle- and upper-class Americans searching for personal creativity with political reverberations.

Moosewood and the other cookbooks listed were popular. Chatty and idiosyncratic, they wound stories of family, friends, politics, and poetry around recipes. Similar in their antiglitz, primitive print, and illustration style, each was inimitable. Woodblock images could be associated only with *Laurel's Kitchen*; handwritten recipes and line drawings solely with Katzen's *Moosewood Cookbook*; stripped-down visuals and zen koans with Ed Brown's *Tassajara Cooking*. Using food to express a joyful and socially responsible life—a potent fusion distinctive to postsixties radical thinking—these cookbooks broadcast the natural foods message more nationally than had co-op pioneers. While their vegetarianism served different masters, these authors all planned to change the American diet. Targeting either its blandness or its ethical badness, this group of cooks compared themselves and their cookery genre with their common enemy: the richly marbled prime cuts of meat and instant/processed/artificial supermarket fare of their youth.

It is understandable that while declaring their own worldview, youth defectors felt the need to throw off their parents' culture. It is less obvious why food came to be perceived as so central to their self-expression and fulfillment. Something must have been horribly wrong with American plentitude that dissidents called for a food fight against, in all honesty, their mother's cooking. For countercultural cooks, their childhood meals carried symbolic and material consequences.

JELL-O SALADS AND JUICY STEAKS: PROCESSING AND PLENTY IN THE 1950S

Cookbooks are tricky historical sources. They rarely reflect the food and cooking diversity in America's kitchens. Indeed, according to food historian Mary McFeely, they tend to "project mainstream expectations and assume a middle-class lifestyle."[6] Yet, as one of the most popular forms of modern literature, they often showcase a period's cultural-culinary gestalt. Natural foods cookbooks certainly mirrored the revolutionary drives of their sixties and seventies readers.

With celebratory gluttony, fifties cookbooks, on the other hand, exuded postwar nationalism. With photographic centerfolds of platters groaning with fat cuts of beef swimming in their own juices, French fried potatoes, vegetables smothered in butter or rich cheese sauces, and cakes, pies, and sweets of every sort, these cookbooks enticed Americans to imaginatively indulge after decades of Depression and wartime self-denial.

Great Depression cookbooks—such as Cora Rose and Bob Brown's *Most for Your Money Cookbook* (1938) or Ida Bailey Allen's *Money Saving Cookbook* (1940)—instructed women to make a "career of thrift, nutrition, and family." Abiding by this charge, wives and mothers, and the cookbooks setting new ideals of womanhood, used meat organs and innards, stretched protein with soybean supplements, and put low-cost soups, stews, and casseroles on regular rotation.[7]

Wartime rationing followed this spartan culinary decade. During the 1940s, coffee, butter, cheese, fresh fish, meat, and sugar supplies dwindled. While the less wealthy were accustomed to frugality, tightened food stocks affected middle- and upper-class American kitchens during World War II. Magazines, government propaganda, and cookbooks counseled women to uphold family nutrition. In the name of duty, American women grew "victory garden" vegetables, baked cakes and pies with corn syrup and molasses, and made due with margarine and canned processed meats. But they did so only "for the duration" and were happy to wave goodbye to arduous home production at the war's end.[8]

The bounteous postwar meat market symbolized the nation's shift from dietary discipline to unrestraint. In the introduction to its meat chapter, the *Better Homes and Gardens New Cook Book* (1953) asked: "When you're puzzling over what to have for dinner, the first question, more often than not, is, 'What meat shall we have?'" This popular fifties kitchen guide suggested, "Serve a steak—a tender, delicious steak—and you can count on dinner being a huge success, especially with the men."[9] "Variety" meats (that is, organs), game, and poultry still made the cut in early fifties cookbooks, but the meat section's queen was a plump beef roast or prime cut of steak. Women could choose to braise a grizzled chicken neck or bony veal shank, but many no longer had to out of necessity.

Although American women, especially in the middle class, entered the work force in unprecedented numbers after World War II, the ideal-typical fifties female became a doting housewife and mother, cooking, socializing, and raising her family in a suburban tract home. Her hearty roast published her family's freedom from want and her devotion to their appetites.[10] The new gender and consumption paradigms translated into a rise in beef sales from 63 pounds per capita in 1950 to 85 pounds per capita by 1960.[11]

Sugar, like meat, was loaded with symbolism. Settling for corn syrup, molasses, and honey sweeteners in recipes through the war period, postwar cookbooks responded to pent-up longings for sweets. *The Culinary Arts Institute Encyclopedic Cookbook* (1950) featured a chapter devoted to "Your Desserts" but also included chapters for "Pies and Pastries," "Your Cakes," "Refrigerator Desserts," "Your Cookies," and "Your Candies." This popular cookery manual devoted seven of its thirty-one chapters to sweet foods. Moreover, the sweet treatment was not reserved for end-of-the-meal dishes. The *New Cook Book*'s salad chapter opened with a sticky fruit concoction, "Cinnamon Apple Salad," which consisted of apples, red cinnamon candies, sugar, water, broken nuts, dates, diced pineapple, and salad dressing. Even such salads as "Vegetable Salad Loaf" suspended sweetened green beans, pimentos, cauliflower, carrots, celery, and radishes in two packages of lemon-flavored gelatin.[12] Desserts indisputably appeared in earlier cookbooks, but they took a back seat to nourishment and survival in the 1930s and dutiful rationing in the 1940s. In the 1950s, housewives indulged their families' sweet whimsies on a daily basis, because they could and because it showed their fulfillment of the era's domestic ideology.

If meat and sugar-sweetened salads and desserts signified postwar fortune, the decade's processed foods denoted the period's veneration of convenience, science, and modernity. With supermarket shopping rising from 30 percent of food sales in 1950 to 70 percent in 1960, a wide array of industrially manufactured and marketed premade foods found their way into America's pantry. Beginning in 1946 with instant mashed potatoes, the list grew. Margarine, freed from a butter lobby–supported tax after the passage of the Margarine Act of 1950, became standard in supermarket dairy sections.[13] Canned, frozen, or freeze dried, premade foods exuded modern glamour. National supermarkets, filled with industrial foods that could be transported from coast to coast, freed the American kitchen from the parochial selection of the town butcher, baker, or farmer's roadside stand. Equipped with affordable new appliances and a cupboard of premixed cakes, breads, and canned soups, the modern housewife could approach meal planning, as the *New Cook Book* enthused, "with a spirit of adventure rather than duty."[14]

An internal paradox bubbled underneath this domestic puffery. At the same time that popular magazines, television sitcoms, sociological studies, and cookbooks framed motherhood and housewifery as the actualization of every woman's dreams, these same mass media insisted that time spent as cook, cleaner, and mother should be easy and short in duration. Following *The Culinary Arts Institute Encyclopedic Cookbook*'s "Quick Dinners for the Women in a Hurry" or Polly Cannon's *Can Opener Cookbook* (1951), she should make supper a casserole, the icon of fifties shortcut cooking. As *The New Cook Book* recommended, "Park dinner in the oven to look after itself while you greet guests, catch up on your mending, or just relax a little."[15]

Fifties cookbooks' commercial sponsorship also influenced their message. Supported or produced by food industries—*Betty Crocker's Picture Book* by General Mills, *The New Cook Book* by Better Homes and Gardens, and *The Culinary Arts Institute Encyclopedic Cookbook* by 100 different companies—made them cookery manuals and boosters for newfangled merchandise. As promoters of novel food and kitchen technologies, cookbooks tried to reconcile the ease of premade food and electrical appliances with fetishized domestic dedication. They did so by symbolically complicating and materially simplifying food.

Boxed cake mixes would be used, but the final confection must be frosted and candy studded into an expression of feminine artistry. Vegetables could come out of a can or freezer, but only if decoratively served in potato chip cups, swimming in a cream soup sauce, or brightened by canned pimento strips. Even when cutting corners, the cook of the house had to make her meal appear to have taken time. Promoting ready-made ethics, distinct gender roles, and celebratory postwar affluence, fifties cookbooks steeped modern cooking and eating in a complex of social and commercial expectations.

Early fifties cookbooks most represent these culinary-intellectual trends. Classic cookbooks, such as Irma Rombauer's 1951 *Joy of Cooking*, attempted to balance a conventional home cooking approach with "quick 'n' easy" recipes. This attitude changed when Irma's daughter, Marion Rombauer Becker, took charge in the late 1950s; she seemed unconvinced that expedience and old-time cooking could be reconciled. Preferring chefs who "spend the small additional time required to make food wholesome and delicious," Rombauer Becker disdainfully dismissed the "group of cooks—if they can be dignified by that title"—who "followed the gray-flannelled pied-pipers who offered TV dinners, an infinity of packaged mixes, and frozen pie-in-the-sky."[16] Later in the early 1960s, Julia Child and Craig Claiborne would chime in against America's artless cooking with high-minded admiration for foreign foodways, particularly French haute cuisine.

Marion Rombauer Becker's sardonic disapproval of processed foods anticipated the counterculture's cooking defection. Where most consumers saw wealth and progress in pantries brimming with quickie inventions, countercultural natural foods cooks—forgetting the lean decades that contextualized unbridled postwar excess—saw absence of nutrition, quality, ecological awareness, and soul. Eating overprocessed foods seemed tantamount to swallowing modern alienation. Conversely, the smells, tastes, and creation of whole foods conferred authenticity and oppositionality on the cook and the eater, according to natural foods champions.

They did not arrive at their mistrust of the postwar meat, Minute Rice, and Duncan Hines diet independently. Scientific studies on the relationship between high serum cholesterol and cardiac illness seemed to prove the dangers of indulgent fifties delicacies like *The Encyclopedic Cookbook*'s "Savory Ham Pie," described as "flaky cheese biscuits float[ing] atop rich gravy in a savory ham pie fit for a king."[17] The Department of Nutrition at the Harvard School of Health, the Rockefeller Institute, and U.S. Public Health Service studies verified increasing rates of arteriosclerosis among the nation's meat-eating men and the connection between heart attacks and Americans' high serum cholesterol diet.[18]

Throughout the 1950s and into the early 1960s, nuclear testing stirred another nutritional worry: food purity. With radioactive fallout discovered in rainwater in Chicago in 1955 and rising levels of strontium 90 detected in milk samples taken by the Consumers Union in 1958, civil disquiet over food safety intensified.[19] Rachel Carson's 1962 *Silent Spring* concentrated this unease. Both the excretions of Cold War weaponry and consumer modernization seemed responsible for a poisonous waste stream that flowed straight into the environment and American kitchens and bodies.

Raised within the potent postwar brew of anxiety, abundance, and commercial hype and reaching adulthood in a countercultural climate, Laurel Robertson, Mollie Katzen, and others pursued natural foods cooking for self-protection and cultural emancipation. Published by small, independent presses, their cookbooks took critical stances on meat eating, processed foods, and the overconsumption and convenience codes backing fifties food culture. The cookbooks of the incipient natural foods movement express the shared principles and utopian fervor of a largely white middle and upper class who decided that their eating and shopping mattered. These books detailed recipes for a new world—serving up social prescription and cooking instructions on the same page.

The moralizations of whole foods explorers percolated into mainstream consciousness, making homemade meals both the cause (when neglected) and the cure (when upheld) for various social ills, including obesity, adolescent rebellion, divorce, ecological deterioration, and more. They aestheticized and politicized private life, placing the home under the microscope of national appraisal. As sensation workbooks—of touch, taste, and smell—loaded with cultural and political directives, natural foods cookbooks elevated nature and natural ingredients to talismanic heights. Establishment food advertisers recognized the emblematic might and versatility of natural foods and from-scratch cooking and spun both back out into the marketplace, creating a circuit of consumer and manufacturer food sacralization.

REVIVING THE HEARTH IN LAUREL'S KITCHEN

The connection of female domesticity to national welfare is a standing trope in America's gendered history. From Republican motherhood to the fifties "feminine mystique," wifely and motherly ardor has been portrayed as women's patriotic, economic, or cultural duty. In the late nineteenth and twentieth centuries, the nontraditional New Woman, the flapper iconoclast, and the Great Depression and World War II working woman tested gender custom. These alternate designs attempted to defy, if not defeat, social housekeeping and obligatory motherhood.

Interestingly, at the end of the restless 1960s, when second wave feminists loudly petitioned against women's homebound invisibility, the authors of *Laurel's Kitchen* reinvested the kitchen and mother with moral and countercultural significance. Following nineteenth-century temperance activist

FIGURE 3. Contented hippie homemaking as depicted in *Laurel's Kitchen*. From Laurel's Kitchen, © 1984; reprinted by permission of The Blue Mountain Center of Meditation, P.O. Box 256, Tomales, CA 94971. For more information about The Blue Mountain Center of Meditation and Eknath Easwaran, its founder, please visit its website at www.bmcm.org.

Frances Willard's edict to "make the whole world homelike," Carol Flinders, Laurel Robertson, and Bronwen Godfrey utilized natural foods in their version of *true* homemaking.[20]

The authors of *Laurel's Kitchen* first met at a 1967 antiwar organizing meeting. Although Flinders recalls feeling an allegiance to San Francisco's radicalism, she had not found "something that would draw out the resources, the obscure strengths that I could feel percolating away locked inside me."[21] After joining a meditation group, she began to reflect on America's consumption treadmill. Meditation helped her to see her family's entanglement in commercialized food, which steered eating and cooking away from its "original all-important function . . . to nourish the body."[22]

Flinders took baby steps by replacing sugar, "the wicked white granules," with more "natural" sweeteners and by swapping out frozen and canned vegetables with fresh.[23] *Diet for a Small Planet* convinced Flinders that meat had to go too. Describing the social benefits of a vegetable diet, she wrote, "If significant numbers of people like us would change their eating habits, adequate protein could conceivably be put within the reach of everyone in the world, for a fraction of the cost of meat. What a privilege to be able to give such a gift." Vegetarianism exempted her family from hormone- and pesticide-fed mass meat and from inflationary seventies supermarket prices. Her meditation teacher's vegetarian diet sealed the deal. As this mentor and his eastern spirituality influenced her family's life, Flinders and her husband agreed, "Our experimentation was over. We were vegetarians for life."[24]

Flinders's natural foods interests developed further when she ran into Laurel Robertson at Berkeley's Organic Foods Co-op. She knew little about the co-op when she first arrived but loved the store's look and feel. "Everything was beautiful: earthen-colored and completely free of cellophane wrappers, alluringly tactile," she gushed.[25] For Flinders, the co-op's noncommercial straightforwardness and food-in-the-raw displays represented a moral and sensuous alternative to the supermarket hard sell.

After confessing her natural foods ignorance, Flinders was guided by Laurel Robertson through the co-op ropes—teaching her the difference between kefir and yogurt and "ogling" calimyrna figs and dried pineapples along the way.[26] This meeting led to many others, as Flinders, Robertson, and, eventually, Bronwen Godfrey fine-tuned their natural foods cooking skills and cookery books together.

Flinders saw Robertson as *the* prototype of countercultural womanhood. Carol Flinders, and women from similar white, middle-class backgrounds, felt that materialist hype had contaminated motherhood and housewifery. To break thorough the mainstream's excessive femininity, second wave feminists strove to overturn gender maxims. On feminism's radical end, where the Bloodroot Collective, authors of *The Political Palate*, stood, this meant obliterating heterosexual monogamous coupling. In the more liberal middle, it meant elevating women's public work and political empowerment over, or at least equal to, motherhood and housewifery. In the introduction to *Laurel's Kitchen*, Flinders disclosed that, although she could not admire the domesticity of her mother's generation, she worried about the feminist attack on homemaking and the nuclear family. Even though housekeeping had been commercially twisted, it had purposeful and emotionally fulfilling functions, from her accounting.

For Flinders, who seemed culturally unmoored and perpetually seeking, Laurel Robertson's motherly serenity exemplified instinctual natural living. Her directedness shone through in their first encounters at peace rallies, but Flinders believed her friend truly settled into her skin after she married. Commenting on this transformation, Flinders mused, "She looked radiant—one of those women, I was sure, who doesn't completely come into her own until she has someone to take care of."[27] In a prime example of the lavishness that Flinders and other seventies nutritional aesthetes attached to natural foods, Flinders breathlessly reviewed Robertson's lunch box preparations for her husband: "I saw the sandwiches: thick slices of dark rye around an egg salad sparked with sweet red peppers and parsley, so thick she had to cut the bread in half before assembling the finished product . . . A fragrant barley soup with translucent pieces of zucchini, celery, and mushrooms went into a wide-mouthed thermos carefully preheated with boiling water, and a tiny packet of grated cheese went in alongside to be sprinkled on top of the soup. She rinsed lettuce and cherry tomatoes and put them in a plastic container with a tiny bottle of herb dressing, then got out a cantaloupe and cut it in half in perfect zigzags, scooped out the seeds, and packed one of the halves with cottage cheese and a sprinkling of toasted sunflower seeds."[28] Added to this hefty load were two thermoses (one coffee, the other hot malted milk), a deftly scored orange (to help him fight off a cold), and homemade protein bars (to boost his weight) consisting of "milk powder, honey, wheat germ, ground sesame and sunflower seeds, soy powder, dates and carob."[29] The meticulous zeal of Robertson's homemaking entranced the far less expert Flinders. In overheated descriptions like this, natural foods writers initiated a fetishization of food, cooking, and particularly whole ingredients that every natural cooking book would imitate.

Natural foods campaigners also romanticized any period or culture that preceded the tuna casserole, TV tray 1950s. Seventies cultural explorers who were settling down and starting families (or communes) invoked traditionalism in home canning, steer plowing, baking from scratch, peasant attire, and with gender orthodoxy. Premodern nostalgia spurred Flinders to envy Robertson for her handed-down cooking culture, gained as a child at the knee of her "Pennsylvania Dutch grandma," a culinary history that Flinders lacked.

Since the 1960s, those concerned about American eating have blamed mass production and, often, women's careerism for obliterating cooking and food know-how. Flinders evoked this sideways antifeminism as she effused over Robertson's wifely acumen. Laurel Robertson, she observed, wielded "strong intuitive powers" in the kitchen—powers trained to sustaining her family's well-being with delicious and nutritious vegetarian cuisine. Longing for this kind of homemaking ease, Flinders turned to Robertson to learn the craft.[30] Her initiation began with whole grain baking by hand.

The industrial white bread loaf was sixties rebels' arch foe. Social critic Lewis Mumford, in the 1962 essay "The Human Prospect," described white bread as a "devitalized foam-rubber loaf, laden with additives and substitutes, mechanically sliced for built-in staleness that boasts of never being touched by human hand."[31] Contrarily, according to Crescent Dragonwagon in *The Commune Cookbook* (1972), "Baking a loaf of brown bread in this society [was] revolutionary."[32] Laurel Robertson agreed and believed that Carol Flinders's natural foods baptism could begin only when she started baking bread.[33] This turn of events resulted in a lengthy chapter on bread making in *Laurel's Kitchen* and in their second cookbook, *The Laurel's Kitchen Bread Book* (1984).

As they did with other natural ingredients, countercultural cooks made whole grains a golden calf. Backing Lappé's protein complementarity, whole grains inspired "Zucchini Oat-Flake Loaf," "Potato Carrot Kugel," and even the whole wheat pastry dough of "Banana Cheese Pie," in Robertson, Flinders, and Godfrey's first book.[34] By the time they published their second cookbook in 1984, their fidelity to whole grains had ripened to a "balmy reverence" for "the precision with which unrefined cereal grains reflect actual human nutritional needs."[35]

As Robertson and Flinders became part of California's emerging spiritual movement (moving to the Blue Mountain Center of Meditation in rural Northern California by 1986), they soaked whole grains in cosmic significance. Flinders suggested this connection in the *Bread Book* as she wondered whether whole grains' completeness might be a "sure, small sign of some larger benevolence hidden deep behind the appearance of things."[36] Her starry-eyed description of unhulled cereals echoed a nature spiritualization present in the New Age and environmental movements and in cultural/nature feminism. From the perspective of *Laurel's Kitchen*, left to its own devices, divine nature produced flawless nutriments. Processing wasted the healthfulness contained within the whole barley, wheat, or rice grain.

Echoing gender essentialism implied in the spiritual vein of seventies feminism, Laurel Robertson believed that teaching Flinders breadmaking reconnected them both to an "ancient art" that "is in our very bones for it seems to be something we somehow remember rather than have to learn."[37] A certain innate woman's wisdom surfaced as they became more expert. This wisdom, she argued, disappeared once machines started making bread. Diminished to quaint nostalgia and tagged as unhip and unmodern, from-scratch cooking and the housewife's nobility had also gone missing.

Robertson's baking lessons helped Flinders settle more deeply and seriously into what she believed to be her womanly role. Her untapped talents, neglected in earlier activism and searching, bloomed, as bread baking required intelligence and invention. Flinders's new avocation also transformed her family, she observed. When a loaf was in the oven, everyone stayed at home. Her baking acted as "a strong counterforce" to outside distractions that typically separated the modern family. This intimacy mimicked traditional societies, she argued, where "everyone took part in producing and everyone knew he or she was needed."[38] Her son, Ramesh (notice the Hindu name), kneaded or mixed dough and, meanwhile, gained a new appreciation for the kitchen as "a place where unquestionably important things go on and where everyone has a contribution to make."[39] Flinders wouldn't have to lecture her son to respect women and reject sexism, because he experienced the significance of women and their work firsthand. He might even become a bread baker himself, she opined.

Carol Flinders's idolization of domesticity connotes a noteworthy difference between the cookbooks in the first half of the twentieth century and those from the seventies natural foods movement. As part of the countercultural overhaul of American norms, the most popular natural food cookbooks show men as welcome and present in the kitchen, chatting, advising, helping out, if they chose. In woodblock illustrations in *Laurel's Kitchen* and *Laurel's Bread Book*, kids, cats, dogs, men, and women crowd the kitchen—a beehive of home production and sociality. Even though *Laurel's Kitchen* explicitly recommended housewifery over women's other options, Flinders and Robertson mention their husbands frequently, not simply as spouses to please but also as partners and pals.

The sixties/seventies cultural Left, on the whole, had not committed to gender equality. In fact, sexism ran as rampantly through the counterculture and the New Left as it did through "straight" society.[40] However, there was at least a stated "movement" goal to rethink divisive dualisms such as male versus female, love versus hate, nature versus culture. The open partnerships portrayed in *Laurel's Kitchen* approached this goal at the family scale.[41]

Obviously, for Robertson and other countercultural women cooks, encouraging male presence in the kitchen was not meant to destabilize traditional gender roles; it just better integrated the family. Men participated in women's cooking and childrearing, and women listened and counseled husbands in their career trials and tribulations. Despite *Laurel's Kitchen*'s cheerful woodblocks depicting coequal parent-partners—listening intently to one another or cooking side by side—this upgrade implied an imbalance of possibility. Men were invited into customarily feminine spaces, but women were discouraged from seeking entrance into the conventionally male work world.

Robertson and her co-kitchen innovators asserted, with a dose of sex-role naturalism, that their unmodern food production struck at the very heart of corporate capitalism. Baking their own bread and cooking whole foods for their families and neighbors, they believed that they were making "revolution from the bottom," similar to Gandhi's anticolonialist battle against England. In the authors' retelling, Gandhi's movement asserted "authentic self-rule," by boycotting British goods and depending on the indigenous Indian cotton-spinning industry, ending India's dependence on modern production and British goods.[42]

With women's hands picking, pouring, stirring, kneading, and slicing the "Sour Corn-Rye" bread, "Vegetable Bean Noodle Bake," and "High Protein Granola" for their families' now wholesome and anticorporate diets, they would foment radical transformation, they predicted. "The crucial point where [women's] efforts will count the most, is not in business or professions, which tackle life's problems from above, from outside, but in the home and community, where problems start," they argued.[43] Applying the ripple affect theory of change held by other natural foods idealists, Robertson, Flinders, and Godfrey opined that as more families converted to vegetarianism and whole foods cooking, the demand for meat and mass-produced foods would decline and more equitable worldwide food distribution would follow. Rejecting both partisan politics and mass protest, the authors of *Laurel's Kitchen* returned to a time-tested American tradition of maternal uplift.

EATING FEMINIST AT BLOODROOT RESTAURANT

As adversaries of patriarchy, the women of the Bloodroot Collective celebrated liberated womanhood in their cookbooks and at their Bridgeport, Connecticut, restaurant, Bloodroot. Like Laurel Robertson and her friends, the collective lionized women's traditional skills and ancient wisdom, positing in their cookbooks that worldwide patriarchy crushed premodern, earth-loving matriarchies. Trapped within this misogynistic culture, the only viable choice was divorce from the mainstream. As member Noel Furie explained, "Separatism was a big deal when we started Bloodroot, and that was to give us the space to grow and to flap our wings and to learn who we are."[44] In 1977, with the help of a down payment loan from the parents of restaurant founder, Selma Miriam, the collective created a safe and expressive space for all women, but specifically for lesbians who suffered under homophobia *and* sexism.

Forever the outsiders, and proud of it, such countercultural operations as co-ops and lesbian feminist restaurants avoided confrontation with the conventional food system. The ideological constancy of their cuisine and their businesses became their revolt. This righteous separatism played a part in solidifying a conceptual and consumer divide between conventional and alternative eaters. The importance of countercultural operations to the natural foods movement's longevity cannot be understated.

Vegetarian Feminism at Bloodroot Restaurant

Communal ownership and operation seemed a natural choice to Bloodroot restaurant's founders—Selma Miriam, Noel Giordano (later Noel Furie), Samn Stockwell, Betsy Beaven, and Pat Shea. Group stewardship, they believed, starkly counterbalanced the heterosexist, androcentric mainstream. Moreover, their unconventional structure released the collective from the combative rat race, a work world, they noted, that hardly invited or encouraged women's full participation anyway.

Reiterating the counterculture's critical review of the modern labor/leisure dyad, the Bloodroot Collective wrote: "We have all learned to separate our lives into divisions/fragments: work during week in order to be able to play during weekend; work to earn leisure; work to earn money to buy things that are supposed to make us happy. Living for the real in the present means giving up the plastic world we're used to."[45] Instead, the collective built a supportive reserve for themselves and other lesbian feminists to explore and incorporate their own gynophilic culture of music, literature, mythology, and spirituality into their daily lives—and, of course, to serve and enjoy a vegetarian, seasonal menu.

To broaden feminist vegetarianism beyond the restaurant, their cookbooks offered a detailed accounting of the politics that stirred the collective. Chock-full of quotes from notable and unknown women and multicultural recipes, these cookery manuals surpassed what the collective believed to be patriarchal America's homogenized/commercial cuisine. The food world they presented venerated "real" American women and their distinct culinary histories. "Collard Greens, Black-Eyed Peas and Corn Bread" paid homage to black women's cooking; "Fassoulada" celebrated Hope Zachariades, Selma Miriam's former Greek neighbor; and the "Kasha Platter" doled out a mélange of Jewish delicacies with vegetarian renovations.[46]

In a formulation embraced by the cultural and political Left in the 1960s and 1970s, the collective concluded that ethnic cultures that produced these foods, while often materially deprived, had vegetable-rich gastronomic legacies. With ethnic recipes and foods, the collective inserted itself and its cookbook readers into the putatively more female-centered and unadulterated "spiritual" cultures of less privileged women. Adopting the ecological and culinary good sense of these "poor" women not only "honor[ed]" them but also grounded their feminism in practical applications, the collective concluded.[47]

For Bloodroot's restauranteurs, vegetarianism was feminist for several reasons. Duplicating the gender orthodoxy of *Laurel's Kitchen*, they surmised that seasonal vegetarianism reestablished all women's inborn, but devalued, connection to the earth. With "Harvest Vegetable Platter" in late autumn, to replace the traditional Thanksgiving turkey feast; "Dandelion Salad" in early spring; and "Beach Plum soup" in the later summer, the Bloodroot Collective retuned eating with the cycles of the earth, rather than the mainstream food world's profit motive.[48] A lunar seasonal calendar ordered the recipes in *The Political Palate*. Jewish or Christian holiday foods, which the collective deemed as antiwoman, were not included. An apple and cream dessert, "Witches Froth," would ring in the pagan and woman-honoring holiday of Halloween. In December, when the world outside engaged in "the obscenity of noise and false jollity" of Christmas and New Year's, the Bloodroot Collective enjoyed a hot bowl of "Hupi Pollivka," a traditional Slavic mushroom soup for winter solstice.[49]

The collective applied a simple moralistic dualism in its judgment of meat eating versus vegetarian societies. Carnivorous peoples constructed what Carol Adams, author of *The Sexual Politics of Meat: A Feminist-Vegetarian Critical Theory* (1990), referred to as the "Blood Culture."[50] Vegetarian societies, from the collective's perspective, "celebrate a model of the wonder of life—in its cycles of growth and decay, blossom and seed, wherein death and life appear as transformations of a single superordinated, indestructible force . . . harvest instead of violence, harmony with slow change of seasons rather than territoriality."[51] This Manichaean review of food and human history increasingly shaped Bloodroot's menu and writing; its first cookbook rejected all flesh-based recipes except for a few fish dishes. By *The Second Seasonal Political Palate* in 1984, even fish was off the table as the collective purified its commitment to "other species and the survival of the earth . . . Those who wanted fish would have to go elsewhere."[52]

Like other seventies experimentalists, the Bloodroot Collective was less concerned with the direction that the outside world took than with its perseverance. As Noel Furie explained, in the restaurant's first decades, she felt surrounded by patriarchy. Only at Bloodroot, in its "subculture within the larger culture," could she "escape."[53] By 1984, with its radical vegetarian feminism well developed, the collective bent neither to market forces that made flesh-based dishes profitable nor to what was perceived as meat-eating feminists' failings. With a network of trusted regional vegetable and food purveyors, along with a few national natural foods producers, the collective remained fairly free of contact with the mass food system.

The collective set itself apart not only from the carnivorous mainstream, but also from the alternative foods movement which it perceived as not socially conscious or resolutely feminist enough. The health discourse, bringing more adherents into the natural foods fold in the 1980s and 1990s, struck the collective as, at the least, narcissistic and, at the worst, antiwoman and elitist. Commenting on the nation's new obsession with personal stress and health, it lamented that "no one seems to ask about stress suffered by poverty and starvation, by rape, by torture and murder, by the death of one's children, by twelve hours a day working on computer chips. 'Stress management' is a luxury of the privileged."[54]

Disturbed by customers' dietary rigidity, the collective returned, again, to the wisdom of "traditional" societies. "We assume," it wrote, "that foods people have eaten for many centuries are likely to continue to be nutritious and that foods lower down on the food chain are less likely to contain concentrations of pollutants."[55] The health and physical fitness fads of the early 1980s manipulated women, convincing them to hate their natural shapes and sizes, "an especially oppressive masochism expected of women in recent years."[56]

The Bloodroot Collective's food choices decreed its radical lesbian feminist values. Ethical vegetarianism established a bright line between its restaurant, bookstore, cookbooks, and selves and what was thought of as a meat-eating patriarchy outside. It reassociated eating with seasonality, reinvigorating the agricultural and cooking knowledge of ethnic women. It pushed the collective to rely on local farmers and ecological food producers, because "the sterile world of pre-packaged supermarkets" rarely stocked quality, season-appropriate vegetables.[57] Finally, ethical vegetarianism distinguished the collective's food choices from less politically astute natural foodists, who also rebelled against mainstream foods but whose health and weight monitoring diluted their diet's critical edge.

More than the other natural foods cookbooks, *The Political Palate*, *The Second Seasonal Political Palate*, *The Perennial Political Palate* (1993), and *The Best of the Bloodroot, Volumes I and II* (2007) described eating and living as wholly apart from conventional America. For this reason, most of the other natural foods cookbook authors covered in this book had broader readership. However, the collective had a large enough following to win *New York Times* restaurant and book reviews and to keep its doors open into the twenty-first century.

Betsy Beaven, Noel Furie, Selma Miriam, and Pat Shea devoted every moment of their lives to a feminist space. As the Bloodroot Collective wrote, "We live our work and work our lives. Our rewards are daily because we live what we believe."[58] At a local level, the collective sustained a business and an intimate community that actualized radical lesbian feminism. Things became more difficult when the collective tried to affect the larger patriarchal order and expand the feminist utopia beyond the restaurant's doors. Noel Furie pondered the difficulties of influencing American society in an interview with *Off Our Backs*: "I'm aware that in this women's structure, whatever I say is put on the table and it's looked at by peers, judged by peers, gone over by peers, and so I get a sense of myself within this community. It's very different than the sense of oneself out in the community."[59] Nevertheless, at the turn of the twenty-first century, the collective's food—its seasonal, local, and animal rights standpoint—became the axis around which a more widespread and commercially sophisticated ethical eating discourse began to turn.

FIGURE 4. Collectivists Noel Furie, Selma Miriam, and Pat Shea pose in front of Bloodroot Restaurant's self-serve counter. *Photo by Robert Giard; Copyright © Estate of Robert Giard.*

COUNTERCULTURAL CONNOISSEURSHIP

All natural foods cookbooks shared *The Political Palate*'s aim of right-minded living, but each interpreted this obligation differently. For Mollie Katzen, author of *Moosewood Cookbook*, and Anna Thomas, *The Vegetarian Epicure*, the pleasure and fulfillment of cooking first-rate vegetarian dishes was the ultimate objective. These women believed American cuisine most lacked quality ingredients and respect for "at-home" cooking, not feminist consciousness or family-sustaining values, although they would be unequivocally sympathetic to and occasionally make reference to those mores.

Laurel's Kitchen's and *The Political Palate*'s narratives read as, first, dogmatic and, second, gastronomic. The exact opposite applied to Katzen's *Moosewood Cookbook* (1977) and *Enchanted Broccoli Forest* (1983) and Thomas's *Vegetarian Epicure* (1972) and *Vegetarian Epicure: Book Two* (1978). More precisely, their gastronomy was their ideology. They shared, with other natural foods cooks, an enthusiasm for self-expression, in lives lived as close to one's honest talents as possible, and an antipathy toward the commoditized food stream. But Katzen and Thomas were not cutting themselves off from conventional society or renovating gender norms or the nuclear family, at least not directly. Elite consumers and national food marketers found Katzen's and Thomas's whole ingredient and stovetop sensualism irresistible. Their natural foods refinement foreshadowed and aided farm-to-table, artisanal connoisseurship at the beginning of the twenty-first century.

Vegetable Love

Mollie Katzen concluded *The Enchanted Broccoli Forest* with the following thoughts: "If more people can feel welcome in the world of careful, expressive and healthful (not to mention, delicious) food preparation, we won't need to turn to junk food out of lack of information about anywhere else to go. We will have someplace wonderful to go, and we can all discover ourselves as artists on the way there."[60] If this could be done alongside Middle America, and possibly seep into suburbia, all the better. If not, no problem. Perhaps Katzen's and Thomas's status as artists—Katzen, a painter, illustrator, and pianist; Thomas, a documentary filmmaker—helps account for their nondoctrinal points-of-view. They already believed a good and rich life necessarily included aesthetic delight and that human existence would improve dramatically if everyone followed a creative calling.

Instinctively individualistic, Katzen and Thomas narrowed their agenda more than that in *The Political Palate* and *Laurel's Kitchen*. They would teach others to make tasty, visually pleasing dishes. They would create a real substitute cuisine for those dissatisfied with the standard American diet and the convenience ideology that inspired it. Natural food values would not disappear; instead, they would be slipped into alternative culinary cultivation.

The necessity of personal expression comes through loudly in the most commercially successful natural foods cookbook of this period, Mollie Katzen's *Moosewood Cookbook*.[61] Katzen's wariness of the counterculture, from her first engagements with it at the Moosewood Restaurant, may explain the book's marketability. In 2002, she considered her dilemma with the Moosewood Restaurant, which she began with her brother and five other people in the early 1970s: "I was always in conflict with the counterculture, and I never fit into a collective. My heart was in the idea of sharing, but I found that a creative impulse was best. And that's a very autocratic impulse, which is not about sharing."[62]

While she may not have realized this defining personality trait in the days when she lived, ate, and breathed the Moosewood Restaurant, her cookbook—supposedly reflecting the food labor of the founding group of owners—was clearly her baby. The restaurant's creators and origins get a nod in the preface, but the cookbook's main protagonists are Katzen's art and recipes. The hand lettering and illustrations, along with the witty stories introducing each section and recipe, come from Katzen's imagination. Moreover, her presentation of natural foods cooking as a fun, exciting, and decidedly *not* an overly serious event shines through as counterpoint to natural foodist somberness.

Moosewood, while containing natural recipe standards—vegetable soups, marinated salads, stir fries, and casseroles—nudged the reader to be inventive, to put an original stamp on this cuisine. Katzen made flexibility and improvisation her cooking style's dictum. In the conclusion to *The Enchanted Broccoli Forest*, Katzen prodded her readers to mess with the rules: "There is always something new to say in any expressive medium. Sure, many cookbooks have been written. Paintings are painted, and poetry is composed; people keep finding new ideas to express and new ways to re-express the

Cauliflower Marranca

If grain is pre-cooked:
1 hour to prepare,
including baking

5-6 servings

1 lb mushrooms, sliced .... sauté in butter
1 large onion, chopped   with juice of 1 lemon

1 large head cauliflower, ... sauté with 3 cloves
         in flower pieces   crushed garlic, basil,
                                salt and pepper

3 cups cooked brown rice or millet ... salted,
                                       buttered.

2½ cups grated cheese of your choice

Combine Everything.

Bake, covered, ½ hour at 350°.

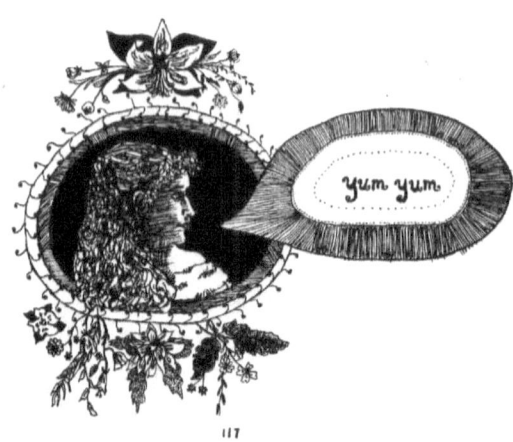

FIGURE 5. Mollie Katzen's inimitable artistic imprint on *Moosewood Cookbook* (1977). *Courtesy of Penguin Random House, LLC.*

timeless ones. Cooking can be a very personal statement, whether you follow a recipe or vary it, or invent your own altogether."[63]

Katzen poked fun at the pretentiousness of natural foods. On her readers' behalf she questioned the "accumulation of mystique surrounding" soufflés, exclaiming: "I would like to deflate this mystique (without deflating the Soufflé), and to encourage all mortal beings to understand just how the making of This Thing can be accessible to us." She also debunked the embroidering of French foods, such as quiche, describing it as an easily constructed "staple" of "the humble provincial kitchens of its native France."[64]

When venturing into unfamiliar and, for many folks, unappealing foodstuffs like the natural foods idol, tofu, Katzen humorously coaxed her readers: "So what is this stuff called Tofu? (Are you afraid to ask, because it seems that Everyone Else Knows and they think you aren't cool?)" As a friendly Sherpa, she explained why soybean curd was the answer to everyone's protein-substitute prayers with recipes for tofu sukiyaki and tofu, spinach, and walnut loaf. She even devoted a section to "Tofu for Children," drolly listing the things that children might rather do with tofu than eat it, such as "squeezing it until it oozed out between their fingers ... throwing it on the floor and stepping on it [and] chasing it around their plate with a spoon."[65]

Her trust in a reader's wisdom and basic skills distinguished Katzen's books from both mainstream cookbooks' exacting instructions and natural foods authors' vegetarian evangelism. She accepted that the quality of the ingredients and her palpable enthusiasm for an ecologically friendly, plant-based diet would incite her readers' creative impulses.

Like *Laurel's Kitchen*'s authors, Katzen tried to enchant readers back to the stove. She sharply contrasted the "minute rice, Campbell's soups, Velveeta cheese" integral to her mother's everyday meal preparation with the yeasty, rich challah she baked every Friday for Shabbatt. On those days, Katzen "was enthralled, and would come in from wherever [she] was playing just in time to help her braid it."[66] Katzen's *Moosewood Cookbook* depicted women's workaday kitchen compromises that got food on the table in the 1950s and 1960s as inauthentic and thoughtless. Her mother's home-baked challah, on the other hand, exuded realness and handed-down wisdom.

Mollie Katzen would never forthrightly assert that preserving her baking skill was the most radical contribution that she could make to society, as *Laurel's Kitchen* lectured. She didn't seem interested in home-bound housewifery. Her cooking, not her family, was *her* art. She was blithe and witty on "movement" self-seriousness. She took a laissez-faire attitude toward the foods and practices given the greatest political measure by natural advocates. On handmade bread she wrote: "It is difficult to talk about bread-baking without lapsing into sentimentality. One is tempted to go on and on about how exhilarated and connected to the universe one feels, about how the kitchen atmosphere acquires sublime soulfulness, about how born-again breadmakers are magical, charismatic individuals . . . etc. However it is not my place to promise you a transformed existence. What I offer you is one with more bread recipes in it. The rest is what you make of it."[67]

Like others in her class and age cohort, Katzen took to the instantaneous gratification of quality consumption and self-expression through shopping, cooking, and eating naturally. Her pleasurably bendable vegetarianism proved far more open to commercial commodification than the moral high-handedness of *Laurel's Kitchen* and *The Political Palate*. Indeed, *Moosewood Cookbook* is the only text in the natural foods collection that holds a position on the *New York Times* top ten best-selling cookbooks in American history, alongside such greats as *The Joy of Cooking* and *Betty Crocker's Picture Cookbook*.[68]

A countercultural hankering for holism and credibility stirred Katzen's critical appraisal of ordinary food. But for her, although nothing was wrong with indulgence or materialism, something was wrong with the premade lifestyles sponsored by General Mills, Duncan Hines, and Swanson frozen foods. This natural foods vision was a far cry from the hippie communalism of the Moosewood Restaurant in the early 1970s, perhaps explaining her split from Moosewood five years after it opened.

If Katzen's adjustable cooking standards detached natural foods from sixties movement defiance or feminist stridency, Anna Thomas's culinary arts floated even further away. In the introduction to *The Vegetarian Epicure* (1972), Thomas wrote, "This book is about joy, not pollution. I hope that even if you are still in the habit of eating meat and fish, you will try some of the different ways and means of cooking suggested here. You might find yourself gradually and happily seduced."[69] In an interview with Robert Ebert in 1996, Thomas remembered: "What I saw were cookbooks about vegetarianism. I didn't want to write about any kind of 'ism.' There's no percentage in trying to tell anyone how to eat. Everybody finds their own way. Live and let live. But you can offer them delightful choices."[70] Putting natural food thinking and politics before taste, according to Thomas and her gourmet followers, resulted in inelegant bowls of mushy brown rice coated with murky bean slop.

Thomas instead made quality a morality, using vegetarianism to draw cultural and class boundaries between natural foods aesthetes and both the uncultivated masses and hippie polemicists. In the natural foods movement's early stages, with its zealous people's food of bean sprouts and lentil loaves, gourmet snobbery was unthinkable. But Thomas, along with other chefs—such as Chez Panisse's Alice Waters and Jeremiah Tower—tried to dignify the movement and its fare with old-fashioned European gentility. It would take time, but by the second decade of the twenty-first century natural foods ingredients and idealism would be defining characteristics of bourgeois epicureanism, in part owing to the foundation Thomas and Katzen laid in the 1970s.

NATURAL FOODS STYLE

Born in Germany to Polish parents who moved to the United States in her infancy, Anna Thomas's family prized serving home-cooked delicacies to friends and family. In a move replicated by many young Americans in the 1970s, Thomas reclaimed her familial heritage from the erasure of post–World War II conformity. By cooking and socializing in the European tradition, she fashioned, what she believed to be, a more grand cuisine than that in popular magazines and hippie kitchens.

Thomas's first cooking book oozed Eurocentrism. Recipes appeared as part of multicoursed meals, including all the requisite features of French cuisine: an aperitif and hors d'oeuvre starter, main course, salad course, desserts, coffee, and a postprandial fruit and nut or cheese plate. Readers were told to consider how each course and dish would complete the other, how "hot and cold set each other off, as do heavy and light, mellow and piquant, and colors play on the senses all the while."[71]

Her first two cookbooks resound with culinary anti-Americanism. Listing the ingredients for "Pizza Rustica," Thomas commented, "This is not a pizza you're likely to find in this country: it is an *Italian* pizza." Nothing this good could be found in North American, she implied. Discussing cheeses, Thomas instructed, "Try to know more about [cheese], for there's a good chance, if you grew up in the average American household, that you have barely made its acquaintance," having only come in contact with "horrifying" supermarket "assortments" of "spreads," "processed cheeses" and "cheese foods." In an uncensored moment, Thomas confessed her outright disdain for what was her own country's standard fare: "The sad truth is that America has never really developed a cuisine of her own." She believed that there was, luckily, a "gastronomical movement" under way that would "abandon the often foul and always tedious world of 'convenience' preparations and return to the enjoyment of natural foods."[72]

Each chapter and recipe in both books of *The Vegetarian Epicure* told the tale of Thomas's fabulous parties. Reading her cookbooks is like peeking in the windows of the most popular house on the block. The one with the hippest people traipsing in at cocktail hour and out in the morning. The one with alluring scents wafting out of a kitchen where a beautiful (Roger Ebert described Thomas as a Greta Garbo look-alike) and talented filmmaker-chef holds court. For Thomas, this enviable lifestyle founded on her thoughtful vegetarian cooking could replace the "rigidly standardized" American culture and the nation's diet with its "lack of imagination."[73]

By the late 1970s, Thomas's deep longings for indigenous gastronomic contact could not be sated by her European connections. All the vegetarian cookbooks of this period searched outside the United States for innovative recipes and ingredients, but only Thomas packed up and left. As a bohemian bon vivant, she became apprentice and anthropologist, digging into the cafes, tapas bars, beer halls of Europe and the Middle East, and Mexican cantinas. This immersion course, which she recapped in *The Vegetarian Epicure Book Two* (1978), affirmed her estrangement from American food and solidified her epicurean internationalism. Tucked inside of Thomas's (and mainstream gourmets') admiration for foreign cuisine was an exoticization of "premodern" peoples and cultures.

In Spain, she sang the praises of the paseo, an evening social stroll where "school girls, linked arm-in-arm, merchants and office clerks, mothers pushing prams and whole families come out to take in the air" and to enjoy the abundant tapas in bars along the way.[74] In Italy, she got "caught up in the spirit of people who have a talent for enjoying whatever life happens to throw their way, who take everything seriously enough to do it well but nothing so seriously that they get stuffy about it." The "exuberantly flavored tomato sauces" on Neapolitan pizzas, the wild mushroom gnocchi in Bologna, the "scrumptious tiny roasted eggplants" on the antipasto table of a Florence trattoria substantiated their culinary virtuosity. Italians did not lament the unreliability

FIGURE 6. Countercultural vegetarian merriment as depicted in *The Vegetarian Epicure* (1972). Courtesy of Penguin Random House, LLC.

of their trains, Thomas enviously decided, because "the opera and the cappuccino were unsurpassed."[75] Finally, in Mexico and the Indian restaurants of England, wearing primitivist goggles, Thomas surveyed two foreign cultures purportedly grounded in ancient ritual and mythos. According to Thomas's interpretation, Mexicans ate tortillas because in the Mayan origin myth, the *Popol Vuh*, corn and man spiritually fused when the gods decided to mold man out of corn. The religious association between Mesoamericans and the god world dawned on her one morning at the breakfast table of family friends in central Mexico. Watching the family cook, "the quiet Indian Nacha, patting out perfect little circles of corn masa with deft flicks of her hand," Thomas dreamily wondered whether "maybe people were made of corn."[76]

When considering the Indian curries she devoured in London, Thomas began by celebrating India's pre-Christian roots. Indians, who had a thriving culture well before "the onslaught of Western Civilization," held cooking in the "highest esteem," even making curry preparation "close to a religious rite," she decided.[77] India and Mexico lacked the aristocratic lilt of France and Spain, but they had something of equal or greater worth to this globetrotting aesthete and others like her. They were frozen in time (at least from her recounting), bound by ritual, sheltered from modernity and its secular and shallow food ways. Where were the origin myths behind the American cuisine? Where were the religious intonations of Campbell's soup and Kraft macaroni and cheese? she implied.

Returning from abroad, Thomas became a loyalist to real ingredients and expert preparation. Her Indian-spiced dal had to include homemade ghee and hand-blended curry powder. Tortillas should be made from masa harina as she had seen the servant, Nacha, use in Mexico. Italian pasta would have to be cooked al dente rather than committing the American blunder of boiling noodles to a pulp. Commenting on America's bastardization of oldworld foodstuffs like parmesan cheese, Thomas sniffed, "That gritty business in the plastic container is hardly more than a thief of its name." Presented with this affront, she instructed, "Walk out of the supermarket where [processed cheeses] commonly cohabit with poor imitations of noble lineages and search out a cheese shop, a good delicatessen, or one of the ethnic groceries or specialties stores."[78] Others joined Thomas's quest for a gourmet alternative. In the 1960s and 1970s, Julia Child's *Mastering the Art of French Cooking* (1961), James Beard's *American Cookery* (1972), and periodicals such as *Bon Appétit*, first issued in 1975, and *International Review of Food and Wine*, first issued in 1978, formed the outlines for an American haute cuisine. Although an elite concern with what Alice Waters described as "formality and beauty and deliberation" framed Thomas's cooking practice, in the seventies, *The Vegetarian Epicure* stood apart from the culinary aristocracy of Child and Beard.[79]

Natural foods dishes, such as "Soybean Croquettes," "Herbed Soybean Casserole," and such whole grain fare as kasha, positioned Thomas's cooking with the natural foods movement (and ecological protein complementarity) rather than Julia Child's goose-liver pâté.[80] And references to marijuana smoking, as an appetite enhancer before dinner and relaxant afterward, correlated her more with the counterculture than with James Beard blue bloods. Hippie style faded in her second cookbook, when the élan of Europe spoke to Thomas more than groovy sixties subculture. Nevertheless, her two cookbooks, while less bellicose than *The Political Palate* or *Laurel's Kitchen*, negatively assessed American food not only for its lack of style but also for its reinforcement of modernity, efficiency, convenience, mechanization, and conformity. For her middle- and upper-class followers, who for aesthetic reasons did not really identify with the "Lentil Nut Loaf" of *Laurel's Kitchen*, and for egalitarian reasons shunned *Gourmet*'s beef wellington regality, Thomas's nomadic, cross-cultural cuisine presented a fresher, hip option, not of self-deprivation, but of vegetarian natural foods suavity which had lasting effect on America's cooking culture.

ZEN AND THE ART OF NATURAL FOODS COOKING

Ed Brown, author of *The Tassajara Bread Book* (1970) and *Tassajara Cooking* (1973), may have been drawn to natural foods and vegetarianism for some of the same reasons as were Katzen and Thomas. He valued skillfully rendered foods, yet Zen Buddhism grounded his cooking practice. After the heightened anticipations of the early sixties "movement," the political disappointments and shocking assassinations of the late 1960s, the economic unraveling of the 1970s (and, later, conservative backlash against liberalism and radicalism in the 1980s), Brown's accepting and pliable Buddhist philosophy granted readers immediate transcendence from the decade's disappointment and detente with consumer America.

Brown combined his Buddhist and cooking commitments when he accepted the head cook position at northern California's Tassajara Zen Mountain Center in 1967. His books were spiritual manuals as much as cooking texts. Thus Brown joined a popular literary genre—which included such books as Robert Pirsig's *Zen and the Art of Motorcycle Maintenance* (1974) and Eugen Herrigel in *Zen in the Art of Archery* (1953)—that used everyday practice to hone awareness.

As in all Zen Buddhist observance, Brown's cooking elevated process over product. "The way to be a cook is to cook," Brown advised on *Tassajara Cooking*'s first page. "Our cooking doesn't have to prove how wonderful or talented we are . . . Just feed, satisfy, nourish. Enter each activity thoroughly, freshly, vitally. SPLASH!" To explain cooking as Buddhist ritual, Brown's *Tassajara* books devoted inordinate space to the tools and technique of the trade. His first book reserved six pages to precisely detailed instruction on

FIGURE 7. Ed Brown at Green Gulch Zen Farm, 1973. *From* Tassajara Cooking *by Edward Espe Brown, copyright © 1973 by the Zen Center, San Francisco. Reprinted by arrangement with The Permissions Company, Inc., on behalf of Shambhala Publications Inc., Boulder, Colorado, www.shambhala.com.*

types of knives, cutting methods, and knife care. Throughout the vegetable section, illustrated directions showed cutting options. Commenting on this precision, Brown wrote, "Given the opportunity, hands can see quite well for themselves, so the eyes needn't be involved."[81] Brown's meditative observance of details suggested an antidote to the impulsive disregard that natural foodists felt typified ordinary American eating—and living, for that matter.

Thoughtful utensil care received top billing in the Brown cookbooks. Concluding *Tassajara Cooking*, he compared the relationship between the chef and his or her tools to the caring interplay between "good friends." To be a good friend to the knives, "clean and replace them in the knife rack after use." To be good friends with the counter, "wipe it after use and scrub sometimes."[82] In each case, the success of food preparation depended on a chef's respectful relationship with tools. Interestingly, like Katzen and Thomas, Brown's role as absolute expert is downplayed in both books, implying Buddhist reserve, but also signifying agreement with the countercultural "do-your-own-thing" credo. In regard to the role of recipes, Brown advised radical autonomy. "A recipe doesn't belong to anyone. Given to me, I give it to you. Only a guide, only a skeletal framework."[83] After that, Brown alluded, the individual must engage cooking, serve the results, and pass lessons on.

Tassajara's simple recipes encouraged readers' exploration of the minimalism apparent in Buddhist art and practice of bonsai trees and Japanese rock gardens. Horticultural historian Peg Streep suggests that the simplicity of the Zen garden helps the observer to "set aside conventional ways of discursive understanding to invite realization."[84] Brown's recipes replicated this austerity by introducing a vegetable and then identifying cutting styles and cooking variations. In the case of celery, recipes followed for "Orange Celery Salad," which called for three stalks of celery, two oranges, one apple, and salt, or "Quick Fry Celery," which called for oil and salt and then instructed, "Slice celery and stir-fry until tender. Sprinkle on some soy sauce if you like and so forth."[85]

Brown's unadorned ethos appealed to culture critics who believed America was drowning in its own feckless excess. His bread book's introduction proposed stark bread consciousness: "Mix some flour with enough water to form a dough, a touch of salt perhaps; shape it, bake it, the result is bread in its simplest, most fundamental form. Everything else is extra: yeast, milk, oil, sweetening, eggs. Extra to make bread more palatable, more 'civilized,' more chewable and sliceable." Careful attendance to fundamentals was a Zen sacrament; "the extras" he wrote, "only detract from the primitive simplicity of grain-tasting unyeasted bread."[86] First master the elemental components of bread before venturing off into complicated versions and manipulations, Brown advised.

Even when it came to rotten vegetables, Brown saw the plant's inner potential. Cook the yellowed greens and throw them in a soup, he advised. Cut off the slimy parts of a zucchini and mash the rest into stewed beans. "If part of a bean is moldy," he persuaded, "the other sections are nonetheless still good and they'll be sad if you don't make use of them." With honest concentration and modesty, a chef could transform even the most unappealing of foods into something enjoyable, bringing out their natural goodness. For this Buddhist monk, whole foods, minimally altered by man, contained "the germ of life."[87] And maybe, Brown intimated in his *Tassajara* books, they even reflected the transcendent.

Zen Buddhism's stripped-down aesthetic resounded with young and alienated Americans who adopted Eastern mysticism in the 1960s and 1970s. Buddhism countered counterfeit values that drove consumer culture, according to its adopters. With meditation, and perhaps, like Brown, a monastic life, an individual could quiet misspent cravings in the present, without necessarily battling or changing the existing (and disappointing) social structure. The job of the Buddhist was to find the divine in the mundane and to learn to accept the multiple facets of being. Precision cutting, careful attention to tool use and preservation, and mindful vegetarian cooking could break through the materialist illusion, tapping into deeper truths. Or so Brown's cookbooks seemed to suggest.

Like other popular Zen texts, the *Tassajara* cookbooks took neither an optimistic nor a pessimistic stance on the health, economic, and political issues stimulating other natural foods cookbook writers. Brown identified whole grains as necessary for bread baking but then concluded, "Don't let a lack of whole grain products keep you from making bread. Most of the recipes can be made with regular white flour, if necessary." Ingredients seemed less crucial to Brown than immersion in cooking and appreciative delight in the final product. Even when he betrayed his biases, discussing the lamentable lack of natural, whole foods "strikingly unavailable and/or outrageously expensive at most supermarkets," a screed on free market capitalism did not follow.[88] Just do what you can. That was his mantra. Some things are good, some things are bad, but everything has some use. Applying the fourth noble truth of

Buddhism—the Middle Path, which warns against extremes in behavior and expectation—Brown accepted all edibles, processed and natural.[89]

Despite Brown's studied impartiality, he had lasting influence on America's cooking and eating habits. In 1979, after his Tassajara sojourn, he created the nationally acclaimed Greens Restaurant in San Francisco with noteworthy chef Deborah Madison (in consultation with Chez Panisse's Alice Waters). Madison and Brown coauthored *The Greens Cookbook* in 1987. In the early 1980s, Brown became head resident-teacher at Green Gulch Farm, a Zen retreat and communal farm in Mill Valley, California. Green Gulch supplied most of the organic vegetables for Greens and other fashionable restaurants in the Bay Area. The self-effacing Buddhist monk, who used natural foods for Zen discipline at Tassajara in the 1970s, assisted the development of the organic/local vegetarian cookery that spread nationwide in the 1980s and 1990s as California cuisine.

Brown's Buddhist cooking philosophy and vegetarianism did not bar mainstream success. In his 1997 cookbook, *Tomato Blessings and Radish Teachings*, he unapologetically explained, "Zen in America is not like Zen anywhere else in the world."[90] Developing a mindful approach to cooking and eating in himself and his students was Brown's only intention for his cookery books, kitchen, and culinary arts classes. If restaurant success and celebrity followed from this Zen practice, so be it. More people had come in contact with the entirety of his Buddhist worldview after he left the Tassajara cloister. And more people might solemnly consider the source of the food on their plate and make the "right" decisions from this knowledge. In the end though, Brown's worldly natural foods philosophy primarily influenced a certain class of Americans—the affluent, who could afford to dine at Greens, buy organic produce, and eat quality vegetarian foods.

Always inclined to transcendence, Brown seemed unperturbed by the class implications of the natural foods movement of which he was a part. In the spirit of Buddhist humility, he concluded the *Tassajara Bread Book* with the following thoughts: "I was head cook of Tassajara for three summers and two winters, until being completely devoured, bones cast aside, I was finally exhausted of food. Now I build stone walls, which is really not such heavy work after all."[91] Brown's Middle Path—some would call it resignation, others peaceful acceptance, still others enlightenment—appealed to a wide audience. When Brown and his fellow "natural foods" authors forged their culturally formative cookbooks, their generation's faith in America's prevailing social and political systems was on the ropes. Yet, in each successive decade after the 1970s, even the ecological and political alternative that Frances Moore Lappé's vegetarianism promised in Diet for a Small Planet seemed to be losing ground to America's accelerating per capita meat consumption. Since these food writers supposed that big change could start in the kitchen, their commitment to the vegetarian, whole foods movement hardly diminished in the late 1970s to early 1980s when the nation's political temperament moved to the center-right.

IDEAL COOKING AND ALTERNATIVE IDENTITIES IN THE NEW CENTURY

In the decades after the first flurry of vegetarian cookbook activity, American food underwent a flush of innovation. In the conspicuously consuming 1980s, a class of moneyed urban professionals slurped down fine French wine and Japanese sushi, forming what sociologists Josee Johnston and Shyon Baumann describe as an elite "omnivorous" food discourse that valued refinement and worldliness.[92] Natural foods enthusiasts continued to cook up boggy tofu stews through the 1980s, but in hippie (or ex-hippie) obscurity. Yet as the century turned, organic, local, and seasonal reappeared, now as a much more pervasive requirement of upper-class consumption and mass aspiration. The natural foods trendsetters surveyed in this chapter remained active in the food world through this period of change. Their later publications and careers indicate this vanguard's persistent identification as resisters and seekers, even as their cooking convictions became common vernacular.

By 1993, *Laurel's Kitchen* had sold over one million copies. Later cookbooks, *The New Laurel's Kitchen* (1986) and *Laurel's Kitchen Recipes* (1993), expanded and revised the *Laurel's Kitchen* formula—whole vegetarian cooking with an emphasis on nutrition and production by hand. *Laurel's Kitchen Caring: Recipes for Everyday Home Caregiving* (1997) was Robertson, Flinders, and Godfrey's last joint cookbook. Robertson had been working on *Kitchen Caring* when, unexpectedly, Carol Flinders was in a car accident. This personal incident alone did not inspire the new book's focus, but it certainly gave Flinders a reference point for her introduction on the connection between healing, the home, and food. Like other aging boomers, Robertson and Flinders had acted as home nurses or had needed care. With an already established philosophy of healthful living through whole foods and vegetarian eating, they simply expanded this flexible philosophy to their new circumstances.

Their concentration on caregiving also reflected a fin de siècle captivation with wellness, especially among the comfortable classes. These Americans were watching their bodies carefully and investing in everything from middle-of-the-road allopathic-homeopathic combinations to more radical colonics, iridology, Reiki, and alchemy. In a 2007 National Institutes of Health survey, 38 percent of adult Americans had used complementary or alternative medicine (CAM) of one kind or another.[93] For the middle and upper classes, as well as skeptics from all ranks, holistic providers freed them from the "corrupted" medical system, while simultaneously maintaining the care that they expected. Devoted CAM consumers needed intellect, fortitude, and a discerning purchasing eye to monitor and manage their bodies. The holistic framework of *Laurel's Kitchen Caring* folded food into the alternative healing paradigm, making natural edibles, along with medicinal herbs, part of the self-care protocol.

Kitchen Caring also indicated Robertson's and Flinders's participation in another arm of the New Age: the syncretic spirituality that germinated in sixties California and extended throughout the United States in the last decades of the twentieth century. In 1976, when Flinders, Robertson, and Bronwen Godfrey published their first cookery book, they practiced meditation with Eknath Easwaran. Easwaran came to the United States in the 1950s, creating the Blue Mountain Center for Meditation in Berkeley in 1960. In 1970, both Flinders and Robertson moved to Easwaran's ashram in Petaluma, California. Thereafter, spirituality seeped into their cookbooks, informing their vegetarianism, their homemaking, and their simple living.

Flinders, the introductory voice in the *Laurel's Kitchen* cookbooks, later wrote several book on feminism and spirituality, including *Enduring Grace: Living Portraits of Seven Women Mystics* (1993) and *At the Root of This Longing: Reconciling a Spiritual Hunger and a Feminist Thirst* (1998). In a 1999 interview in La Leche League's periodical *New Beginnings*, she clarified her comprehension of the interconnections of feminism, spirituality, and homemaking: "Our homes are holy places and in our work as mothers we have the opportunity to sanctify the everyday." She further noted that "keeping a home or kitchen is not an end in itself, but is useful in terms of bringing about full human unfolding."[94] Spiritualizing the home and the homemaker-cook, Flinders and Robertson seemed to have resolved, for themselves and their fans, the tension between liberated womanhood and gender traditionalism. Indeed, *Laurel's Kitchen*'s home-front revolution resurfaced in such new-century motherly manuals as Shannon Hayes's *Radical Homemakers: Reclaiming Domesticity from a Consumer Culture* (2010) and Raleigh Briggs's "natural housekeeping" handbook, *Make Your Place: Affordable, Sustainable Nesting Skills* (2009). Yet, within the feminist movement writ large, mystified motherhood and femininity remained hotly debated, regarded by some as undermining women's full equality and assisting cycles of antifeminist backlash, a critical perspective to which the Bloodroot Collective remained dedicated.

Bloodroot Restaurant doors remained open in the new century, though with only two original collective members, Selma Miriam and Noel Furie, in the kitchen. In 1993, when Betsy Beaven was still involved, they published their third cookbook, *The Perennial Political Palate*. Always self-consciously on the food ethics cutting edge, the collective's *The Perennial Political Palate*, as well as *The Best of the Bloodroot, Volumes One and Two* (2007), contained mostly vegan recipes. By that time, the remaining collective members eschewed almost all animal products and were quite incensed that others had not gone vegan. After thinking through the interdependence of speciesism, racism, and sexism, they had seen the light. Following their lifelong outsider dispositions, they argued that veganism pronounced their radical feminism much more explicitly than the depoliticized "healthy" vegetarianism popular in the 1990s and 2000s.

As far as its general influence on American life, the Bloodroot Collective purposefully rejected advertising or any other capitalist marketing from the start. Cookbooks were self-published, and although articles by collective members, on topics ranging from breast cancer to herbal gardening, appeared in various books and publications, Bloodroot's separation from the patriarchal mainstream, and sometimes from the not-exclusively feminist progressive Left, has limited its reach into the larger society. The collective would have it no other way; any other path would dilute members' feminist rationale. That being said, new generations of young women (and sometime men) have come to work and eat at Bloodroot Restaurant and have refreshed and updated the animal rights, feminist food politics which the collective created. "Many customers come into our restaurant assuming we are a health place. I know our food is healthy, but we are not interested in the latest health fads. We are animal rights vegetarians, and our intention and pleasure is to prepare and eat delicious diverse meals that change every season, and to share them with our friends,"[95] founder Selma Miriam wrote in 2012 on her blog, *selmaslist*. Ever the firebrand, Miriam insisted on Bloodroot's ethical distinctiveness in the new vegetarian landscape.[96]

Unlike Miriam, Anna Thomas's measure of American food modified and softened with age. After publishing *The Vegetarian Epicure Book Two* in 1978, Thomas disappeared from the natural foods scene. With the book's proceeds, she made her master's thesis film: *The Haunting of M*. In 1983, she and her husband, filmmaker Gregory Nava, cowrote and coproduced the critically acclaimed film *El Norte*. After *El Norte*, she remained in the film industry, her most well-known work being *My Family, Mi Familia* in 1995.

In 1996, she reappeared with *The New Vegetarian Epicure*. Much like her seventies cookery manuals, she organized *The New Vegetarian Epicure* around parties and seasonal gatherings. Thomas's epicurean template stood the test of time with just a few concessions to healthy eating rules in the 1990s. In *The New Vegetarian Epicure* she minimized, if not completely eliminated, the cheese- and cream-infused dishes of the first *Vegetarian Epicure*. On the reduction in fat in her present-day cooking, she wrote, "The first *Vegetarian Epicure*, and its sequel, captured the Geist of a certain time—it was a guilt-free era, when butter and cream were used without a care and when cheese ruled. Today of course our attitudes are different. And I say thank goodness."[97]

The biting sarcasm that she hurled at American cheese, bread, and culture in the 1970s dropped from her newer cookbook. Commenting on the U.S. food scene, she wrote, "As a country, too, we've grown more sophisticated about cooking. Ingredients that were unheard of twenty years ago are now common on supermarket shelves, and farmers' markets are sprouting up everywhere ... American food is not just healthier but infinitely more interesting and varied than it was when I first started to cook."[98] Finally, she seemed to imply, America had caught up to her standards—a change that her vegetarian cookbooks had no small part in making happen.

Like Katzen, Thomas seemed to want to sever her cooking story from its seventies origins. In the introduction to her 1996 cookbook, in interviews, and on her webpage, there were no references to the countercultural milieu from which her vegetarianism and cookbooks issued. It is as though her vegetarianism sprang from her own good sense, not as a response to a specific

American moment. If she had written several cookbooks between 1978 and 1996, then it would not have appeared odd to omit the social context for her seventies vegetarian conversion. Yet, with *The New Vegetarian Epicure* representing her journey from the 1970s to the 1990s, twenty years of living and cooking, it seems amnesiac to not ruminate on the origins of her once-unorthodox vegetarianism.

In part, this erasure can be explained by Thomas's wariness of the countercultural revolt. She agreed with sixties dissenters' estimation of American culture and food as bland, boring, and uninspired, but she never bought into the anticapitalist current that bore communes, natural foods co-ops, and other separatist organizations of the 1970s. Moreover, the barefoot, back-to-nature hippie was not her image of the "new American." Like many countrymen and women before and after, Thomas's grudge against America was a very typically upper-class discomfort with the nation's gracelessness. She recommended a "turn to vegetarianism" in her first cookbook for reasons of "enlightened self-interest," not for international nutritional equality, feminism, or even spiritual fulfillment.[99]

Her Eurocentric epicureanism certainly divorced her from the Spam and Jello 1950s and 1960s, but at the turn of the twenty-first century it did not. Her vegetarianism excluded her from the gourmet circles of James Beard in the 1970s. But by April 2003, she was serving Julia Child "Spring Pea Soup" and "Grand Marnier Chocolate Cake" at a luncheon of "a few friends joined by common interests in food and writing."[100] As gastronomy renovated supermarkets and vegetarianism remodeled upper-echelon eating, the United States had become everything that Thomas longed for in her breakout seventies cooking book.

In the introduction to the 1972 *Vegetarian Epicure*, Thomas clarified her views on gourmet eating: "My idea of a fine meal is one in which a fine vintage wine will be happy. That is not to say that this is a necessary test: vegetarian eating is much too various to be thus measured. But cooking and eating (and drinking) my way through this book in that epicurean spirit, I found the possibilities of vegetarian cuisine inexhaustible."[101] This definition remained true for Thomas; what had changed was that many more Americans, as well as the commercial food apparatus, joined the party.

Many more Americans had also become converts to a California culinary inventiveness since the first *Tassajara* cooking books. "Doing the very best we could do with French recipes and California ingredients" with one "unbreakable rule ... the freshest and finest ingredients ... the best of the region," is how Alice Waters delineated "California cuisine" in her 1982 cookbook, *Chez Panisse Menu Cookbook*.[102] Ed Brown joined Waters, Deborah Madison, Thomas Keller, Annie Somerville, and other Bay Area chefs to steer the nation's food future with their American adaptation of French nouvelle cuisine.[103]

Brown contributed to another cultural phenomenon: the spiritual movement, often referred to as the New Age. Brown would not comfortably define himself as New Age. He was a committed and practicing Buddhist well before this movement, which tends to coalesce all religions into "spirituality." Nevertheless, certain components of his life and published works associated with this eclectic confederacy of seekers. In the 1970s, Brown's cookbooks asserted that Buddhist awareness could be sharpened by banal bread baking and vegetable cutting. In the 1990s, his *Tomato Blessings and Radish Teachings* (1997) further defined this doctrine but paid much less attention to food making and more to the spirituality of cooking. The structure of *Tomato Blessings*, with a biographical vignette introducing a list of related recipes, was common to other popular New Age books that used personal experience—everything from quilting to woodworking—to elaborate spiritual points.[104] By the end of the twentieth century, the middle and upper classes journeyed to spiritual retreats, practiced Hindu-inflected Yoga and Buddhist meditation, and read treatises, like Brown's, available in every major bookstore's spirituality sections, in droves. For those who longed to fill their lives with deeper significance, New Age spirituality and California cuisine seemed to provide daily affirmation of the metaphysical purpose of their existence. In fact, the two often intertwined.

This commercialized spirituality is manifested in a publicity web article for a California-based organic produce company, Earthbound Farm, entitled "Zen and the Art of Doing Good Works: Earthbound Farm Helps Zen Center One Scenic Step at a Time." Choosing Ed Brown as the featured speaker for their "Chef Walks" series (and contributing some of the proceeds to the Monterey Bay Zen Center), the advertisement positioned the farm as concordant with the progressive mores held in esteem by its customers. Brown's placement as featured chef spiritualized organic consumption. "Life can be very delicious when we take the time to savor a moment of our experience: sunlight, earth, plants, sights, sounds, smells. All the flavors of experience: sweet, sour, salty, bitter, and pungent. Let's join the feast!" Brown ruminated in the ad's copy.[105]

After reading this advertisement, customers who attended this special cooking class, or even those who just bought the company's products, could imagine that each time they put Earthbound's organic romaine or asparagus in their grocery basket, they maintained their own health, sustained organic farming, helped progressive causes, such as the Monterey Zen Center, and, finally, made contact with Zen Buddhist wisdom. A gratifying and heady mixture of politics, spiritual purpose, and healthism was all wrapped up in the simple deeds of purchasing a head of lettuce or attending a weekend cooking class.

Mollie Katzen, too, continued to shape the U.S. eating scene. Indeed, she did so more than any in the countercultural cookbook cohort. Her books are—hands down—the most commercially successful. She is the most prolific, with twelve publications as of 2016. Her *Vegetable Heaven* received the 1997 International Cookbook Review's Best Cookbook of the Year and was a Julia Child's Cookbook Awards finalist. *Health Magazine* named Katzen—alongside Deborah Madison, Julia Child, Alice Waters, and Martha Stewart—as one of the women "who taught a generation how to turn American cooking into enlightened cuisine." Magazines have described her as everything from "a living legend" to a "visionary" to a "beloved mentor."[106] In 1995, she became the star of her own show on PBS, *Mollie Katzen's Cooking Show*. And in 1999, she opened a website featuring weekly recipes, a gallery of her artwork, and various Katzen books and gifts (posters, cards, calendars, magnets, and aprons).

Katzen's cookbooks, sometimes leading, sometimes following, reflect the eating changes of the middle and upper classes, which have constituted a culinary historical bloc since the 1970s. When the rebelling cultural elite felt estranged from the superprocessed food of its youth, Katzen's *Moosewood* delivered virtuoso vegetarian cooking with ethnic intonations. When butterfat and cholesterol became anathema in the health conscious 1980s and 1990s, Katzen's second editions of *Moosewood* and *The Enchanted Broccoli Forest*, as well as *Still Life with Menu* (1988), provided reduced-fat and cholesterol-free recipes. At the turn of the twenty-first century, as a charter member of the Harvard School of Public Health and Nutrition Roundtable, Katzen led in the period's scientization of health and food. Her diet book, *Eat, Drink, and*

Weigh Less: A Flexible and Delicious Way to Shrink Your Waist without Going Hungry (2005), is just that, a diet book, implicating her and her scientist collaborator, Harvard dietician Dr. Harvey Willet, in the era's valorization of the thin body and health as the paramount personal endeavor.

In her most recent book, *The Heart of the Plate: Vegetarian Recipes for a New Generation* (2013), Katzen once again stood her ground as a counterculinary leader. With millennial food revolutionaries resurrecting a Frances Moore Lappé-esque global justice and animal rights food politics, Katzen's *Heart of the Plate* lightened things up. In a webcast *Talks at Google*, Katzen explained her revived frustration with self-identified vegetarians: "In the forty years in which I've been writing cookbooks, I have found the word vegetarian is always about meat, as in keep it away . . . it has nothing to do with vegetables." Exasperated, Katzen wished that vegetarians just loved vegetables, rather than hating meat. "My definition of vegetarianism," she impatiently sighed, "has nothing to do with meat expect for the fact that in my perfect world when we are all done putting as much beautiful plant food on this reconfigured plate as we want, there isn't much room for anything else . . . I want vegetarian to become an adjective that describes the food on the plate and not a noun that identifies the person eating the food."[107]

Poof! With one fell swoop Katzen unfastened herself and the word "vegetarian" from the ecoglobal responsibility that defined (most of) the countercultural food revolt. In the new-century cognoscente, of which she is a part, vegetable connoisseurship (with a sotto voce nod to animal rights and ecological consciousness) trumped everything. Meat wasn't off the table, just belly-busting Burger King debauchery or pumped-up factory-farm chicken breasts. Always the weather vane, Katzen's politically enigmatic vegetable adoration hit the right cultural notes of the moment. It also indicated the distance vegetarianism, as a practice and a principle, had come.

WITHER THE NEW WORLD?

The vegetarian dissent that seventies cookbook authors recommended never undermined the clout of the capitalist "technocracy" against which they rebelled, as Warren Belasco has persuasively argued.[108] Except for the Bloodroot Collective, most of these cooking innovators just wanted a different flavor of consumerism—a shrewder food and market culture. Their vegetarianism, especially in Anna Thomas's case, was based on some pretty vague ethics (at least Katzen mentioned *Diet for a Small Planet* in *Moosewood*). Thus, rather than weakening commercial capitalism, they handed food producers and advertisers a brand-new buyer: the ecologically watchful, status-striving, organically gastronomic, health-obsessed moneyed patron.

Carrying considerable economic and cultural clout, seventies natural foods cooks and movement leaders initiated an orbit of publications, organizations, and businesses parallel to the conventional food stream. Dining at Alice Waters's Chez Panisse in Berkeley or sitting down to a seasonal farm-to-field supper put on by a local CSA; enjoying Ben and Jerry's ice cream or Earthbound Farm's organic carrots; going to an acupuncturist or a holistic health center: they incubated a lateral world where their daily consumer choices matched up with their spiritual, political, and cultural principles. Mainstream producers replied to this demand substantively with ecological edibles, as well as superficially with organic come-ons. By the late 1990s, organic goods could be found on most grocery store shelves, and by the new century two-thirds of surveyed Americans claimed to buy supermarket organics at least occasionally—a testament to the mainstream food system's successful rejoinder to the counterculture's epicurean coup.[109] As cultural historian Michele Lamont suggests, the elite "frame other people's lives in countless ways." The seepage of the organic and natural cooking imperative into mainstream households certainly confirms this supposition.[110]

CHAPTER 3

"ORGANIC STYLE"
Rodale Press and Mass-Mediated Organics

Distributed nationally, countercultural cookbooks increased attention to natural foods beyond that of neighborhood food co-ops. While not formally coordinated, co-ops and cookbooks created the architecture for a cultural movement—with political and economic implications—devoted to the consumption and distribution of natural foods.

Rodale Press, of Emmaus, Pennsylvania, was another important medium for the proliferation of natural foods ideology. Founded by Jerome Irving (J. I.) Rodale, in May 1942 Rodale Press published the first magazine devoted to compost-fertilized agriculture, *Organic Farming and Gardening*. With little interest shown from what Rodale hoped to be the magazine's target readers—farmers—he renamed it *Organic Gardening and Farming* to entice wartime gardeners. In 1979, the magazine was changed to *Organic Gardening*, which it has remained since.[1] *New York Times* columnist Wade Greene, in a 1971 profile of J. I. Rodale, described early *Organic Gardening and Farming* readers as "a hard core of cranky, generally conservative and often foreign-born gardeners."[2] Throughout the 1940s and 1950s, this small but steady faction of older, middle-class subscribers read Rodale's dense, journal-like publication, with articles from "Hints for the Victory Garden" (September 1944) to "Are Chemical Fertilizers Factors for Undermining Our Health?" (March 1943). To expand its audience, Rodale's *Prevention*—first published in 1950—circulated information on diet and health, the medical establishment, pollution, exercise, and preventive protocols.

During Rodale Press's first two decades in business, *Organic Gardening* and *Prevention* pounded away at postwar science, technology, and the food manufacturing industry, even as the majority of Americans seemed to accept these innovations. After Depression-era and World War II deprivation, chemical agriculture and processed foods had made the United States the best-fed nation on the earth, by popular account. While limited, Rodale's devout audience indicates a discordant current rippling beneath postwar America's celebratory exterior. With newsreels reporting on Hiroshima's flesh-eating consequences and generalized atomic anxiety, Cold War Americans confronted a new sense of bodily defenselessness that distinguished their health concerns from earlier food safety panics.

In a 1954 *Bulletin of Atomic Scientists* article, physicist Ralph Capp disclosed the terrifying transformation that atomic weaponry and its poisonous waste posed. Fallout, he wrote, "cannot be felt and possesses all the terror of the unknown. It is something which evokes revulsion and helplessness like a bubonic plague."[3] Yet, unlike the plague, a biological force exacerbated by man-made conditions, human beings let the atomic threat loose. Nuclear weaponry's apocalyptic capacity destabilized America's sense of its mortality, installing what historian Robert Crawford describes as a psychosocial state of "somatic vulnerability."[4] In a 1957 *Dissent* article, "The White Negro: Superficial Reflections on the Hipster," Norman Mailer described the deep consequences of America's thermonuclear turn: "For the first time in civilized history, perhaps for the first time in all history, we have been forced to live with the suppressed knowledge that the smallest facets of our personality or the most minor projections of our ideas or indeed the absence of ideas and the absence of personality could mean equally well that we might still be doomed to die as a cipher in some vast statistical operation in which our teeth would be counted and our hair would be saved, but our death itself would be unknown, unhonored, and unremarked, a death which could not follow with dignity as a possible consequence to serious action we had chosen, but rather a death by a *deus ex machina* in a gas chamber or a radioactive city."[5]

In the early Cold War, some citizens managed existential dread by following the government's cue—dutifully building backyard bomb shelters and participating in civil defense drills. When these protective measures were later revealed as useless and misleading, atomic angst turned into disillusionment with the private and public institutions implicated in nuclear weapons and chemicals proliferation. Many youth who came of age in this worrisome period found the establishment's duplicity unforgivable.

Disquiet over industrial and military poisons, alongside a mounting mistrust of the government-corporate coupling, triggered the defensive turn to natural foods and chemical-free farming. The organic label, even more than the "natural" moniker, became for many the truest alternative to mainstream processed goods. Untainted by chemicals, fertilized with manure from free-roaming farm animals, nurtured by sunshine, crop rotation, hand and hoe weeding, and beneficial bugs, organic farming glaringly rebutted agribusiness's monocrop, mechanized, chemical methods. Health food stores' imperfect produce affirmed the "natural" inimitability of organic items, especially compared with supermarket vegetables' uniformity.

From the 1940s forward, organic, denoting a type of production and consumption, has served as a malleable container for the consumer cravings and the social viewpoints of middle- and upper-class customers across the political spectrum. Organic shopping has connoted alliance with environmentally sound agriculture; holistic alternatives; decentralized, humanized economics; animal rights; principled consumption; and self-determination. Rodale publications helped connect this pliant organic idiom to the natural foods movement. Although J. I. and Robert Rodale used their notoriety to advocate for national farm policy and to lead agricultural experimentation, in their magazines, three generations of Rodales primarily pitched organic products for personal improvement and health defense. This individualistic consumer outlook was capacious enough to speak across the Rodales' and their readers' differing political persuasions, from J. I.'s conservative populism to Robert's libertarian radicalism, to, finally, Maria's new century green lifestyle. While the Rodales never had complete message control—farmers, agricultural organizations, and shoppers contributed to the meaning and direction of organics—from the 1940s to the new millennium, in the popular imagination, Rodale equaled organic.

THE MAKING OF AN ORGANIC GURU

Rodale Press would have never become the foremost health, fitness, and organic publication company had Jerome Irving Rodale—born Jerome Cohen in 1898 to Polish-Jewish parents on Manhattan's Lower East Side—not always dreamed of writing. In 1930, J. I. and his brothers moved their electrical component company from Manhattan to rural Emmaus, Pennsylvania. Fortuitously, the World War II manufacturing boom made the Rodale brothers rich. As a result, J. I. had the freedom to scratch his writing itch and to follow his new love of nature. "I came under a new influence," he reflected in his autobiography, "living more in the open, thinking more about nature as it affects man."[6] With spare time and unbounded energy, J. I. took his share of Rodale Manufacturing's profits and funneled it into a magazine and book company that, over time, popularized organic farming and food and preventive health and fitness.

After his nature epiphany, Rodale began research on agriculture, which led him to British agronomist Sir Albert Howard. Howard, who worked for the imperial government of India, conducted numerous studies on native Indian cultivation practices, concluding that compost fertilized farming surpassed modern chemical agriculture. In his hallmark work, *An Agricultural Testament* (1943), Howard compared the practices of the "Occident" and the "Orient," asserting that Western farmers' enslavement to machines and chemicals provoked weak health, pest infestation, and soil erosion. "Mother earth has recorded her disapproval in disease in crops, animals, and mankind," Howard related.[7]

Rodale became a booster for chemical-free agriculture after reading Howard's glowing account of salubriousness at a New Zealand boy's school that served only compost-fertilized produce. Sickly since childhood, J. I. had experimented with sundry health regimens, from Bernarr Macfadden's physical fitness program during his adolescence to Swedish massage, chiropractic, and psychotherapy in his young adulthood. Howard's dietary disease theory proved irresistible to a man already prone to health gimmickry and instant cures.[8] Rodale reflected years later: "The impact on me was terrific! It changed my whole way of life. I decided that we must get a farm at once and raise as much of our family's food by the organic method as possible."[9] He promptly purchased a sixty-acre farm in Emmaus and began his first trials with manure-fertilized vegetable farming using his own and his family's bodies as organic laboratories. His "findings" became source material for books and *Organic Gardening* and *Prevention* editorials and articles.

In wartime and postwar America, organic agriculture had many enemies, from J. I.'s perspective. Prior to the Second World War, American farmers applied lead- and arsenic-based chemicals to their fields, but to minimal public notice, except when residues on produce caused the occasional seizure in a consumer.[10] Once the war ended, chemical farming escalated. From 1940 to 1971, synthetic fertilizer use increased tenfold, with DDT—the "atomic bomb of the insect world"—bolstering the reputation of petrochemicals. Popular magazines and scientific journals depicted DDT as the miracle solution to agricultural pests with none of the side effects of prewar arsenic- and lead-laced farming inputs.[11]

In the 1950s and 1960s, normal municipal governance included aerial insect management. The two largest pest control projects targeted gypsy moths in the Northeast and the southern fire ant.[12] Applied by planes, these toxic chemicals could conceivably waft into the homes, lawns, water, and ecosystems of the standard citizen with or without her/his knowledge or permission. In the nervous postwar climate, when Americans felt vulnerable to covert and overt communist attacks as well as internal bodily invasions by tasteless, odorless, radioactive bomb testing fallout, aerial pest control seemed one more menace from the sky.[13]

In his study of fifties pest control programs, Edmund Russell discovered that for many Americans, aerial spraying exemplified the powerlessness of the Cold War citizen against the ascendant military-industrial complex. Zoologist George J. Wallace, in a June 1959 *Readers Digest* article, worried less about rights infringement than what he believed to be the cataclysmic ramifications of massive sprayings: "If this and other pest-eradication programs are carried out as now projected," he wrote, "we shall have been witnesses, within a single decade, to a greater extermination of animal life than in all the previous years of man's history on earth."[14] This apocalyptic prediction displays the panicky, dystopic national temperament during the dawning years of the atomic and chemical ages.

Public outcry over inadvertent chemical and radiation exposure persisted, despite the mass media's buy-in to scientific modernity. In 1958, Congress responded to a vocal antichemical citizen cohort with the Delaney Amendment to the Food, Drug, and Cosmetic Act, stating: "No additive shall be deemed safe if it is found to induce cancer when ingested by man or animal." Yet, in the same year, the Food and Drug Administration (FDA) further sanctioned synthetic food processing by tacking 700 chemical additives to their "generally regarded as safe" (GRAS) list.[15]

J. I. Rodale's magazines; Adelle Davis's nutrition books, including *Let's Eat Right to Keep Fit* (1954); Gaylord Hauser's 1951 bestseller *Look Younger, Live Longer*; and Euell Gibbons's foraging guide, *Stalking the Wild Asparagus*

(1962), which argued for a foraged natural diet—all amassed a respectable following.[16] Nevertheless, from the 1950s to the 1970s, most American shoppers willingly purchased supermarket produce and instant products. They also swarmed the new and clearly not-natural fast-food restaurants such as McDonald's, which in 1958 sold its 100 millionth hamburger, and in 1959 opened its hundredth restaurant.[17]

The American Medical Association attempted to undermine "food faddists" with regular public warnings that health food diets caused "irreversible damage to health."[18] Meanwhile, federal food protection agencies countered public unease with industrialized foods by questioning causal links between diet and illness.

Despite these assurances, Rachel Carson's 1962 groundbreaking study, *Silent Spring*, on DDT's ecological consequences affirmed nascent agrochemical disquiet. Carson found that agricultural DDT runoff and pesticide spraying led to weak bird eggshell formation. She extrapolated her findings on the bird ecosystem to humans, warning that inadvertent pesticide ingestion, through air, water, and food pollution, likely had similarly detrimental influences on human health.[19] Moved by Carson's DDT polemic, President Kennedy instructed his Life Sciences Panel to create a federal pesticide policy. The committee's May 1963 report, "The Use of Pesticides," recommended reducing use of toxic chemicals.[20]

Food and chemical industries immediately began damage control. *Chemical Week*, an industry journal, blasted Carson, claiming that "the sweeping and sometimes unwarranted conclusions she draws will be seized upon by the extremists as vindication of their erroneous tenets." Placing organic farmers in company with what *Chemical Week* designated as "superstition-ridden illiterates," chemical agriculture's champions dismissed popular distaste for pesticides as Luddite irrationalism.[21] They employed this ad hominem strategy through the 1960s and 1970s, while organic food and agriculture gained firmer footing.

The industry-sponsored assault on antipesticide warriors and alternative agriculture did not deter J. I. or his son, Robert, who became president of Rodale Press in 1951. In fact, it motivated them to deconstruct justifications for artificial fertilizers and to confront agribusiness and compliant government agencies. J. I. Rodale was convinced that if the United States Department of Agriculture (USDA) conducted comparative studies of nonchemical and modern farming methods, natural fertilization would prove indubitably superior. Yet the USDA resisted. According to Rodale, "The men in the USDA keep plodding away in their habitual systemic routines, despite the fact that miraculous changes in the soil's capacity to hold the rain water are being wrought on farms run by the organic method."[22] Echoing Herbert Marcuse, William Whyte, and other fifties social commentators, Rodale worried that America's bureaucratization threatened conscientious individualism.[23]

Rodale disliked industrial and agricultural scientists, but he reserved special enmity for medical scientists, whom he attacked more regularly and vehemently than any other professional group. His displeasure with doctors, and particularly with the American Medical Association, stemmed from his fundamental aim: the "conservation of human health" through an organic diet.[24] From this base philosophy, he showed less interest in "saving the earth"—a concept borne from late sixties and early seventies ecological consciousness—than in preventive wellness through nonchemical food production and consumption.

With *Prevention's* 50,000 paid subscribers to its first issue and *Organic Gardening and Farming's* 60,000 readers in 1950, it would be a stretch to portray Rodale's postwar readership as confirmation of pervasive dissension beneath the exultant age of affluence.[25] Nevertheless, the nuclear disarmament activist organization, SANE, civil defense resisters, critical commentary on social conformity and the neotranscendental Beat literary group indicate that a noteworthy segment of Cold War citizens questioned the blessings of the American Century and its military-industrial-commercial culture.

Rodale, his magazines, and his fans can be seen as a health-focused protomovement—a precursor to the more expansive and ideologically complex natural foods movement that sprouted in the revolutionary loam of the 1960s and early 1970s. At the same time, although his magazines and books issued consistent disapproval of technology, science, and consumerism, a reactionary strain made his critiques more reformist than revolutionary. His viewpoint and tone in *Prevention* and *Organic Gardening* was, on the whole, culturally and politically conservative. Perhaps, Cold War McCarthyism forced Rodale to take a cautious editorial tone, which later he never revised. Or, perhaps, he was simply conforming to his rural Pennsylvania community's antiliberal tendencies. Either way, for Rodale, U.S. society was largely sound. Only bureaucratic lethargy and governmental acquiescence to corporate farming stood between America and the organic promise.

Rodale's circumscribed political imagination demonstrates the restrictions on social criticism and alternative thinking in the 1950s and early 1960s that the next generation set out to smash. At the same time, the details of J. I. Rodale's health idyll—harmoniously aligned with nature, modeled on primitive and ethnic lifeways, with a premium set on independence from the medical establishment through dietary self-health—marked continuity between his postwar manifesto, the countercultural food movement of the late 1960s and 1970s, and the holistic organic consumerism of the early twenty-first century.

J. I. Rodale's Organic Health

Youth malcontents in the 1960s and 1970s may have found Rodale's position on technology a bit fuzzy. In a 1950 *Prevention* editorial Rodale simultaneously instructed readers to retreat to nature while accepting technological progress: "We must go back to nature if we wish to live long. We must garden and go barefooted. If we live in New York we must go searching for four-leaf clovers in Central Park, and no policeman will arrest you if you do it barefooted... We do not have to stop the advances of technology but we have to learn to live with these forces... We must not industrialize or technologize our own bodies."[26] They may have also found his longing for recognition by establishment institutions confusing, if not outright objectionable. Yet they concurred with Rodale's nature romanticism.

Reminiscent of nineteenth-century preservationists and foreshadowing eco-utopian thinking in the 1960s and 1970s, Rodale endowed nature with a transcendental aura. Reflecting on the sublime, almost mystical, "gleams" of nature in *The Organic Front* (1949) Rodale wrote: "It is breath-taking to behold the beautiful interplay of natural forces and the biological activities going on in old Mother Earth as these gleams of life go about their task of manufacturing plant food. Without the aid of this micro-organic world man would cease to exist."[27] Standing at the edge of the Grand Canyon, he conjectured: "If we could force our politicians to pass laws as they sit at the rim of the canyon I believe our statutes would be more in the public interests."[28] Rodale believed so thoroughly in nature's restorative potency that contact with wilderness would even enliven world-wearied civil servants.

Rodale attributed the midcentury rise in chronic diseases, such as diabetes, heart disease, and cancer, to America's detachment from nature. Living in concrete jungles, eating machine-processed supermarket foods containing "tooth-cracking phosphorous acid" and innumerable invisible and tasteless chemical insecticides, fungicides and additives, modern individuals lived recklessly.[29] Traditional peoples, such as Rodale's model primitives, the Hunzas of the northern tip of India, suffered no such maladies. The Hunzas' general well-being, versus America's chronic unwellness, proved natural living's efficacy. Primitive cultures, working-class peoples, and ethnics possessed a magical immunity to the angst and illnesses of the civilized world, according to J. I. Rodale. Guided by necessity and instinct, premodern peoples did not fuss over their diets, at least from Rodale's amateur-anthropological standpoint. This primitivist hypothesis, which surfaced in gender traditional counterculture cookbooks, such as *Laurel's Kitchen* and *The Political Palate*, steered Rodale's simple and tautological disease analysis in *Happy People Rarely Get Cancer* (1970). The Hunzas' health-promoting habits kept them robust and optimistic. Thus, primitive and ethnic peoples were happy because they were healthy, and happiness, along with an unadulterated diet, ensured a salubrious life. The civilized world lacked both happiness and a "natural diet," and its citizens suffered. Cancer had steadily increased over the twentieth century from 3.7 percent of deaths in 1900 to 15.7 percent of deaths in 1955.[30] Linked in various scientific studies to radioactive fallout and the unprecedented use of chemicals in food production and agriculture, this disease looked like the hellish penance paid for convenience foods and Cold War militarism. Rodale recommended primitivism as a cure.[31]

According to Rodale's findings, a few special cultures within the industrialized United States possessed exceptional health. Dubiously, considering Native America's desperate rates of poverty and malnutrition, Rodale rosily suggested that American Indian women who stayed true to native ways—"an out-of-door life of activity with plenty of fresh game and wholesome food and clear water, with healthful teepees for homes"—enjoyed easier childbirth than most American women.[32] Even urban African Americans'"simple" working-class life ensured protective health benefits.

In a spectacular exhibition of the racist presumptions behind his and other primitive romanticists' happy-healthy-noble-natives thesis, Rodale, after studying African Americans' lower cancer rates in 1964, concluded: "Negroes should get less cancer than whites, for the Negro race is a happy race. True, there is their problem of segregation, but the Negro nature being what it is, I think a Negro sings just the same, and is not going to let segregation dampen his spirits as much as a similar problem would do to the white person."[33] Like another fifties racial sentimentalist, Beat writer Jack Kerouac, who "wished" he could "exchange worlds with the happy, true-hearted, ecstatic Negroes of America,"[34] J. I. Rodale believed that even unenviably segregated African Americans lived better and more healthfully than did white suburban denizens.

Rodale idolized the Hunzas and black Americans not because they confronted modernization but because they, purportedly, remained untouched by it. Run-of-the-mill Americans thoughtlessly indulged in convenience, science, and technology and had to work their way back to Eden. "The atom bomb has its atomic fallout. An ordinary heating system sends death-dealing smoke into the atmosphere, as does the automobile. Foods are sold preserved with poisonous additives, and the food processors and government biochemists nod their heads in approval"—the challenges were many, Rodale warned.[35]

For J. I. Rodale, as well as the environmentally alarmed in the 1960s and 1970s, the social and economic entities responsible for this mess seemed without national constraints and impervious to legislative control and citizen outrage. Against such ghostly adversaries, Rodale recommended the only viable solution: "We must question every generally accepted health tenet or dogma, as rooted as it may be in the public's mind. You must observe the effect on you own bodily processes of your basic daily actions. Make your own interpretations." He advised radical self-conservation.[36]

In the high-stakes Cold War, Rodale connected the nation's future to its people's diet. "A sick nation is a weak nation. Is it patriotic to live so poorly, to weaken your body so much that you pass on a poor physical heritage to the next generation?" he asked.[37] Rodale did not question America's pursuit of Cold War dominance; he just wanted to fortify the "troops" with healthy food. Despite an impatience with deep-rooted powers, Rodale was, finally, a patriot. Indeed, his obedient nationalism did not contradict his organic rebellion. He adopted an organic diet and farming because, from his accounting, compost-fertilized agriculture promised relief from a life plagued by dizziness, headaches, and heart troubles. While the early twentieth-century popular front echoed in his 1949 book, *The Organic Front*, and in his denunciations of big business, the cornerstone of J. I. Rodale's organic agenda—self-protection through diet, exercise, and organic gardening—was a traditionally American, individualistic approach to a systemic economic and agricultural predicament. This conservatism, although challenged when

FIGURE 8. J. I. Rodale eating one of his favorite organic cure-alls, sunflower seeds, 1970. Courtesy of Co Rentmeester/The LIFE Picture Collection/Getty Images.

countercultural radicals seized organic farming for their antiestablishment environmental insurrection, remained a subterranean script that patterned future natural foods movement thinking and action.

In 1971, J. I. Rodale's directorship of the organic mission ended when he unexpectedly passed way from a heart attack on the *Dick Cavett Show*, ironically after bragging that he would live to one hundred years old. Son Robert, who had worked at the press since his early twenties and who, as a baby boomer, was more generationally connected to the sixties uprising than was his older father, took the wheel and steered Rodale organics through the tumult, experimentalism, and economic deflation of the 1970s.

REINVENTING ORGANIC IN THE REVOLUTIONARY 1970S

Nineteen seventy-one was a banner year for J. I. and Rodale Press. Between 1968 and 1971, countercultural readers increased circulation figures for *Organic Gardening* from 390,000 to 720,000 and for *Prevention* from 520,000 to 920,000.[38] This spike in subscriptions, as well as organic agriculture's increased popularity, motivated the *New York Times* to run Wade Greene's feature on J. I. Rodale titled "The Guru of the Organic Food Cult." Other popular magazines, including *Penthouse, Women's Wear Daily,* and *Smithsonian*, also covered Rodale and the organic story in the same year. Inopportunely, as many young Americans became *Organic Gardening* subscribers and Rodale enthusiasts, and as even more Americans took *Prevention*'s self-health message seriously, J. I. Rodale died. Yet, Rodale's circulation figures continued to rise, indicating an organic and dietary health camp blossoming as a vital counterforce within U.S. culture.

This bloc, along with scientific data recommending national dietary reform, slowly pushed the federal government to act. In 1966, President Johnson's FDA began a thorough review of food additives. Nixon's administration followed suit with the first White House Conference on Food, Nutrition and Health in 1969 and by creating the Environmental Protection Agency in 1970, the year of the first Earth Day. At the same time that the federal government responded to citizen push-back, organic and natural foods proponents, lacking trust in government and politician intervention, built their own food infrastructure.

The creation of the National Organic Farmers Association in 1971 and the International Federation of Organic Agriculture Movements in 1972 is a prime example of organizational stays that made organics a permanent feature of the American and global economy. The appearance of natural and organic food companies, such as Arrowhead Mills (established 1960), Erewhon (1966), Eden (1969), and Celestial Seasonings (1978), along with the growth of health food stores from 500 in 1965 to 3,000 in 1973, testified to a burgeoning alternative food market.[39] In 1980, John Mackey's Whole Foods Market tried organics and health foods on a grander scale and succeeded as the first health food supermarket in the United States.

The increased demand for organic and natural foods can partially be attributed to pop health books, such as James Turner's *Chemical Feast* (1970), Judith Allen and Gene Marine's *Food Pollution: The Violation of Our Inner Ecology* (1971), and Jacqueline Verrett's *Eating May Be Hazardous to Your Health* (1974), that substantiated widespread worry over food purity. As Anne Colamosca wrote in the *New York Times* in November 1974, "Suspicion about the established major food producers in the U.S. runs so deep among a sturdy core of middle-class consumers that they are willing to continue to pay high prices for what they consider to be purer and more nutritious even when times are hard."[40]

Natural foods gained national momentum in the 1970s, a significant turning point. Alternative food producers peddled and promoted their wares within their growing, but still outsider, economy of retail stores, co-ops, food conspiracies, and small-scale organic or health food industries. Like other rebels building communes, co-ops, and experimental operations, excited natural foods consumers and producers were convinced that the obvious good of their products would push the nation toward ecological and principled consumption. One at a time, each shopper, small retail establishment, and organic vegetable producer would undermine the supermarket system. The Achilles heel of this snowball theory of social change was that until the natural foods tidal wave hit the shores, the movement presented no blocks to or protections from corporate food and the agricultural industry's human and natural damages. Nevertheless, natural foods participants seemed satisfied that they were doing the right thing daily—setting an example for others to follow.

The seventies counterculture, and its natural foods movement, brimmed with energy and (a measured) hopefulness in the very period when the nation fell into political cynicism and economic deflation. With the Organization of Petroleum Exporting Countries (OPEC) embargo and resultant oil crisis of 1973–74, stagflation setting in, and a body of literature announcing the earth's inherent limits, such as Paul Ehrlich's *Population Bomb* (1968) and Barry Commoner's *Closing Circle* (1971), many Americans felt that the United States must alter its consumption habits and move toward a sustainable economy, as E. F. Schumacher argued in *Small Is Beautiful* (1973).

Robert Rodale became a leader in the organic/natural food (and living) movement in this cultural context. Consequently, his organic message expanded beyond the dietary health and organic gardening framework established by his father's magazines. With seventies progressives beginning to "think globally," Rodale's organic aspirations followed. As the head of Rodale Press, from 1971 until his untimely death in a car accident in Moscow in 1990, Robert Rodale addressed the nation's uncertain economic future and the arcadian impatience of progressive naturalists with his own organic agenda.

COUNTERCULTURAL RODALE

If J. I. Rodale had a guru in British agronomist Sir Albert Howard, his son, Robert, had one in British economist E. F. Schumacher. Bob Rodale (as he was often called) found Schumacher's critique of the capitalist West's "giantism" and inhumanity, in *Small Is Beautiful*, incisive. America's expanding bodies and inflated seventies economy were related, and neither boded well for the country, according to Robert Rodale. To make itself whole again, America would have to quit its addiction to technology and mindless consumption. "I don't mean take a side road. I mean go backwards," Rodale wrote. "Let's stop riding and do some walking. Let's peel potatoes instead of opening a packet of potatoes."[41] Through the 1970s, Rodale, like his father, used his magazines to push his antimodern designs.

In an article comparing city dwellers to "organic people"—who "observe and try to understand the web of life that nature weaves"—Rodale opined that "people who live in cities, without gardens, are orphaned from the organic family. They don't have an opportunity to link their lives directly with a natural system."[42] Reckoning back to an abiding American anti-urbanism, with precursors in Jeffersonian yeoman idealism and early nineteenth-century transcendentalism, dissenting Americans who shared Rodale's intolerance of technology and modernity aligned with this urban critique.

This was all new for Rodale Press. J. I. Rodale, a native New Yorker, kept an apartment in Manhattan his whole life. He loved Broadway and for a time owned his own theater, primarily because no company would stage his clumsily written, didactic health-themed plays. Although he occasionally excoriated city living and prescribed daily contact with the sun and the soil, the founder of the U.S. organic movement did not blame America's metropolises for its predicament. Robert Rodale, and others of his generation, did. And they looked to its rural landscapes for escape.

"WE'VE GOT TO GET OURSELVES, BACK TO THE GARDEN"[43]

Seventies "back-to-nature" and "back-to-land" pioneers joined a historical procession of American rebels who left the city for the putative satisfactions of farming and self-support. Back-to-the-lander Bob Light explained his motives to *New York Times* columnist Roy Reed in 1975: "We don't want to support the system. We don't want to support the factories belching out the smoke. It's not our goal to make money. I've decided that I'm never going to pay taxes again under the system this country has." To distinguish the seventies back-to-land movement from the more-threatening sixties communes, Reed remarked, "Unlike the earlier drug-oriented and somewhat escapist youth movement of the nineteen-sixties, the self-sufficiency movement is characterized, at least in its cutting edge, by enthusiasm, optimism and hard work, especially work done with the hands."[44] Reed's and the nation's anti-hippie bias colored his characterization of sixties communes as hedonistic hideaways. Nevertheless, there was some truth in the comparison of these two stages of countercultural motion. Postscarcity unrestraint let sixties radicals focus on self-actualization with sex, art, music, food, drugs, and spirituality. Personal lifestyle choices and cultural expressivism carried equal weight with seventies radicals. But as the abundance bubble burst, countercultural adventurers and organic leaders felt the need to bring purposeful sobriety to their endeavors.

Columnist Tom Monte detected this seriousness when visiting Rodale's experimental farm and offices: "One gets the distinct impression that these people are gearing up for the apocalypse, the coming apart of a technology they maintain will ultimately cause its own destruction."[45] Cognizant of the global environmental and national economic crises brewing, seventies organic mavericks constructed alternative livelihoods based on needs, self-sufficiency, and global ecological mindfulness.

Unlike his father, who wanted to be the spur in the mainstream's hindquarters, pricking its government agencies and institutions into organic reasonableness, Robert Rodale, influenced by the era's antistatism and separatism, saw rural organics as a means to a detached economic and cultural other end. To advance organics, he bought 333 acres of land near Kutztown, Pennsylvania, renaming his father's Health and Soil Institute as the Rodale Institute. Echoing radical ecologist Wendell Berry, who described gardening as a "complete action" that would "lead to other solutions," Rodale saw a straight line from backyard farming and gardening to profound social renovation.[46] "We're beginning to sense how vulnerable our complex economic system is to threats from within and without," he warned. The United States must "begin to work for more personal independence," breaking its subservience to already dwindling foreign fuel sources with domestic alternative energy.[47]

In the wake of the OPEC oil embargo, Presidents Nixon and Ford supported nuclear power and domestic oil development. During his one term, Jimmy Carter nearly pleaded with Americans to conserve by lowering their thermostats and wearing sweaters. In 1978, unsure of citizen buy-in, he introduced an energy bill to Congress that would force reductions through increased oil prices. While Carter's self-denial ethos fell on many a deaf ear and Congress passed only a diluted version of his bill, his message did ring true to environmentally aware Americans already converting to solar, wind, and wood-powered energy.[48] Throughout the 1970s, *Organic Gardening* backed energy alternatives in pieces on wood-burning stoves and nonrefrigerated food storage systems.

In contrast to his father, Robert preached local economic autonomy along with a global environmental overhaul. Under his direction, sizable portions of the company's profits were funneled into international research and development. In one case, five million dollars of Rodale revenues was put to agricultural research for an African hunger relief program. Reflecting on his use of publishing profits for foreign organic agriculture interventions, Rodale commented, "It's true that we're very good at selling our magazines and books. We see that skill as a necessary one to help us fulfill our missionary function."[49] From the mid-1960s forward, an issue-driven, à la carte politics (rather than party or class fidelity) appealed to environmental liberals as well as social conservatives. Rodale's international "mission" coordinated with this ecumenicalism. His Cornucopia Project for reconstructing American food distribution, as well as his agricultural work in Africa, fit the postsixties civic imaginary.

Robert Rodale liked to tell a family story that he believed predicted his future as an international leader. On the day he was born, his mother saw "WW" in her mind's eye and asked J. I. what this sign could mean. J. I. prophetically guessed, "Worldwide; this boy is going to be worldwide in his outlook."[50] Despite this folksy explanation, Robert Rodale's planetary perspective stemmed from the geopolitical and cultural influences of the era.

Cheap jet air service in the 1960s opened the world to more Americans than ever before. For disenchanted middle- and upper-class youth, globetrotting was a must. Young boomers saw the world through adventure travel and also as the Peace Corps first agents. In the United States, the 1965 Immigration Act, which threw off an older Eurocentric quota system, exposed white America to the world's diversity. On the political front, the Vietnam War verified the reach of the United States' military-industrial-technology complex, convincing the political Left that its target should be home front capitalism and American imperialism abroad. Decolonization struggles across the globe inspired the revolutionary designs of late sixties radicals, such as the Weathermen and the Black Panthers. Finally, the emerging science of ecology, which depicted humankind and nature woven in biological interaction, required eco-conscious Americans to view their most individual decisions as globally germane. As radical ecologist Wendell Berry claimed in his 1976 tract, *The Unsettling of America*, "The use of the world is finally a personal matter, and the world can be preserved in health only by the forbearance and care of a multitude of persons." Berry's personalized environmentalism confirmed the era's redefined citizenship and activism.[51]

For Robert Rodale, who came into adulthood working for America's only publishing company devoted to organic gardening and preventive nutritional health, late twentieth-century globalism was formative, as was Berry's individualistic environmentalism. In the 1970s, and especially in the 1980s when the appropriate technology movement floundered, Rodale traveled to China, Africa, India, and (in the early 1990s) post–Soviet Russia to build organic organizations and crop development networks in places more in need of or at least more receptive to his message than was the United States.

While Robert Rodale spent his time on international projects and other social reconstruction schemas—such as his plan to localize the American economy and food in "regeneration" zones—his executive staff used *Prevention* for a more modest target: individual health.[52] Rodale's *Prevention* tied the private to the public by arguing that chemical and food industries buried evidence on the toxicity of their goods. Individual citizen consumers, with far less capital and political authority, suffered the consequences by directly and indirectly ingesting agricultural chemicals and synthetic additives. *Prevention* drove this point home regularly by citing alarming statistics about the links between chemical exposure and male infertility, cancer, and the like. But health, according to Robert Rodale and *Prevention* columnists, was a matter of individual choices. When all was said-and-done, Rodale believed health was a "talent"—acquired over time through discipline and moderation. In his clarion call for rugged self-sufficiency, he argued: "We must look for health freedom beyond the law and into the workings of our own minds. Anyone who does not believe firmly that health is something we create for ourselves by the way we live will never have health freedom, under any set of laws . . . Changing some laws will take the locks off the doors to those self-created cages. But it's going to be up to you to open the door and walk out."[53] Following his father's diagnostic tradition, Robert Rodale used his own conditions and successful at-home treatments to prove the self-help health strategy. Leg ulcers? Use zinc. Hypertension or heart disease? Eat garlic. Constipation? Follow the diet of "Africans and other primitive people," who "rarely get any of these diseases because of the unabsorbable fiber they consume every day."[54] Robert's health remedies were not a far stretch from J. I.'s *Prevention* protocols or from the fears of somatic vulnerability that stimulated interest in postwar dietary therapies.

Much like his father, Robert Rodale believed that organic agriculture's merits would win over the doubting public. Yet, as seventies insurgents strived to spread the simple living and back-to-the-land antimodern revolution, the general electorate became disenchanted not only with the "hippie" lifestyle but also with Great Society liberalism by installing a succession of conservative presidents from Nixon to Bush. Exhausted by the fraternal battle of the Vietnam 1960s and frightened by the economic and racial divisiveness of the 1970s, many Americans, even some loyal New Deal Democrats, invested in the conservative certainties of God, country, and family.

The new conservatism seemed the polar opposite of sixties movement radicalism, but striking philosophical intersections associated the natural foods counterculture to rising Republicanism. Both organic believers and Nixon and Reagan Republicans deeply mistrusted *bigness*. Conservatives blamed bloated government and social help bureaucracies for producing a class of slothful Americans living off the public dole (paid by working families' hard-earned tax dollars). Counterculturalists also believed that everything big and modern—cities, industry, technology, the military, government—threatened human and environmental health and devitalized the public forum. As Paul Cowan, the author of *The Making of an Un-American* (1970) commented in a *New York Times* interview: "This nation is too big for any group to govern it humanely ... Living in smaller, self-governing regions, Americans ... might become decent citizens of the world."[55] For cultural dissenters and environmentalists, organic farming, appropriate technology, and preventive health furnished small, human-scale alternatives that might lead toward Cowan's proposal. For conservatives, voluntarism, deregulation, and states' rights assured protection from overtaxation and secular social reforms. Both sides of the postsixties ideological aisle hoisted the flag of self-determination as its own, but for different ends.

These shared standards worked to Rodale Press's advantage. As the 1970s turned into the 1980s, Reagan's conservatism overshadowed Democratic reformism, and yuppie conspicuous consumption supplanted countercultural homemade frugality. For many progressives, this national rearrangement made in-the-streets revolution seem less compelling and possible.[56] If Rodale Press had remained confined within the organics, solar energy, and environmentally sound home technologies (like Robert's pedal-powered grain grinders) milieu, its magazines and books would have faded into the ether as did such various alternative publications as the *Berkeley Barb*, the *East Village Other*, and the *Whole Earth Catalog* (even though this magazine would be revived later). To avoid this fate, by the end of the 1980s, Rodale discontinued journals like *New Shelter* and *New Farm* created in early seventies do-it-yourself and survivalist zeal. Healthism, on the other hand, now engrossed the comfortable classes of all political persuasions. *Prevention* and Rodale's sports and fitness magazine acquisitions checked the company's descent into anachronistic irrelevancy.

PREVENTIVE HEALTH AND HEROIC FITNESS IN THE AGE OF LIMITS

Always attuned to the next health trend that might catch its elite readership's attention, Rodale publications aggressively cornered the fitness magazine niche, acquiring or creating *Bicycling* (1978), *Cross Country Skier* (1985), *Superfit* (1985), *Runner's World* (1985), *Mountain Bike* (1986), and *Backpacker* (1988) for its new sports department. Sports and athletics fit easily into Rodale Press's health philosophy. J. I. Rodale had taken daily walks up steep hills for his heart and prodded his readers to follow. For his son, Robert, exercise, along with organic gardening, alternative technology, and simple living, supported ecological self-sufficiency. In fact, Robert Rodale believed exercise served dual purposes.

At a personal level, exercise improved cardiovascular activity, assisted in weight reduction, and increased muscularity. If practiced regularly, Robert Rodale believed that exercise freed average Americans from the medical establishment and reinforced wellness. On a national scale, walking and biking were environmentally sound substitutes for fuel-inefficient and polluting cars, trains, and buses. Always willing to prove his theories through example, he rode or walked to work every day, regardless of the weather.

The ordinary seventies fitness partisan did not take up exercise with these earth-friendly applications in mind. Instead, most Americans began running, biking, swimming, and walking to improve their health, vitality, and attractiveness. Kenneth Cooper's *Aerobics* (1968), the first popular exercise book of this period, crystallized the relationship between exercise and heart health. A Texas doctor and exercise physiologist, Cooper recommended aerobic activity as recuperative therapy for heart attack patients. Exercise's exact cardiovascular rewards remained a point of debate among doctors and medical scientists throughout the twentieth century. But by the early 1970s, jogging and running, seen by many as the preeminent preventive exercise, attracted such widespread acclaim that hundreds of jogging clubs popped up nationally. The New York City Marathon, traditionally run by Olympic athletes, jumped from 125 participants in 1969 to 11,500 in 1979. By 1975, the Department of Health, Education, and Welfare found that 5 percent of the population over twenty jogged or ran.[57]

Running perfectly suited the 1970s and 1980s middle and upper classes (the segment from which most runners came) because it required discipline and hard work—traits long respected by this social strata. In the early 1970s, when the nation confronted the natural limits of its oil-driven consumer economy, restraint and ambition seemed all the more necessary. Running also appealed to this class because it melded work and leisure. In communes, homesteads, co-ops, and other alternative enterprises of the 1960s and 1970s, counterculturalists (generally from the same class as runners) tried to break down what they believed to be the artificial boundaries between labor and leisure. Communalist Albin Wagner described this holistic approach to work at his group home, Drop City: "Droppers are not asked to do anything. They work out of the need to work. Out of guilt or emptiness the desire to work, hopefully, arises. If it is no longer work, but pleasure [sic]. Doing nothing is real work. We play at working. It is as gratifying as eating or loving. We are based on the pleasure principle. Our main concern is to be alive."[58] Instead of infusing play, flexibility, and excitement into their work environment, runners in the 1970s and early 1980s poured work into their off-hours, making their existence a test of self-regimentation and endurance. Their toned muscles, "healthy" heart rate, and improved running speeds proved that they made better use of their spare time than the rest of couch-potato America. Daily exercisers' grandiosity on the social, psychological, and spiritual capacities of running rivaled Rodale on the power of the bicycle, which he described as "the most efficient machine the mind of man has ever created."[59]

In *Running and Being: The Total Experience* (1978), Dr. George Sheehan depicted running as a heroic journey. On a particularly arduous run, Sheehan exclaimed: "I am fighting God. Fighting the limitations he gave me. Fighting the unfairness. Fighting all the evil in me and the world. And I will not give in. I will conquer this hill, and I will conquer it alone."[60] Seventies culture critic Christopher Lasch found in these extravagant reports, and all seventies self-improvement schemes, America's devolution into egotism.[61] Sheehan's overheated testament that "once I discovered running, it became the key that unlocked all my energies . . . [It opened] the world beyond health, fitness and wellness—the world of maximum human performance," demonstrated Lasch's point.[62] At the same time, the self-realization language Sheehan used signaled a genuine yearning by many Americans to keep the excitement and meaningfulness of the 1960s and 1970s going in the next decades of their lives. Exercisers' lofty language and self-perception as dissenters from mainstream indolence and suburban obedience loosely tied their routine to the counterculture projects of expressive individualism and authentic living.

Robert Rodale may have imagined fitness as a catalyst of broader social change. But in all truth, his company jumped on the fitness bandwagon for economic basics. With *Prevention* and *Organic Gardening* suffering double-digit advertising losses in the early 1980s, Rodale executives attached the company to the exercise craze to abate financial bleeding. A wise move, for by 1982 one-third of U.S. adults testified to exercising regularly. These numbers only increased in the decades after, as exercise and bodily fitness became a required insignia of elite standing (especially for middle- and upper-class women). As scientific evidence validated the relation between health and exercise, a morally intoned health discourse compelled every class of Americans to "be fit." In the same period, Rodale's core executives determined to bring all parts of the company more into the mainstream, revamping its publications to respond to the revised needs of its 1980s and 1990s readership and to widen the commercial opening for health and fitness products.

From 1950 to 1979, *Prevention*'s advertising revenues came from vitamin and natural supplements companies. During that period, *Prevention* never associated with products that the editors deemed questionable, such as tobacco, alcohol, and automobiles. In line with its natural health mission, the magazine refused commercial contracts for "laxatives, reducing aids, pain killers, refined flour or sugar, or anything containing artificial flavoring, coloring or chemical preservatives."[63] These stringent regulations distinguished *Prevention* from more commercial magazines and for many readers confirmed the press's organic faithfulness.

In 1985 Rodale's advertising team stepped away from this policy, accepting over-the-counter drugs and processed food commercials for its popular health publication. This was a dramatic departure from J. I. Rodale's monthly dunning of doctors and drugs in the 1950s and 1960s and Robert Rodale's antipharmaceutical, self-health edicts in the 1970s. At the beginning of the 1980s, Robert Rodale and his executive staff acknowledged *Prevention*'s advertising custom but, due to market exigencies, lightened its preachiness and loosened its promotional conventions. Without these amendments, Rodale executives worried they might lose a new baby-boomer target audience of largely female "health management specialists, executives concerned with health and fitness ... and parents."[64]

Under the same pressures, Rodale Press refashioned *Organic Gardening* to catch a new high-profit segment of nesting baby boomers and Gen Xers. With glossy and stylish *Flower and Garden* already on the magazine racks and *Fine Gardening* coming to press in 1988, Rodale designers continued to reorient *Organic Gardening* to a "well-off baby-boomer aesthetic." This meant more lifestyle features and even the possibility of automobile advertisements, which *Organic Gardening*'s publisher Bennett Zucker believed would be a "terrific category" for future ad growth.[65] The contemplation of automobile copy in Rodale's *Organic Gardening*, the popular clearinghouse for organic discussion and information from the 1940s onward, marks a pivotal transition within the U.S. organic movement. In the 1970s, Robert Rodale faulted automobiles for America's energy crisis. He and other food systems critics believed the nation must end its petroleum-fueled transportation and food distribution system. Stirred by this goal, Rodale created the Cornucopia and Community Regeneration projects, recommending local organic consumption. By 1988, Rodale publications entertained the possibility of placing car advertisements in the major mouthpiece of the organic movement, *Organic Gardening* magazine.

Robert Rodale was apprised of these style and structural changes. Yet, it seems that as organic gardening and preventive health and fitness swept the United States, his focus (as always) drifted across the world. Through the 1980s, he busied himself with multiple projects: the Regeneration and Cornucopia projects, and trips to Zimbabwe (at the behest of the U.S. ambassador) and to the West African Rodale Institute office. In 1989–90, Rodale directed the publication of the first experimental organic farm and farming magazine, *Novii Fermer* (*New Farmer*), in Russia. It was in Moscow, in September 1990, that Rodale died in a traffic accident. Always on the go, in the last decade of his life, he no longer wielded as pervasive an influence over his family's publishing company. Those in charge, while respectful of the Rodale organic mission, had money, publicity, and success on their minds.

Robert Rodale's writings in the 1980s do not indicate any overt discordance between his imagined international organic future and *Prevention*'s and *Organic Gardening*'s more monetarily pragmatic direction. His editorials in both magazines adjusted with the times. Responsive to the growing influence of New Age holism, Rodale incorporated spirituality into editorials.

Yet he never shook the worldwide outlook that his father assigned to him at birth. He doggedly devoted his heart and his time to a global agricultural revolution, as suggested by his posthumously published famine-relief treatise, *Save Three Lives: A Plan for Famine Prevention* (1999).

Interestingly, Rodale's last book did not insist on voluntary simplicity or a national retooling to energy-efficient technologies. Rather, he directed readers to what some critics cynically dubbed "checkbook activism." An earlier Rodale had argued that resonant social change necessitated self-control and sacrifice. But now he recommended that readers address global famine by donating to relief organizations, writing letters to elected officials, traveling, educating others, and visiting the Rodale Institute—no interruption of personal accumulation or consumption required.

Perhaps Rodale backed away from self-sufficiency because he recognized that many Americans were feeding materialist hungers (enhanced by marketing and cultural cues) that had been tamped down by the voluntary poverty of the countercultural 1960s and the economic restraints of the recessionary 1970s. As Reagan conservatism redirected American politics and society, Robert Rodale and his organic compatriots, who had made *Organic Gardening* such a hit in the early 1970s, were forced to confront the unlikelihood of economic revolution. As former hippies settled into long-term social services, environmental, consumer advocacy, and academic careers (as well as straight white-collar jobs), fomenting change from within and alongside the existing capitalist system seemed much more effective than rural separatism and intentional privation.

While these heretofore outsiders established themselves in mainstream power positions, the Rodale project, organic farming and food, moved out of the countercultural margin to one center of a segmented marketplace. Between 1971 and 1981, the National Organic Farmers Association increased its membership from 135 to 1,000. And by 1984, a trade organization, Organic Foods Producers of North America, served an expanding corps of organic food producers. Rodale's organic certification program assisted these developments. In 1981, further substantiating the organic way, the Rodale Institute began an experimental comparison of conventional and organic agriculture known as the Rodale Institute Farming System Trial.[66] On the West Coast, California and Oregon instituted their own organic certification organizations, California Certified Organic Farmers (CCOF) and Oregon Tilith. Constant consumer demand since the early 1970s stimulated these infrastructural advancements.[67]

By 1989 a Harris poll, conducted at the behest of *Organic Gardening*, found that 84 percent of Americans surveyed would buy organic if priced the same as conventional produce. Fifty-eight percent stated they would buy organic regardless of price.[68] The year this poll was taken, evidence of carcinogenic Alar residues on apples caused such widespread and "middle America" consumer outcry that its producers pulled the chemical off the market. When contemplating the Alar scare, John Haberen, director of Rodale's Agricultural Research Center, remarked, "The public is carrying the big stick now."[69] For many within the pro-organic community, the successful Alar protest proved the potency of consumer choosiness and portended a bright and potentially mainstream commercial future for chemical-free foods.

The federal government's slow but eventual involvement in the organic argument further endorsed Americans' antipesticide partiality. Since the 1940s, J. I. and Robert had regularly implored the USDA to fund a comparative study of conventional and organic agriculture. The federal government ignored their request until the late 1980s, when pressure from newly powerful environmental and public interest organizations and a consolidated organic agricultural constituency made a reflexive renunciation of organics impossible. In 1979, Carter's USDA began a countrywide investigation of organic farming, resulting in the Low-Input Sustainable Agriculture Program, known as LISA. When Reagan came into office, his USDA put LISA on the back burner. Yet, owing to constituent and lobbyist pressure, Congress revived LISA in 1988, allocating $3.8 million for organic research and development. A tiny portion of the U.S. federal agricultural budget, LISA nonetheless signified organic consumers' reach.[70]

The 1980s organic movement's momentum culminated in 1990 with the attachment of the U.S. Organic Foods Production Act (OFPA) to that year's Farm Bill. Robert Rodale passed away before OFPA's enactment, but its very existence denoted a tectonic shift in governmental attitude toward organic agriculture. If Robert Rodale had had time to reflect on the status of organics at the end of his life, he would have found much about which to be hopeful. The merging governmental and mainstream recognition of organic foods meant more demand and a burst of commercial growth.

On the other hand, the commoditization of the alternative food and agriculture movement threatened to muffle the criticism of consumer society that motivated the 1970s and early 1980s organic reaction. Julie Guthman explains in *Agrarian Dreams* (2010) that federal standardization of the organic label mostly addressed the needs of large interstate merchandisers, such as food processors and livestock farmers. Organic movement formalists, who cultivated small plots for a local market using "agroecological methods" and who believed in the environmental correctness of a decentralized marketplace, did not want a federally mandated organic standard. In fact, they worried such intervention would deflate the critical environmental and, sometimes, anticapitalist foundation from which the countercultural natural foods and agriculture movements sprang.[71] Standardization and incorporation promised that other, more imaginative ecological, social, and cultural alternatives to established food and farming practice would be quickly forgotten and overshadowed by a singular monetized definition of organic.

For a simple-living organic proponent such as Robert Rodale, commercial recognition of his lifelong cause must have been met with a certain degree of excitement and an equal measure of misgiving. But in the year of his death, no one could really predict where nascent organic consumerism would take Rodale Press. Rodale executives had spent the 1980s soft-pedaling antimaterialism and organic radicalism. They had positioned the company to be a significant sponsor of exercise and health consumption. What would become of Rodale Press and the organic enterprise, in the absence of its most influential advocate, was yet to be determined.

FROM ORGANIC IDEALISM TO CONSCIOUS SENSUALISM

Rodale Press did not disintegrate into leaderless turmoil after Robert's death. During the last decade of his life, Rodale spent most of his time abroad. When he returned to Emmaus, he would bombard Bob Teufel, the press's president, with a barrage of new article and magazine ideas, then he was off to Africa or Latin America. Thus, when Robert passed away suddenly, the publication company was already accustomed to running without a Rodale at the helm.

Robert's wife, Ardie, took temporary control after his death, and the press profitably cruised on without much family influence. *Men's Health*, a mid-1980s creation, exceeded all expectations with a circulation rate of 1.5 million by 1994, beating out the combined sales of *Esquire* and *GQ*.[72] By 1998, *Men's Health* was the third most popular American men's magazine, following *Sports Illustrated* and *Playboy*. The miraculous success of this self-help, male grooming and exercise magazine meant that Rodale had won a new readership: white middle- and upper-class men eager to conform to the fitness and fashion benchmarks defining late twentieth-century American manhood.

In addition to inventing the men's health magazine genre in the 1980s and 1990s, Rodale Press upped newsstand sales of *Prevention* from 662,386 in 1986 to 811,801 in 1996 with a total circulation of more than 3 million—a feat unmatched by the top 20 national magazines, all of which experienced a newsstand downturn in the same period. Editor Mark Bricklin attributed *Prevention*'s success to the company's intentional relaxation of the magazine's "hard-core health message filled with warnings about how you had to follow the straight and narrow."[73] Rodale's book department also cashed in on the swelling alternative health fad, selling 10 million copies of *The Doctors Book of Home Remedies* between 1990 and 1994 and ending the decade with $200 million in books sales in 1999.[74]

Fortunately for Rodale, Inc., when the metaphysically intoned long-distance running bubble of the late 1970s–early 1980s popped, exercise did not go the way of Erhard Seminars Training (EST), the smiley face, pet rocks, and other seventies fads. One exercise regimen after another followed on running's heels—aerobics in the late 1980s, the StairMaster and spinning in the 1990s, and by the turn of the twenty-first century an obsession with the precisely defined and muscular female and male body, as the unparalleled sensation of *Men's Health* (crucial to popularizing the washboard abs) made plain. At the same time that many Americans set aside unprecedented portions of their leisure time sculpting their physique and honing their target heart rate, another portion asserted bodily mastery with holistic and preventive health, making alternative therapeutics a substantial sector of America's health care economy. Rodale Press simply absorbed these newer manifestations, as well as cyclical diet fads, into its already well-liked health and fitness magazines.

Organic Gardening, on the other hand, suffered an identity crisis. Three months after Robert Rodale's death, Stevie O. Daniels, managing editor, left *Organic Gardening* and was replaced by Mike McGrath. McGrath, a self-described former "hippie" and *Rolling Stone* correspondent, restyled the magazine to appeal to the die-hard home gardener. Organic methodologies, while always a pragmatic must for McGrath, earned less philosophical or political rumination under his editorship. Typical of other more conventional gardening magazines, from 1990 to 1997, McGrath offered hard-boiled green thumb tips on growing the biggest, the best, and the brightest flowers, tomatoes, and lawn.

In a noteworthy departure from Robert Rodale's unequivocal commitment to fuel-efficient petroleum-independent farming and gardening, McGrath regularly touted the benefit of power equipment. His boyish fascination with machines culminated in an annual guide of petroleum- or electric-fueled garden and lawn tools. In a common postsixties manipulation of "movement" phraseology for promotional purposes, McGrath "playfully" entitled this issue "Power to the People."[75] McGrath's irreverent humor and garden machismo won him a faithful following, but over the course of his editorship, *Organic Gardening*'s audience dwindled from 1.3 million to 600,000—a reduction which got him fired in 1997. Thereafter, the magazine floundered under one editor after another, each with his/her own creative design for *Organic Gardening*.

Organic Gardening's decline could certainly be attributed to the absence of its most determined in-house believer, Robert Rodale. At the same time, the magazine's trials connoted the ideological disarray of the postseventies organic movement as a whole. By the last decades of the century, sixties antimodernism and seventies countercultural self-reliance, the bases of the earlier organic argument, had gone underground. After a decade of ostentatious accumulation and indulgence under Reagan, and the idolization of dot-com billionaires under Clinton, gratuitous scarcity no longer resonated culturally, even for many environmental activists. At this historical crossroads, Robert's daughter Maria Rodale stepped up to the plate to, once again, rewrite Rodale's organic mission.

MARIA RODALE'S ORGANIC STYLE

Robert's youngest daughter, Maria, was working in the circulation department of *Backpacker* magazine when her father died in Moscow in a car accident. At age twenty eight, she had limited experience in the company and little desire to step into the leadership role designated in her father's will. In the mid-1990s, she hired herself as creative director. This job, which required hands-on involvement in the press's fiscal records, allowed Maria to unearth what she claimed to be a financial mess. *Organic Gardening*'s reader attrition was only the tip of the iceberg, as far as she could tell. To stop the company's hemorrhaging, Maria hired consultants, who after studying the business extensively, affirmed her suspicions. Armed with this knowledge, Maria began to make moves to renovate the company, all of which met resistance from inner-circle executives who had worked closely with Robert Rodale and who, in the decade after his death, had turned the company from a "100 million dollar magazine company to 400 plus million dollar multimedia juggernaut."[76]

Making no headway with what she described as a "culture of entitlement," Maria took a break in 1996 during which time she, like every Rodale before, wrote her own organic tract, *Maria Rodale's Organic Gardening* (1998). A year later, she rejoined the company, announcing her intent to integrate "healing" into Rodale's preventive platform. Finding continued recalcitrance to her leadership, she began firing executives, one after the other. In 2000, either through resignation or dismissal, the book and magazine division presidents, the editor in chief/publisher of *Men's Health*, and his two successors left Rodale. Most significant, the company's president, and Robert Rodale's right-hand man, Bob Teufel, chose (or was forced) to take early retirement. For Maria, her family, and her hired consultants, the inertia and resistance to change that came along with Teufel's leadership outweighed the rewards of keeping him. With the slate cleaned, Maria and her family could finally, according to a local paper, put the "Rodale back in Rodale, Inc."[77]

Maria's first goal was to hire a president media-savvy enough to lift Rodale out of its stodgy book and magazine format. After much searching, in April 2000 she named Stephen Pleshette Murphy, formerly a Disney publishing executive, the new leader. With an impressive objective of doubling revenues in five years to one billion dollars, Murphy wasted no time, quickly reshuffling the magazine company into multimedia content groups: Women's Health, Men's Health, Sports and Fitness, and Organic Living. Thusly arranged, *Prevention* could promote a health-related Rodale book or video on the Rodale website or at a fitness fair. While Murphy and Maria Rodale believed in this cross-format organization, the reorientation resulted in 148 layoffs, the largest in Rodale history. Needless to say, these changes dampened company morale, with many wondering whether Rodale had "lost its soul" by hiring a president who knew much about profits but little to nothing about compost (Robert Rodale's specialty) or marathon running (former president Bob Teufel's avocation).[78]

Murphy noticed these rumblings but pressed forward with plans to utilize Rodale's customer database of twenty-five million in acquiring new advertising contracts. This database, which Murphy named the Rodale "village green," contained readers' product preferences and information about individual subscriber's health problems—a ripe resource for drug companies and preventive health products. By 2001, Murphy's maneuverings—the total of which resulted in $40 million in cost cutting—brought Rodale out of a financial decline that began in 1999. This success sealed Murphy's position at Rodale, until 2009, when he departed to become chief executive officer of Christie's auction house.[79]

With the ship righted, Maria Rodale transferred her attention to leading the *Organic Living* sector. In Maria's eyes, organic farming was a Rodalian idea. Thus, in addition to prioritizing healing and what insider John Griffin described as extracting Rodale from its track that was "too male, macho, too athletic and sweat-oriented," Maria determined to put her DNA on American organics. Yet, unlike her father and grandfather, who pursued national agricultural reform, Maria's organics mostly targeted home hobbyists and natural aesthetes.[80]

In 1999 she began this modification by firing *Organic Gardening* editor, Nancy Beaubaire, placing herself at the top of the masthead. Beaubaire had come to *Organic Gardening* in 1998 from *Fine Gardening* and *Country Living Gardener*. With Maria's approval, she stripped *Organic Gardening* of Mike McGrath's motor-head, bigger, better, brighter vegetable format and replaced it with glossy spreads of spontaneously natural, but perfectly groomed, flower gardens. She also added stories to appeal to the elite "foodie," such as visits to a "cozy California inn" to "discover how the garden's bounty inspires an exquisite organic cuisine."[81] Beaubaire's monthly columns entitled "The Healing Garden," "Healthy Eating," and "Herbs that Heal" demonstrated her compliance with Maria Rodale's directive to make healing a thematic component of all Rodale publications.[82]

Despite her obedience to Maria's editorial vision, reader complaint, especially from Mike McGrath loyalists, led to Beaubaire's dismissal. In May 1999, Maria Rodale took over *Organic Gardening*. As editor she made McGrath an at-large columnist and mixed his vegetable mania with Beaubaire's high-end flower fashion and organic lifestyle. Despite her acknowledgment of McGrath's popularity, it was clear from her introductory editorial that Maria Rodale's *Organic Gardening* (newly named OG) would distinguish itself not with more of Mike McGrath's vegetable "Tall Tales" but by instructing readers on enjoying an "organic lifestyle beyond the garden." With "organic foods, restaurants, and resorts popping up everywhere (like wildflowers)," Maria encouraged readers to use OG as a lifestyle primer.[83]

Organic Gardening readers recoiled at the pricey organic initiative under Beaubaire's editorship: Maria's OG received the same shocked outrage. Reader Joseph Vincze expressed the betrayal longtime Organic Gardening readers felt when Rodale's green way of life invaded his gardening monthly: "What are you doing to my Organic Gardening magazine? It is becoming some sort of generic holistic publication. I originally signed on with Organic Gardening back in 1992 to keep informed of the organic movement . . . so I don't need the "Healing Garden," "Healthy Eating," and any other cooking articles . . . Please stay focused to the mission of the magazine to promote organic gardening."[84] Enough readers shared this writer's indignation that Rodale realized she needed a separate magazine for her organic vision. A short two years after placing herself at the editorial helm, Rodale slipped away from OG to create Organic Style.

Organic Style's target audience was women like Maria: thirty-something-going-on-forty wealthy women with tastes for pampering but a nagging obligation to the preservation of wild nature, the conservation of the earth's limited resources, and an imprecise awareness of social justice issues. With organic product sales (including health, beauty, and food items) growing 20 percent annually from 1996 to 2001 and with organic food sales at $6.4 billion in 1999, early twenty-first-century America seemed primed for a hedonistic organic magazine.[85]

In public relations releases preceding Organic Style's premiere, Rodale argued that with so many natural and organic options, the organic consumer no longer had to endure deprivation as proof of moral determination. Her audience of "conscious sensualists" who "want to do the right thing for their health and the environment, but not at the cost of living well," could turn to Organic Style for guidance on chic eco-conscious beauty, fashion, diet, exercise, food, health, and vacations tips.[86] Organic Style lasted only from 2001 to 2005. In 2015, it was relaunched with J. I. Rodale's flagship publication, Organic Gardening, and branded as Organic Life. Despite unsteady readership, Rodale's "style" magazines anticipated and contributed to the direction of the natural foods movement in the new century.[87]

Maria Rodale never seemed tormented by the question of what Organic Style's commercial sensualism would do to the antimaterialist doctrine touted by her father throughout the 1970s and 1980s. When asked about the friction between her eco-immoderation and her father's organic minimalism, in a moment of either defensive reaction or outright ignorance, she remarked that her family rarely advanced the countercultural worldview with which it was often associated.[88]

While no one would have mistaken her soft-spoken, socially conservative father for a hippie or a political extremist, he certainly used his magazines and the Rodale Institute to broadcast incontrovertibly countercultural ardors, such as alternative energy and rural liberation. In 1971, Robert Rodale described his magazine company's position within U.S. society to *New York Times* columnist Wade Greene: "We are afraid of becoming legitimate. We have a lot of freedom now. We can say a lot of things knowing that our readers look at us, you know, as sort of oddball. So I'm comfortable being in a small minority and I don't know how to operate if we're in a majority."[89]

Maria Rodale's disavowal of her family's and its magazines' relationship with sixties and seventies protest denoted an ahistoricism in postsixties consumer culture. Early on, corporate advertisers understood the seductiveness of the baby-boomer rebellion and quickly inserted its gestalt into teenager-targeted products and marketing. By the end of the century, rebellion became so central to American culture that, counterintuitively, individuals used carefully chosen acquisitions to mark disgust with hyperconsumerism. This paradox appeared most frequently among the elite, who had strong inclinations to distinguish themselves from the compliant masses, the ability to do so, and leftover countercultural compulsions to have their "stuff" proclaim their originality.

A close study of *Organic Style*'s organic facelift—making this agricultural method, in Maria Rodale's words, "hip not hippie"—displays how its well-off female audience negotiated the contradictory push and pull of early twenty-first-century pecuniary culture. Following the green indulgency set by *Organic Style*, this consumer group satisfied its requirement to uphold environmentally conscientious divestment, while lavishing in sumptuous merchandise.

The *Organic Style* Trinity

Organic Style seemed to operate on three rules: please yourself first, do your best, good will follow. The magazine repeatedly suggested mutuality between the right thing to do and the right thing for you, thus its subtitle, "The Art of Living in Balance." In a fluffy bastardization of the feminist and countercultural "personal is political" credo, a Maria Rodale editorial outlined the holistic relationship between the private and the public: "The best choices for you are often the best choices for nature. Choices that preserve all that you love and need. Choices that help you live a healthier, more beautiful life. Choices that give you a clean conscience and a happy heart."[90]

Organic Style warned against self-flagellation. No dogmatic rigidity here, and above all no need to settle for bland food, unshapely clothing, or drab home furnishings just because they were organic. Owner of the first certified organic restaurant in the United States, Nora Pouillon elucidated this malleable organic ethic in an *Organic Style* feature on her Washington, D.C., eatery, Nora: "You don't have to be into macramé and Birkenstocks and eat brown rice and tofu. The only difference is that you really have to think about what you consume. If you buy a piece of paper, choose the unbleached kind. If you buy cleaning stuff, why buy all those things with a big sign that says Warning: Keep out of reach of children?"[91] Paralleling Pouillon's accommodating organic "politics," in a 2001 *New York Times* feature Danny Seo, author of *Conscious Style Home* (2001), green-celebrity watcher and adviser to *Organic Style*, explained the nondoctrinaire attitude he brought to his own "conscious style." "I'm not a purist. A lot of people think you have to do everything 100 percent eco, but my bedding line is 30 percent organic . . . It shouldn't be a punishment to live this way." Vaguely referencing the sixties/seventies movement, Seo argued that if the eco-consumer movement holds too tightly to a "militant" approach, it might lose the average American.[92]

In Seo's comments and in Maria Rodale's assertion that organic consumers were "younger people who did not grow up with the stereotypes of what organic is," seventies hard-scrabble, organic simple living was a connection to constantly battle and hopefully, over time, bury. This did not mean total detachment from agricultural and environmental politics.[93] The *Organic Style* reader—guilty over the ecological pressures first world consumption put on the planet and on third world producers—could alleviate his/her conflicted conscience by interpreting spending as social activism of a sort.

Maria Rodale's editorial ruminations on organic coffee exhibited this invention. Confiding her own feelings of impotency in the face of global environmental decline, Rodale offered that by simply spending eight dollars a month on a can of organic coffee (rather than three for a conventional coffee), a mere sixty dollars a year, readers could do good: "Before dismissing the idea, ask yourself this: Would you write a $60 check to a charity if you knew that almost every cent would go to helping Third World children get healthy and educated? Would you spend that amount knowing that you could be saving warblers, parrots, toucans, and other species from extinction? If your answer is yes, great! Switch to organic coffee now."[94] No boycotting or reduction in individual pleasures to tread more lightly on the earth for Maria Rodale. She simply implored her readers to pick the best of everything, and the best always meant organic. Nonorganic production methods fouled the environment, threatened individual health, and were inferior in taste and quality. How could the actual taste of, for example, beef (a topic covered in *Organic Style*'s March 2004 issue) differ if cattle grazed on the open range? Well, besides the obvious links of conventional feeding sources to diseases like mad cow, the difference was more about belief then taste. For devoted organic consumers, if a food was made with "old-fashioned" techniques, in harmony with nature, if the animal had the opportunity to roam freely and was not confined to cell-like stalls, the product simply tasted better.

Ostensibly, the organic method may have culminated in more tender and delectable cuts of beef. Nevertheless, the natural consumer's image of the cattle's life—chomping on prairie grasses, roaming in the sunshine rather than penned up in smelly stalls, slurping from a fresh pond rather than a "polluted" barnyard trough—informed his/her taste buds' response just as much as the beef's actual consistency and flavor. As Eatwild.com's website creator, Jo Robinson, claimed, "When I eat grass-fed meat, I have a sense that I'm eating the kind of food I'm designed to eat."[95] The certainty that organic farmers, grocers, and food producers shared consumers' dedication to the environment and local food systems was another component of the organic-quality supposition in Maria Rodale's signature magazine.

Organic Style reinforced these presumptions with in-depth profiles on wild salmon fisheries in British Columbia; a family-owned "natural meat company" in Bucks County, Pennsylvania; a tea emporium in Los Angeles; an organic winery in Mendicino County, California, to name a few. In each story, readers were privy to the company's business ethics and to its owners' inner lives: his/her homes, children, and personal history were all part of the organic ambience.

Organic Style humanized and miniaturized the global food system. The consumer became a participant in a like-minded gang. The food people showcased in *Organic Style* were just folks, like the reader. Sometimes they lived more glamorous lives than the average reader and had a lot of money, as did the owners of Applegate farms meat company, Stephen McConnell and Jill

Kearney (a former film producer), who rambled around their 250-year-old farmhouse in an old-money region of eastern Pennsylvania, or New York City tea connoisseur, Kelly Tisdale, who owned a Manhattan tea emporium, "Teany," with musician Moby. Yet, despite these "minor" differences, the organic people featured juggled busy work and family lives and were, like the reader-voyeurs, convinced of the right-mindedness of organic and natural foods, but were not nitpickers. This clubby intimacy with celebrities and beautiful people was common in other new millennium women's magazines, such as *Martha Stewart Living*, *O*, and *Real Simple*. All these publications seemed to adore the practiced and understated style that privilege allowed.

The organic fellowship depicted in *Organic Style*, on the surface, imitated the enclaves of awareness and activism promoted by Robert Rodale's 1970s–1980s *New Shelter* and *Organic Gardening*. In his regional "islands of purity," Rodale had urged: "We must start a personal, do-it-yourself program of analysis and action to find out how vulnerable we are, and also to protect us as best we can against the small amounts of poisons that now infuse almost all of our air and water."[96] Robert Rodale's solution to America's despoiled environment combined both public work and personal behavior modification. As he said, "It would be wrong to blame only industry. We have wanted, even demanded, some of the products that caused the creation of the wastes now soaking through our water supplies." The fundamental task lay not simply in identifying the problem and creating protective "islands of purity," though. Rather, he argued, preserving the earth called for action. "Will we be willing to give up some of the conveniences we have come to feel are our right in exchange for the health of future generations?" Robert Rodale circumspectly inquired in 1981.[97]

Twenty years later, Robert's daughter answered this question with a resounding no. No, her *Organic Style* readers would and should not delay delight nor fuss over the propriety of nonessential spending. But, yes, they would remain ecologically diligent and would use *Organic Style* as a guide to consuming alternatively. Traveling to Asia, a reader could follow in the footsteps of Sharon Collins (a lawyer, profiled in *Organic Style*, who tossed her career to travel and photograph Asia) and learn the life-altering lessons of Buddhist "calmness, openness, and generosity."[98] With such lofty aims and metaphysical souvenirs, a reader could justify a similarly expensive trip as a "spiritual quest," lifting the venture above the draining of natural resources and tacky resort getaways. By situating any improvidence within a discourse of deliberate and authentic living, *Organic Style* relegitimized the ostentation so anathema to Robert Rodale's 1970s–early 1980s back-to-the-land tenets.

This is not to say that seventies rebels did not enjoy their own version of consumerism. Self-sufficiency devotees pieced together outcast identities with survivalist and outdoors merchandise, such as canning equipment, home pickling and beer-making kits, earth shoes, kerosene heaters, and camping gear. Thus, to a certain extent, because Robert Rodale's magazines put so much political stock in individual shopping, eating, and home habits, they created the conceptual template for *Organic Style*'s postseventies construal of swanky organic spending as dissension. At the same time, in the 1960s and 1970s, natural consumerism, still a stripe of accumulation, was carried out in a marginalized, noncorporate retail network with definite social-environmental results in mind.

The rekindling of status spending in the 1980s and 1990s seemed to prove that the market economy was far too powerful and ingrained to be turned over by a handful of hippie businesses and self-sufficiency boosters, no matter how impassioned. Given that capitalism wasn't budging, oppositional citizens had to come to a détente with the system. At the dawn of the twenty-first century, shelling out the bucks for the hip, delicious, and amusing organic and natural goods flooding the market was a no-brainer. The righteous logic of sixties/seventies antimaterialism did not put the delight of wanting, getting, and having nice things to rest.

While *Organic Style* regularly reinforced this positive picture of organic living as fulfilling and honorable, in the background of each magazine lurked the long-lasting Rodale concern with toxic contamination and somatic vulnerability. Articles that asked "How Toxic Is Your Zip Code?," "Is Pollution Preventing Your Pregnancy?," and "How Healthy Is Your City?" reminded readers that safety remained elusive.

Although *Organic Style*'s writers and editors understood the social-structural mechanisms generating toxic health threats, their solutions were primarily self-defensive and local in scale. Rather than launch a citizen's campaign to press Congress or the FDA to control certain chemicals, the kind of public campaigning J. I. and Robert Rodale both did as national organic leaders, *Organic Style*'s self-protective strategies duplicated late twentieth-century activism known as NIMBY (not in my backyard). Both NIMBY activists and *Organic Style* writers and readers fixed on a specific pollution catastrophe in a certain locale; they generally did not formulate macrostructural responses to late modern industrialization. More often, they set their sights on a particularly negligent factory owner or baldly unresponsive politician.

The issues that *Organic Style* took seriously—chemical food additives, breast cancer, pollution—were treated as "backyard" problems. Concluding its consideration of school environments, *Organic Style* listed helpful hints in articles titled "Help Keep Your Child Healthy" and "Make Your Home a Smoke-Free Zone," "Fight Fungi," "Care For Your Linens," "Get the Lead Out," "Preempt Pesticides," "Cut Out Chemical Cleaning Products." An article that identified toxic conditions in schools nationwide—in Georgia, California, New Jersey, and Illinois—with a "protect your own" conclusion indicated a resignation to industrial irresponsibility and government torpor.[99]

Overwhelmed by unsound land use and corporate negligence, it seems that the elite's sense of public effectiveness, even with its cultural clout and class and racial entitlement, narrowed to what Ulrich Beck calls the "politics of self-preservation." According to Beck, without any countervailing stops, the international free market's wreckage continued unwatched, and disempowered citizens recoiled to safeguard themselves and their families from its unstoppable march.[100] Examples of this process abound in post–World War II America. Antibiotics, chemical pesticides, and food additives, originally revolutionary and beneficial inventions, turned into public health hazards once released to the market. For the individual citizen, Beck argues, the "global risk society" is an exceedingly perilous place with very little to depend on. Traditional partisan politics are an insipid rejoinder to the reach and independence of technology and global corporate dominance. Governments are paralyzed by nonstate enemies. And for the United States' political Left, temporary work, migrant labor, and multinational businesses made the point around which it historically built collectivity—the working class—immaterial.

The sixties New Left and the seventies counterculture understood these tendencies of late capitalist societies and erected collectives of conscience to stanch fragmentation and civic disempowerment. For a time, their organizations, political coalitions, communes, collectives, and businesses offered a genuine alternative, even when countercultural rebellion often meant consumption of the unorthodox stripe. Yet, the nation's persistent materialism and political right turn in the late 1960s challenged their relevance. *Organic Style* revived the countercultural battle against the "global risk society," arguing that a fatalistic surrender was simply not an option, at least for America's well-off. To effectively serve its early twenty-first-century affluent female readership (and striving imitators), *Organic Style* had to affirm its alternative organic identity, but not so much that it sounded politically zealous or, most important, frumpily unstylish. And it had to make capitalism—the thing that brought America processed, additive-saturated foods, petrochemical agriculture, and drug-driven medical science—seem less of an adversarial titan.

For its short moment in the sun, Maria Rodale's *Organic Style* (and its reboot, *Organic Life*) did this by characterizing the commercial sphere as a responsive and fluid partner. Thomas Frank describes this postsixties interpolation of capitalism as "market populism"—a belief that "markets expressed the popular will more articulately and more meaningfully than did mere elections."[101] But, in fact, although Frank describes this pro-business orientation as a by-product of America's rightward tilt, the natural foods movement was in the vanguard of commoditized politics. From its co-op and cookbook inception, it favored market and home front solutions for municipal problems.

Maria's grandfather and father both believed that, if united, Americans would direct the market and the federal government to organic agriculture and foods. J. I.'s populist anticorporate leanings and Robert's countercultural antimaterialism made them far more suspicious of the market than were Maria and her generation, especially of advertising agencies that manufactured needs in the buying public. For Robert Rodale and other critics of postwar consumer culture, stuffing grocery stores with gourmet organic foods and expensive alternative herbal remedies was a stopgap measure. In the end, what the market sold was more the symptom than the cause of the affluence disease. Each month he advised *Prevention*, *Organic Gardening*, and *New Shelter* readers to ignore shopping's siren song. If anything, Robert and J. I. wanted the readers of *Organic Gardening* and *Prevention* to shake loose from supermarket and supermall manipulations.

While their opinions diverged on consumerism's role in the organic movement, three generations of Rodale did agree on modernity's toxicity and the merits of organic foods. They concurred that a nonchemical agricultural system should act as a model for all human endeavor. And they agreed that personal lifestyle decisions were central to the organic project's success. From this core covenant, the Rodale organic ideal transformed to address the trials of each era—J. I.'s sunflower seeds, bonemeal, and organic vegetables to shield the body from fifties atomic poisoning; Robert's rural retreat and solar energy for self-sufficiency and observant living in the recessionary and experimental 1970s; and, finally, Maria's hip green consumables and NIMBY protest to mark alternativeness and control in the global hypermaterial new millennium. In 2018, after years of floundering and financial decline, Rodale, Inc. was purchased by Hearst, thus ending the family's dominion over American organics.[102] Nevertheless, for over seventy years, the Rodales had helped nature-revering and health-attentive readers bind their angst, buffer their bodies and homes, and author their interaction with the media-commercial giant.

CHAPTER 4

DR. ANDREW WEIL AND THE POSTSIXTIES PROMISES OF FOOD

In a 2002 survey of natural foods consumers, the Natural Marketing Institute found that more than half of those interviewed cited health and wellness as the stimulus for their food purchases. Only 8.3 percent cited "environmental concerns."[1] The Hartman Group, a health and wellness marketing firm, uncovered similar trends in its analysis of natural and organic shoppers.[2] According to Laurie Demerritt, Hartman's executive vice president, healthism, not environmentalism, was expanding the "green marketplace." In fact, "there was never a very large environmental market" she concluded. "There was a lot of talk, but not a lot of dollars on the table."[3] Demerritt's sweeping generalization might have missed the complexity of shoppers' desires. Yet, in the first two decades of the new century, health—while sometimes seen through an environmental lens—remained an outstanding reason for organic purchases.[4] The commercial success of natural goods, documented in myriad studies, would have been unlikely had these previously countercultural products not been swept up in the expanding multimedia commercial complex and the popular health craze.

As the new century's most well-known alternative health personality, Dr. Andrew Weil contributed to the commoditization of natural health and foods. One of the first televised self-health gurus, Weil created the model of populist adviser that others followed. Yet, unlike Deepak Chopra, Dr. Oz, and other superstar "docs," Andrew Weil's career and life followed the historical curve of the counterculture and the natural foods movement. A mutinous medical student in the late 1960s who published controversial studies on the effects of marijuana and treated tripping hippies at the Haight-Ashbury Medical Clinic; an off-the-beaten-path ethnopharmacology researcher and altered-states expeditionary in the 1970s; a holistic healer in the 1980s; and an empire-building, natural health luminary at the turn of the twenty-first century, Dr. Andrew Weil helped implant countercultural precepts into the defining natural and consumer trends of the period.

BECOMING CONSCIOUS AND COUNTERCULTURAL

Like other acclaimed sixties personalities, Andrew Weil diverted from a promising medical career when the period's strong winds blew him off course. A Harvard biology undergrad from 1960 to 1964, Weil heard about the psilocybin studies of Timothy Leary and Richard Alpert in Harvard's Center for Research in Personality and volunteered. Leary declined, abiding by the university's prohibition against undergraduate participation. Instead, he advised Weil to conduct his own mescaline trials, which the curious student did with a group of classmates. Weil's exclusion from the Leary-Alpert project only further piqued his interest. He followed their investigation closely, eventually writing several provocative *Harvard Crimson* articles on it. *Look* magazine noticed the *Harvard Crimson* pieces and commissioned Weil to write an insider's report, the results of which appeared in 1963 under the title "The Strange Case of the Harvard Drug Scandal." The *Harvard Crimson* and *Look* exposés pitted Alpert and Leary against Harvard, eventually resulting in Leary's resignation and Alpert's dismissal by 1963.[5]

The Harvard psychedelics experiments initiated Weil's lifelong preoccupation with consciousness. In the 1960 and early 1970s, he and other altered-states advocates used the mind and the body for nonconformist experimentation. They became convinced that mass exposure to hallucinogens would incite a consciousness revolution, making business as usual untenable. Theodore Roszak, in *The Making of the Counter Culture*, described this psychedelic conjecture as a "simple syllogism: change the prevailing mode of consciousness and you change the world . . . universalize the use of dope and you change the world."[6] For psychedelic revolutionaries, the battle was never for the streets or for Congress—it was for the nation's mind. The seat of consciousness was the individual. The revolution, therefore, must begin inside each American's head.

After the 1960s, when it became clear that the psychotropic new age wasn't coming, Andrew Weil did not give up on converted consciousness. Nor did he waver from his investment in the individual as *the* change agent. Instead, he translated his earlier drug-induced insights on reality into the practicable venture of consciousness attuned to diet, exercise, and stress reduction. The conventional medical mindset, according to Weil and other critics, did not account for patients' inner reality (a reality cherished by counterculturalists) or for the mysteries of the cosmos. With sharpened physiological awareness, individuals could make contact with their own biological truth. Physicians' formulaic medical analyses paled in comparison with this "systemic reflective awareness," according to the holistic perspective that Weil and other alternative healers developed.[7]

Introducing into the mainstream health debate the culturally loaded term "consciousness," which for many conjured up a montage of stoned hippies, head-in-the-clouds countercultural idealism, and feminist rap sessions, required considerable rhetorical and historical finesse. Through various media, Weil loosened consciousness from the drug subculture, presenting the trained mind as a tool for calm and healthy adjustment to the drains of modern existence, rather than a prerequisite for battle with the "system."

In the 1970s and 1980s, the holistic promise of health through a natural foods diet, "subjective consciousness," and nontraditional remedies appealed to counterculturally influenced Americans who already distrusted dominant institutions.[8] As Weil explained in one of his first advice books, *Health and Healing* (1983), liberated from medical authoritarianism, patients could "learn their body's normal patterns ... recognize early signs and symptoms of illness ... experiment with simple methods of treatment and be wary of the pitfalls of unthinking confidence in professional doctors."[9] New discoveries in conventional medical science reinforced Weil's anti-expert approach. As Peter Carroll observes, when postwar medical research affirmed environmental and social explanations for modern diseases, such as cancer, heart disease, diabetes, and neurological disorders, illness and health looked far more under individual control than was previously thought.[10] Freedom from external expertise, and the obligation of self-definition, meshed perfectly with the countercultural libertarianism of the average holistic adherent.[11]

As Maria Rodale's *Organic Style* exemplified, by the twenty-first century, this individualized health code had been turned into a widely sought commodity, as much as a state of being. Healthfulness became a personal accomplishment and a show of middle- and upper-class standing, won through willpower and observant consumerism.[12] Dr. Weil's star rose as many postsixties Americans made physical well-being the foremost human purpose and whole foods and natural health the means to that end. Weil's corporate complex—which includes a website, a Facebook page, a Twitter account, a blog, best-selling books, several PBS series, and many eponymous natural food lines—guided wellness consumers through the alternative health labyrinth. In a nation with a centuries-old dedication to self-reliance, his do-it-yourself wellness marketplace attracted many.

FROM MUSHROOMS TO BOARDROOMS: BECOMING A HEALTH GURU

Andrew Weil entered Harvard Medical School after completing his biology degree in 1964. Despite this seemingly conformist choice, Weil remained an altered-states aesthete. As a medical student, he continued experimenting with natural and synthetic psychedelics. In his last year at Harvard, Weil decided to challenge the academic world again by proposing a study of the effects of marijuana on human consciousness. Informed by Leary's and Alpert's missteps, Weil safeguarded his project by partnering with Harvard psychiatrist Dr. Norman Zinberg and conducting the experiment at the more flexible Boston University. Securing a nonillicit marijuana source remained the only glitch in Weil's plan. Eventually, his lobbying and his adviser's reputation convinced the Federal Bureau of Narcotics to send Weil a trial supply.[13]

According to Weil, in the drug-paranoid 1960s, little evidence supported government warnings about marijuana's dangers. To scientifically dispute unfounded alarmism, Weil and his associates, Dr. Zinberg and Boston University Ph.D. student Judith Nelson, collected a group of experienced and marijuana-naive subjects, had them smoke the drug, and then put them through a series of tests. From this data, Weil's team concluded that marijuana was not a hallucinogenic drug (a claim espoused by many medical professionals), nor was it addictive. Importantly for Weil's later ruminations on the relationship between consciousness and bodily health, subjects who were marijuana novices experienced a less pronounced "high" than did regular users. For Weil this proved the drug's pharmacological mildness. It also signified that "set and setting" (an idea borrowed from Timothy Leary) could determine the effect of the drug on the subject. Experienced users, who knew they might get a placebo or the real thing in this double-blind experiment, could not trigger a psychological response to the drug. They demonstrated all of the physical effects—red eyes, increased heart rate, dryness of the mouth—but displayed no "subjective response."[14] *Science* published these findings in the 1968 article "Clinical and Psychological Effects of Marijuana in Man." The study's controversial conclusions garnered much media attention, making Weil a minor celebrity.

After finishing medical school, Andrew Weil spent a year in a clinical internship at Mount Zion Hospital in San Francisco, volunteering his spare time at the Haight Ashbury Medical Clinic treating causalities of the drug scene. Thereafter, in lieu of military service, he fulfilled one year of a two-year contract with the National Institute of Mental Health (NIMH). Enervated by conflicts with NIMH officials over his acclaim as a marijuana expert, Weil decided to leave the "straight" medical establishment and record his thoughts on America's drug culture. *The Natural Mind* (1972) was this record.[15]

In *The Natural Mind*, Weil argued for a more sophisticated national response to widespread youth drug experimentation. Drawing from his medical education and his observation of the psychedelic subculture, Weil aimed to deflate mainstream antidrug hysteria by proving the human need for altered consciousness. Naively, he recommended that Americans recognize drugs as "keys to a better ways of using the mind." As he optimistically predicted, "We are living in the midst of a revolution in consciousness that will transform human society. Stoned consciousness is spreading through our population like a chain reaction; it cannot be stopped. At some critical point, most of us will be experiencing our perceptions in a stoned way all of the time. What will happen to external reality at that point is anybody's guess."[16] Taking his part in this imminent uprising, Weil applied for and won a fellowship from the Institute of Current World Affairs. With institute monies, he conducted research, in Mexico and Latin America, on "altered states of consciousness, drug use in other cultures and other matters to do with the complementarity of mind and body."[17] In *The Marriage of the Sun and Moon* (1980), Weil recounted his investigations.

Weil's overarching goal during the fellowship was to test a hypothesis that South American "New World Indians" had a healthier drug culture than that in the United States. Because Indians had "ritualized [their] use of drugs in positive ways under careful social controls," Weil surmised that he would find little evidence of addiction and abuse in Latin America and Mexico. Like other world-curious counterculturalists, Weil idolized the indigenous peoples of South America and Mexico, who seemed to possess effortless authenticity. Specifically, Weil imagined that native communities, because of their long history of psychoactive plant use, fully accepted intoxicants and nonordinary consciousness.

His results varied. In Columbia, searching for *yage*, a plant-based hallucinogen mythologized by Beat author William Burroughs in *The Yage Letters*, Weil met opportunists posing as yage medicine men. These charlatans plied jejune hippie tourists with the native whiskey, *aguardimente*, and then served an ersatz yage concoction, which for Weil only produced diarrhea and incessant nausea. In exchange, the Indian imposters acquired cash and ample supplies of aguardimente.[18]

Weil had better luck finding Indian drug wisdom in the tiny Columbian village Cubeo. Cubeo men tucked wads of roasted and pulverized coca leaves, the plant from which cocaine is made, in their checks on special occasions and when doing arduous work. Weil marveled at the wise use of this intoxicant, and he praised the "natural way" they prepared it. Contrasting the two experiences, Weil recounted, "I saw no evidence among these Indians that coca use was addictive or dependence-producing, nor that it was injurious to health."[19] In fact, Weil concluded that the coca nourished the Cubeos' psychological and physical health.

Why had Western cocaine, derived from the same coca plant, created addicts and violent drug trafficking? For Weil, the simple answer was Western culture and consciousness. "The Indians I know who use coca respect their drug," Weil concluded. "They honor Mama Coca by treating her plant reverently, preparing it for use carefully, and guarding its power by saving it for occasions when they need it."[20] Native Cubeos respected nature and the coca plant. They did not extract its most potent element and imbibe it but harvested the entire leaf, roasted it, pulverized it, and mixed it with ash to create a mild paste which provided a pleasantly mild high. Unlike Americans who used cocaine for psychological escape or for ego enhancement, the Cubeo only expected coca to induce relaxation and well-being.

Ruminating on American versus Cubeo treatment of intoxicants, Weil concluded, "The choice seems to be ours: Drugs become useful or dangerous depending on how we view them and how we use them."²¹ With the correct frame of mind, Weil argued, everyone could experience highs, even without chemical or botanical stimulants. After several years of travel and contemplation, Weil affirmed that altered consciousness came from within. Given the right set of expectations and cultural frame, a consciousness seeker, allegedly, could shift mental attitude simply by munching on fiery chilis or surrendering to the stimulating influence of a solar eclipse. In his future career as an integrative practitioner, he would weave these insights into his theories on mind-body interaction.

Andrew Weil's South American expedition and his posttravel conclusions about intention and consciousness follow his generation's evolution from wild countercultural youth to mainstream adulthood. While traveling, Weil became a bohemian scholar/explorer. He willingly drank, sniffed, smoked, and ate any psychoactive substance that came his way, in the name of science and heightened consciousness. At the end of his vision questing, he deduced that psychic transformation resided within. His celebration of nonchemical intoxication in *Marriage* seemed to be his way of negotiating his youthful exuberance for physical and mental exploration with his more serious intention of reforming America's approach to the mind and body. For his message to reach beyond the sixties drug culture, he had to find licit demonstrations of his point. His project had to transcend countercultural self-exploration and psychic titillation. This reorientation took time. After he returned from South America in the mid-1970s and settled in Tucson, Arizona, he spent the rest of the decade crusading for drug enlightenment. He cowrote an encyclopedia of illegal and legal drugs for parents, *Chocolate to Morphine: Understanding Mind-Active Drugs* (1983), with children's book author Winifred Rosen. And he became an adjunct professor of addiction studies at the University of Arizona.

On the whole, Weil's campaign to depoliticize drug use and to regularize altered states failed to convert America. Like many other countercultural strategies for social evolution, "straight" Americans found his message either laughable or threatening. Former vice president Spiro Agnew and Senator Paula Hawkins denounced *Chocolate to Morphine* and argued that Weil's books be banned from schools and libraries.²² Government policy, especially during the "just say no" Reagan 1980s, continued to demonize and criminalize drugs and drug users. American society, despite the continued use of psychoactive substances, never accepted Weil's equalization of the rational and irrational mind. His unconventional pro-drug message also failed to penetrate the increasingly consumerist culture stream. His authority as a radical drug expert could not easily be used to launch other products, ideas, or institutions or to enhance his celebrity.

By the end of the 1980s, Weil began to pack away his psychedelic ambitions, turning his intellectual energy to the "new models of healing and alternative medicine."[23] Nevertheless, he resolutely clung to his nonconformist and rebel identity. As he, and other alternative healers, worked to substitute the hospital-physician-pharmaceutical agglomerate with what they pitched as a kinder and more natural holistic system, they created a new target for the antiestablishment motif of the sixties. Like natural foods innovators, holistic critics decided to form a separate circuit of natural health practitioners and therapeutics for patient independence. This natural health movement enjoyed success because it comprehensively satisfied the needs of the middle- and upper-class individuals who had come into adulthood in the wave of the sixties movement. A skeptical generation, they mistrusted vested power. A searching generation, they determinedly sought new lifestyles and unorthodox spiritual and secular philosophies. A nonconformist generation, they invested personal stock in individualism and, what they believed to be, righteous, antimaterialist self-expression. Concurrently, as the first broadly affluent generation, they expected and sought exceptional healthfulness, youthfulness, and comfort. What they could not know or predict was that the holistic emphasis on self-diagnosis and personal responsibility made them subject to health advice from an even more commanding institution: the multimedia consumer complex.

BUILDING AN INTEGRATIVE EMPIRE

Weil's first popular diet and health treatise, *Health and Healing*, enjoyed greater success than his three drug reform and consciousness manifestos. But it did not propel his stardom. As far as his literary agent, Lynn Nesbit, was concerned, Weil satisfactorily served a niche audience of alternative medicine aficionados. Consequently, she made little effort to grow his market presence. In the early 1990s Nesbit famously gibed: "If Andy Weil really wants to make it, he's got to shave off his [hippie] beard."[24]

Since his earlier years as a mutinous medical student researching marijuana, Andrew Weil had wanted to make his mark on American culture. As the media consumer system made celebrity the key to social influence in the 1990s, he decided to find an agent who would give him the recognition and access to the masses that he felt he needed for his health mission. Richard Pine was this promoter. After being hired, Pine implemented the key change that launched Weil's career: he got him on television.[25]

In regular appearances on PBS, either in segments on his book or as a holistic talking head, Weil became recognized as an alternative authority. Simply by having his face on TV, Weil sold more books: a perfect publicity loop. By 1997, the *New York Times* designated Weil "America's best-known doctor," and the University of Arizona named Weil director of its new integrative medicine program. Mixing visual and print exposure with administrative duties at a mainstream medical school gave Weil a level of respectability that other popular healers and the holistic movement as a whole lacked.[26] Although Weil repeatedly asserted that he hired Richard Pine to more effectively transmit his alternative health and natural diet message, the trajectory of Weil's career and celebrity development, after Pine was onboard, suggests otherwise.

An essential step in Weil's advertising advance was the creation of his website, AskDr.Weil.com in 1996 (later revamped and named drweil.com) and its Time Inc. acquisition in 1997. A Time representative matter-of-factly stated that they signed Weil because "our strategy is a brand name strategy, and he's a brand in the health area."[27] With this industry leader overseeing his website, Weil acquired access to a larger portion of the web health market.[28]

Weil's decision to establish an internet foothold in the mid-1990s presciently anticipated the new-century social media explosion. According to a Nua and Pew 2002 internet survey, six million North Americans used the web as a medical directory. On an average day, 93 percent of health surfers researched particular diseases, 63 percent engaged in more generalized browsing on "nutrition, exercise, and weight control," and 48 percent sought information on "alternative medicine." With health becoming a national fixation, Nua and Pew predicted that by 2004, "E-healthcare" would grow to a $10 billion industry.[29] Seizing the spirit of the times, Dr. Weil's corporation, Weil Lifestyle, LLC jammed his website with dietary health information and what his promotional team described as "Best in Breed" products.

Weil did not jump immediately into commercialism. Originally, he forbade his web staff from placing any endorsements on his site except for Weil Vitamin Advisor, his Polaris Matcha Green Tea, and his online lifestyle management service, "Optimum Health Plan." Over time, side panel pop-up ads for "OrganicBouquet.com," *Natural Health, Body and Soul,* and *Eating Well* magazines (in which Weil was a regular commentator), Evoluzione clothing, Fungi Perfecti medicinal mushrooms, and Vital Choice salmon products found their way into the daily e-letter Good Morning from DrWeil.com. In the 1960s and 1970s, like other young dissidents, Weil disdained American consumer culture for its falsity. Yet, as part of the first fully consumerist generation, his bohemianism depended on countercultural commodities—rock 'n' roll, natural foods, hippie clothing, and the like.[30] In the postsixties context, Weil balanced these seemingly dueling signals by crafting an alternative marketplace chock-full of holistic, natural, and organic goods imbued with the social-spiritual uplift and self-actualization touchstones which resonated so meaningfully with middle- and upper-class consumers.

As Weil's mission statement projects, "My primary purpose in creating *Weil Lifestyle* is to provide a funding platform to support educational research and programs that will ultimately improve health care and empower individuals to make better health choices by following the principles of integrative medicine."[31] His team's merchandise selections supported these elevated goals. Weil Lifestyle's cochairman David Stoup explained how the company achieved commercial-scientific synergy: "By partnering with philosophically aligned and best-in-class companies, we're accelerating the adoption of Dr. Weil's integrative approach to health and health care. The products combine good science, innovation, understanding of the mind-body interaction, and respect for health education and individual empowerment."[32] Despite this exalted self-description, as with other websites, visitors to Weil's internet space were subject to about as much product placement as actual health information.

Weil Lifestyle's online *Weekly Wellness Bulletin* and his monthly *Self Healing* paper newsletter only promoted Weil trademarked products. Each month his followers, who paid $29.95 a year for his preventive advice, received a publication packed with inserts and commercial flyers—all with Weil's face prominently displayed. This commercial copy solidified, over and over again, the link between Weil's friendly, ruddy face and consumer yearnings for physical vitality, correct eating, mental serenity, and Weilian optimum living.

All of Weil's recommended products were backed by findings in his "serious" health articles. Like advertorials which pose as serious journalism, the overlap of Weil-branded product placement, "hard" dietary advice, and scientific scholarship blurred the lines between commercials and objective nutritional commentary.³³ The lead story in the May 2005 issue of *Self Healing*, "Stocking a Spring Medicine Chest," exemplifies this imprecision. While Weil did not plug his own vitamin company in the article, almost every other newsletter came with an insert for his supplement line. Convinced that his/her sinus trouble, stomach ailment, or general fatigue would be remedied by a medicinal herb featured in *Self Healing*, a Weil reader could search the Vitamin Advisor to buy the recommended and trademarked supplements. Weil's website need not make a direct endorsement; it was implied.

Weil's coverage of nutritional studies tilted toward infotisement as well. The "scientifically proven" healthy habits that his studies recommended could all be achieved with a Weil trademarked or endorsed product. Occasionally, even his newsletter, framed as his website's most academic and scientific segment, disregarded the thin veneer between endorsement and evidence by unblinkingly plopping Weil goods down in the middle of a serious column. Concluding an article on the influence of sound on human health, Weil plugged, "If you'd like to try a form of sound therapy to help relax, I've recently released a CD with my friend and colleague Kimba Arem called *Self Healing with Sound and Music* (see the enclosed brochure)."³⁴

Weil is able to pull this off because he and his handlers made him the guardian of integrative health. In his books and on his website, Weil presents himself as a fallible confidant, openly confessing his weaknesses along with the secrets to his visually publicized good health. In a December 30, 2015, Amazon.com "top positive review" of *Health and Healing*, a Weil fan effused, "Dr. Weil tells you exactly how to eat and what to supplement to cure it [a health condition]. He talks in terms of himself often. He is compassionate. He speaks of his own anxieties so to tell you that it's okay for you to have them too." James Twitchell suggests that celebrity endorsements work so effectively because they promise a contagious transmittal of whatever extraordinary qualities the consumer attributes to the famous face in the advertisement. Such an endorsement guarantees that "if you use this product, if you touch this stone, if you go to this holy place, if you repeat this word, you will be empowered because the product, stone, place, word . . . has been used [or recommended] by one more powerful than you."³⁵ Weil's observations on his own celebrity confirm Twitchell's analysis: "Having become a public personality as a result of books and television programs, and the fact also that I'm fairly recognizable, I have to be aware that whatever I'm doing, people are watching. If I'm in an airport eating a frozen yogurt, a lot of people are going to come and over and say, 'Well, I guess it's all right to eat frozen yogurt.'"³⁶

The extra enchantment of Weil products and media, beside his notoriety, is that they are attached to nontraditional medicine and self-health, which are lures for his baby-boomer disciples and the generations following in their footsteps. Weil devotees are voracious health consumers, particularly of holistic formulas that they perceive as less invasive, less toxic, and more self-directed than is standard medicine. At the same time, Weil enthusiasts,

FIGURE 9. Andrew Weil practicing what he preaches, in a publicity photo. *Courtesy of Joe Mc-Nally Photography.*

who have an ingrained nonconformist instinct, enter the marketplace warily. Nervous about the media-consumer complex's dominance and capitalism's continual destruction of the biosphere, they seek merchandise and companies that serve a greater god than the almighty dollar.

Weil's products and personhood address these warring impulses within his market base. His corporation has skillfully used branding, supersaturation, commodity fetishism, and merchandise integration to sear in his readers' minds the purportedly noncommercial objective of his work and health corporation. In point of fact, Weil Lifestyle, LLC does turn all after-tax profits into the Weil Foundation. Doing so, it appears to have grabbed the reigns of consumer capital and trained them to serve human need rather than human greed. It ostensibly fulfills, in the present, the revolution that proved so frustratingly unreachable to social progressives in the 1960s. Recalling a phone conversation with a business consultant in the 1980s, who then informed him that "sixties values are dead in the water," Weil reflected: "I hung up and I was thinking, What were 60's values? They were optimism and community, you know, and that they should be dead in the water didn't seem to me to be right! It was an amazing time the 60's, partly because of a sense we had that we could change everything. The irony, of course, is that it's only now, because my generation is moving into positions of power in society, that a lot of those ideas can actually be made possible."[37] From this former hippie's perspective, filling the marketplace with well-vetted health goods, educating America about preventive health and stress management, and developing the organic and natural foods industry constitutes the revolution. Commenting on his roles as an integrative health physician and commercial personality, Weil explained: "There are a lot of physicians out there who are very popular with consumers, who have no credibility in the profession. I think I've been able to walk in both worlds, and I will continue to do that. I feel that both of these worlds are necessary, because without the consumer movement none of this would be happening."[38]

In her 1997 Sunday magazine feature, *New York Times* columnist Larissa MacFarquhar abided by this self-characterization, describing Weil as the noble "Shaman, M.D.," an image that other journalists followed. Framing Weil as a humble alternative doc with an important message on his mind, MacFarquhar opined: "For Weil, the financial aspect of his popularity has never been the point. He is not the kind of guy who wants a lot of money. He lives in a non-descriptly furnished old ranch house in the desert 45 minutes outside of Tucson. He drives a 1994 Toyota pick-up truck."[39] When asked about his appearance on QVC hawking his best-selling books, *Spontaneous Healing* and *Eight Weeks to Optimum Health*, Weil explained that the healing message was his "calling." It hardly mattered, he seemed to suggest, how he delivered the wellness word.[40]

Weil's ability to reconcile counterculture and consumer culture is attractive to his age cohort, who want to preserve the outsider edge they acquired during their rebellious youth, while simultaneously indulging in their later prosperity. He knows his consumers' most secreted fears about their bodies, health, and morals. He also knows their civic yearnings, because he is one of them. Maybe he is even better than them, an authentic hippie who survived the 1960s and is still "making a difference." When the psychedelic upheaval never materialized, Weil had to find a way to live authentically within the confines of the very same society that he and his countercultural comrades, had, in Howard Brick's words, "promised to challenge totally."[41] He did so by becoming the nation's alternative health rabble-rouser. Dr. Andrew Weil made a grand promise to America of maximal existence through integrative health and natural foods magic.

With diet at the center of his website and online subscription management program, "My Optimum Health Plan," Weil elevated natural eating to a new level of cultural and commercial magnitude. With selective scientific evidence and market saturation, Weil's company soaked specific natural edibles, such as green tea and soy foods, in an alluring brew of health, environmental, psychological, and spiritual signs. In so doing, Weil's multimedia business contributed to the redefinition of natural foods from vehicles of countercultural dietary contest to implements of psychic satisfaction and self-conservation. The natural foods corporate apparatus assisted this refinement by publicizing every shred of health data and styling every food with even the vaguest health associations as the next lifesaver.

DRINKING THE ORIENT: GREEN TEA MEDICINE AND MAGIC

Like any commercial apparatus, Weil's platforms had to generate constant health hype. One month Weil followers should avoid carbs, and the next, use holy basil to reduce stress. Yet for several decades certain foods, such as green tea and soy foods, appeared on his website and in his books with enough frequency that any follower would have at least tried them. According to the good doctor, there were numerous reasons to choose green tea, the first of which was Asia's tradition of treating food as medicine. Asian societies, Weil explained in *Eating Well for Optimum Health* (2000), with their "tradition of healing cuisine ... [blur] the lines between food and medicine" and present a fresh health alternative to the West's bifurcation of eating and health care.[42]

Andrew Weil always found little to praise in the Western diet and Western culture. Western foods, he believed, triggered more illness and bodily discomfort than other culinary cultures. Asian foods and Asian custom, on the other hand, emanated an exoticism that seemed intrinsically more healthful. Unfortunately, culturally debilitating interactions with the West threatened even ancient Asian wisdom. After Western contact, Hawaiian island Polynesians, who, according to Weil's recounting, were "very active and largely free of degenerative illnesses," took to eating "American fast food, especially bread, rice, soda, snack foods, pastries and candy." This cultural collision, Weil argued, caused native Hawaiians' "normal heaviness [to blossom] into morbid obesity."[43] Modern Japan and China exhibited similar health declensions. As American foods swept across these previously insular nations, chronic disease, such as arteriosclerosis, followed. Although interaction with Western dietary habits unsettled Asian traditions, an inner essence remained unperturbed, at least according to Dr. Weil's romantic renderings.

Andrew Weil's long-standing fascination with Asia's putatively indestructible uniqueness comes through in his account of his first encounter with green tea: "I learned to drink green tea in Japan and associate it with good times there: when I inhale its subtle fragrance, I am transported to tatami rooms in temples and country inns, where I sat on the floor with friends, admiring flower arrangements and artfully served food. The experience is sensual and meditative at the same time, and I know that I am giving my body something that is good for it."[44] Culture critic Kim Lau notices that ahistorical idolizations of Japan are routine in the new-century dietary discourse. In health-preoccupied modern America, she argues, disease-free Japanese bodies have become "'icons of a lost past, symbolic representations of the 'natural' and the 'traditional.'"[45] Andrew Weil and his health-seeking contemporaries gravitated toward Asian edibles for the same reasons that postwar Beat writers adopted Zen Buddhism and sixties hippies practiced meditation and read Hindu mystical texts. For countercultural and Beat seekers, spiritual "orientalism" presented psychomystical release from America's secular emptiness. For the postsixties health consumer, the stakes were higher, a life-and-death matter. For them, the "Orient" possessed the secrets of wellness and longevity.

Through the 1990s, scientific studies lauding green tea's healthful attributes only further corroborated Weil's belief in the innate intelligence of Asian culture. Weil argued in his December 2003 newsletter that polyphenols, green tea's antioxidant compounds, may "block the development of prostate cancer," as well as "hinder the oxidation of LDL cholesterol," thus managing "elevated cholesterol and triglycerides." Green tea's polyphenols might also benefit women, Weil claimed in another addition of *Self Healing*, as they may block cancer-causing "free radicals"; sustain "bone mineral density"; and boost the immune system by helping the body make "interferon gamma, an immune system protein."[46] For Weil, green tea packed a double punch: it came from a holistic and spiritual culture, and its leaves carried salubrious chemical components.

Weil's biochemical analysis of tea points to a postwar leitmotif: the banalization of science. In the 1950s, the national government became a financial and ideological sponsor of science with the creation of the Atomic Energy Act in 1946 and the National Science Foundation in 1950. With the 1958 adoption of the National Defense Education Act and founding of NASA, the country's Cold War fate became tied to the advancement of science. Science, then, moved out of the laboratory and into the public forum. From 1950s science fiction to high school science clubs, to *Time* magazine's 1961 appointment of "the American scientist" as the "man of the year," science occupied the nation's imagination. The cultural ascent of science engendered a functionalist approach to eating, according to historian of health and medicine Robert Crawford.[47] As Americans appraised edibles for their cellular health units, food got sorted into chaste and corrupted, natural and unnatural clusters. Judged through this Manichean framework, food's traditional aesthetic, gustatory, and communal traits receded in importance.[48]

Weil's elemental dissection of food replicates the microscopic orientation of postwar science. In molecular biology, subatomic physics, and computer microchips, twentieth- and twenty-first-century science and technology has attempted to unravel smaller and smaller units of matter. Simultaneously, with genetics, viral biology, immunology, and nutrition, medical science exchanged straightforward organ and blood mechanics for complex physiological networks. Outside of the laboratory, cognizance of particulate pollutants, atomic radioactivity, and cellular physiology, as related to disease, generated considerable, albeit superficial, lay awareness of microscopic anatomy.[49] For Weil, the most threatening and inscrutable illnesses of the modern age—cancer, AIDs, diabetes—originated at the molecular level. Based on this presumption, micronutritional responses made sense. With molecular science, described by Crawford as "our primary symbolic order," all aspects of human existence—sexuality, birth, death, criminal behavior, drug addiction, mental disorders, and eating—became biochemical problems to be solved.[50] Consequently, foods became valued for their chemical constituent parts. A tomato is not eaten for its healthful "tomatoness" but for its "lycopeneness." Regular doses of raw garlic are recommended for their natural antibiotic molecules, broccoli for its cancer-fighting antioxidants, and so on.

Medico-populists like Weil, who, since the 1960s, had striven to democratize medical knowledge, contributed to the clinicalization of eating and everyday life and to the dissemination of microbiological dietary consciousness. Translating complicated (and inconclusive) studies into easily digestible health snippets and tossing around molecular wordology, Weil and the popular press turned health-fixated Americans into amateur scientists. Along the way, they contributed to the turn-of-the-twenty-first-century muddling of scientific fact with advertising fiction and of political engagement with self-preservation. Au courant health consumers, even those holistic aficionados who questioned Western rationalism and the scientific paradigm, embraced this scientification of their bodies and culture—demanding more studies, more precise information, and more nutritionally enhanced foods.[51] The food industry happily complied. In the last decade of the twentieth century, food producers and marketers created a group of foods saturated with vitamins, minerals, and chemical components drenched in healthful assurances. Variously described as "nutraceutical," "pharma," "optimum," "functional," or "smart" foods, this commercial food trend inspired companies such as Kellogg's to spend $65 million creating a functional foods division and Campbell to issue a mail-order Intelligent Quisine line.[52]

The tea industry benefited directly from nutraceutical notions, transforming its almost commercially moribund beverage category into a trendy commodity. Prior to 1990, U.S. tea sales slumped to under one billion; by 2003 total tea sales had jumped to 5.1 billion. Concocting ready-to-drink tea products loaded with "medicinal" herbal extracts, companies such as Arizona, Snapple, Tazo, and Sobe led the charge in the renaissance of the specialized tea market. Throughout the 1990s, all types of tea saw improved consumer attention. In 1994, *New York Times* columnist and foodie Florence Fabricant proclaimed tea "the coffee of the 90's."[53] In chichi Manhattan eateries, tea garnered new notice with tableside tea service and pulverized green tea powder sprinkled on gourmet foods as a spice.[54] Industry analysts all agreed that the "endless positive media coverage extolling the health virtues of tea" had given the traditional hot beverage new commercial bearing.[55]

Perfectly poised to cash in on the scientific acknowledgment of tea and wellness consumers' weakness for health potions, every traditional black tea company added a special green tea addition to its lines. Lipton, Salada, Twinings, Bigelow, Davidson, and Harris introduced a green tea product, as did natural tea labels such as Stash, Tazo, Celestial Seasonings, and Good Earth. And they all wrapped their packages in Asian signs, health promises, or a combination of the two.

British tea company Twinings joined the green tea choir with a mix of Asian and health come-ons. According to columnist Jane Pettigrew, this very staid British tea purveyor pumped up its image with a "stylish and very contemporary" package that they hoped would "convey the Eastern aura but retain the endorsement of the famous black and gold Twinings brand." Twinings new green tea box highlighted the important health attributes within, explaining, "Green teas are a natural source of antioxidants which help protect the body from damage caused by free radicals and are naturally lower in caffeine than most black teas."[56] Combining Asian and health codes on its lime-colored green tea package, Bigelow presented a snow-covered mountain and Buddhist temple arch on its frontispiece while prominently announcing in capital letters the "healthy antioxidants" inside.

Celestial Seasonings, which peddled a variety of flavored and fortified green teas, drew in tea consumers with an idyllic tableau of an Indian woman harvesting tea before majestic Himalayan-like mountains. Once sold on this naturalist Asian sensibility, health seekers could flip to the back for a clinical report on green tea. "Studies at Rutgers University and in China and Japan," the package informed, "suggest a possible correlation between antioxidants found in green tea and overall good health." Using medical lingo, tea companies such as Celestial Seasonings, Twinings, and Lipton signaled recognition of the average wellness consumer's fluency in middlebrow scientific health nomenclature.

In 2005, Lipton, detecting a gold mine of promotional possibilities in "sciencey" tags, such as "antioxidants," attached "AOX" to all green and black tea products. According to its webpage, Lipton adopted the "AOX" moniker to "emphasize the flavonoid antioxidants found in both black and green tea [that] can be beneficial to help the body protect itself from the harmful effect of 'free radicals.'"[57] In this same time period, Salada created a spate of green tea varieties, many with "medicinal" infusions, including Green Tea with Echinechea Supplement, Green Tea with Purple Antioxidants, and Green Tea with Ginseng Supplements. Salada conjoined the "Oriental" past and the "scientific" present, invoking the healthy-Asian dyad so persistent in the green tea market on its "100% Green Tea," billed as "traditional from the orient." The package explained, "For centuries green tea has been recognized in Asia for its role in a healthy lifestyle ... Researchers theorize that antioxidants contribute to good health by neutralizing free radicals ... No wonder Emperor Shen Nung proclaimed green tea to be 'heaven sent.'" Salada took the scientific-dietary trope one step further than Lipton and others by organizing its tea and health data in an online *Salada Newsletter*. Mimicking a "true" scientific journal and web health letters like Andrew Weil's *Weekly Wellness Bulletin*, each *Salada Newsletter* was dated and stamped with an issue number. In the fall 2004 *Salada Newsletter* (Issue 10), wellness-questing tea drinkers could find such features as "Tea May Help Blood Circulation" and "Green Tea Extract Fights Liver Damage in Mice."[58]

Beverage companies were not the only commercial institutions that harvested customers through green tea's mystique. Applications of green tea in hand wash, face lotions, and supplements and diet pills surfaced in pharmacies, supermarkets, and beauty supply stores across the United States. As the mass media chased after every drop of positive (or negative) evidence tying green tea's biochemical abilities to cancer prevention, heart health, neurological function, and dental hygiene, the food and beauty industries retooled their products to match.

The relationship between Andrew Weil's health corporation and such mainstream food industries as Salada was not necessarily direct. Most of the best-in-class products associated with his name were made not by blockbuster national corporations but by small retailers and producers. Yet, in the productive and fast-paced information culture of the twenty-first century, new natural food and health data traveled quickly. Green tea rode in this groove with its alleged alchemy broadcast in both print and visual media and through the commercial field. Tofu and soy foods followed the same trajectory. Laden with sagacious Eastern echoes and the microbiological assets discovered by modern Western science, tofu and soy foods exuded a potent mix of cultural and medicinal-natural symbology.

SOY FOODS: VEGETARIAN MEAT AND DAIRYLESS MILK

For Asia-phile Andrew Weil, tofu and soy "facsimile foods"—common in the East as fermented tempeh, wheat gluten, and tofu—radiated untainted Oriental reasonableness. In *Eating Well for Optimum Health*, Weil explained that Japanese Buddhist temple cuisine, known as *shojin ryori*, did not use soy to concoct exact meat replicas but rather applied soy's au naturel goodness in "meals, as beautiful as those of the *Kaiseki* cuisine that evolved as part of the formal tea ceremony." Recalling his first exposure to these soy masterworks, Weil dreamily wrote, "I remember a wonderful *shojin ryori* lunch I enjoyed with a friend at Nanzenji, a famous old Zen temple in Kyoto, on a sunny autumn day looking out over the temple gardens. The soy foods in it were ingenious and delicious."[59]

Late twentieth-century scientific discoveries of cancer-protective phytoestrogens, "as well as the low-cholesterol and low-fat complete protein constitution of soy foods," reaffirmed Weil's already-favorable estimation of these Asian staples. The wonders of soy were many according to Weil's health newsletter, *Self Healing*, and daily health news propagator "Good Morning from Dr. Weil.com." Like green tea, soy had limitless salutary effects, particularly for women. Its plant estrogens contained natural chemical protections from breast, ovarian, and lung cancer in women and prostate cancer in men. They also, according to Dr. Weil, relieved menopausal and menstrual symptoms.[60]

Soy foods were also reliable substitutes for meat—a food type that those concerned with health deemed antinutritional and, some, unethical. Since the 1950s, the correlation between poor health and meat consumption became an article of scientific and citizen faith, reincarnated and reinforced in each successive decade. Postwar nutritional analyses made the connections between America's meat indulgence and the spike in cardiovascular disease and death among American men established science.[61] The seventies natural foods movement, specifically Frances Moore Lappé's *Diet for a Small Planet*, added another layer to antimeat presumptions, proposing vegetarianism as an ecological and humanitarian obligation. In the 1980s, the "Surgeon General's 1988 Report on Nutrition and Health" blamed America's fatty diet for five of the "ten leading causes of death in the United States ... coronary heart disease, certain cancers, diabetes, and arteriosclerosis." Continuing this thread, an influential report compiled by the National Heart, Lung and Blood Institute in the 1990s emphatically warned all Americans to decrease animal fat calories by 7 percent.[62] Although the ecological (and animal rights) framework of the 1960s reemerged at the turn of the century, preventive healthism and food fashion, more than "small planet" politics, evoked much postsixties vegetarianism.

Until the ascendance of the protein-heavy Atkins regime in the 1990s and paleo dietary fads in the early 2000s, the accumulating case against animal fat was an article of faith among wellness consumers. With per capita meat consumption between 1978 to 1998 dropping—beef by 54 percent and pork by 45 percent—America's (particularly affluent female shoppers') decision to go vegetarian, or to limit meat with soy and wheat-meat substitutes, adversely affected the red meat industry.[63] Meats less associated with bloody and fatty carnivorousness, such as seafood and chicken, enjoyed a reverse trend during this period.

Vegetarianism or, more precisely, flexitarianism, the label that Andrew Weil applied to his own eating routine, rose steadily.[64] According to the Vegetarian Resource Group, in the early 2000s a uniquely postsixties vegetarianism was on the rise. While only 2.8 percent of Americans polled considered themselves strict vegetarians, 6–10 percent defined themselves as "almost vegetarian," and an even greater number, 20–25 percent, said they were "vegetarian inclined" and were "reducing meat in their diet."[65] Curiously, a 2002 *Time* survey of U.S. vegetarianism found that of 11,000 people questioned, 37 percent claimed a vegetarian identity, but 60 percent of that 37 percent confessed to having eaten meat, poultry, or fish in the last 24 hours.[66] While this contradictory self-characterization could have indicated confusion about vegetarianism, it could also have connoted the appeal of a meat-free identity and a more fluid interpretation of vegetarianism in which individual whimsy and desire (say for the occasional hamburger) could be reconciled by the "flexitarianism" label.

Ethical justifications, essential to the sixties vegetarian natural foods movement, did not disappear. Yet, at the start of the new century, the true movers in the plant-based dietary sector were consumers (particularly baby boomers) who became "vegetarian-inclined" for health reasons. Politics and morality did not cause the decline in red meat consumption or the precipitous increase in soy-based meat analogues. Self-preservation did. Postsixties "almost vegetarian" and "vegetarian-inclined" health-attentive Americans drove red meat consumption down and the soy foods market up by guiltlessly supping on Fakin' Bacon, Smart Dogs, and Gardenburgers. They voted with their dollars for reproductions that smelled, felt, and tasted as close to the animal flesh (and milk) original as possible. With 2,300 soy products invented by 2001, the food industry answered consumer appeals by churning out one imitation soy meat after another.[67]

Soy food producers and marketers were rewarded for their attentiveness to America's defensive health diligence. Between 1992 and 2002, soy food sales quadrupled from $0.852 billion to $3.2 billion. By 2013, total annual sales had risen to $4.5 billion.[68] Industry insiders agreed, this increase was a boon for supermarkets. Claire Madden, vice president of MarketResearch.com, observed, "Soyfood brands are important to supermarkets, as they give conventional groceries the reputation associated with carrying healthy and trendy products and keep their customers from purchasing soy items elsewhere."[69] Soy's silver bullet reputation made soy-fortified merchandise, such as energy bars, and soy-enhanced beverages and powders strong favorites with the consuming public. The Food and Drug Administration's (FDA's) October 1999 approval of the "soy health claim," that products "high in soy protein . . . may help lower heart disease risk," buttressed the already widespread faith in soy's assumed medicinal attributes.[70]

With a 21 percent "compound annual growth rate" from 1991 to 2001, soy milk was a gainer in the mainstream marketplace.[71] For parents uneasy with industrial milk production and for the increasing number of Americans identifying dairy allergies and sensitivities as the root cause of numerous ailments, soy milk, made from extracted soy bean waters, delivered a "pure" alternative. Andrew Weil, who like other alternative health professionals, asserted that milk proteins caused allergies, digestive problems, and autoimmune reactions, warned "optimum health" followers to steer their families clear from cow's milk. Weil-endorsed calcium-fortified soy milk was pitched as an alternate.[72]

Sales of soy milk, while quite impressive at the century's end, leapt 45 percent in 2001 when White Wave made its *Silk* brand soy milk more user friendly—moving it from the dry goods shelf and positioning its new milk look-alike container in the refrigerated dairy case.[73] In 2003, Peter Golbitz, president of the market research firm Soyatech Inc., estimated that given patterns in soy milk consumption, by 2010, soy milk would account for 5–10 percent of the U.S. "dairy" market.[74]

Curiously, of all the soy foods, tofu, the original countercultural protein surrogate and longtime Dr. Weil favorite, had been left out of the postsixties soy boom. Tofu experienced a mid-1980s spike in popularity, a precursor to the meat-reduction fad, but flattened out by the early 1990s. Tofu, a pressed cake of cooked pureed soybeans, has a distinctive soy flavor and texture that clearly did not appeal to most Americans' palate.[75] Only after the introduction of flavored and ready-to-eat tofu goods that masked its beany character, such as Soy Boy Caribbean Organic Tofu, Melissa's All-Natural Baked Tofu Cutlets, Hearty and Healthy Tofu Steaks, and others, did tofu gain a small slice of the soy consumer pie.

Discussing the health dividends of a soy-rich diet in 1998, nutritionist Nancy Clark recognized the roadblocks between Americans and tofu: "Years ago, folks had little good to say about soy foods. Tofu . . . was maligned as a food for 'nutty' vegetarians . . . Today, however, people are jumping for soy."[76] For most health-attuned consumers, tofu was weighed down by strong historical inflections of hippie invention and flavorless asceticism. In a tongue-and-check feature on tofu, *New York Times* columnist Jonathan Reynolds dryly described the roots of the United States' aversion to this Asian staple: "Cold and uncooked, it's squeaky, with the texture and disposition of a particularly upbeat sponge. In the mouth, it's so darn watery and perky, it feels as though it will clean the enamel off your teeth, suck all the saliva from your mouth and then bounce right out onto the street to do some more good somewhere else. And it's almost beige, the second least appetizing color for food (Blue is first)." A culinary sophisticate such as Reynolds could transcend his ingrained revulsion to tofu by discovering that with a bit of butter and a hot sauté pan, tofu's "outsides crisp pleasantly [turning it into] buttery little French-fried custards."[77] Health hopefuls and Asian romantics, like Andrew Weil, who aspired for optimum health by imitating the exotic other, downed tofu preparations effortlessly and joyfully. The average American eater, even for the sake of soybean's scientifically suggested low fat and cholesterol, and the important-sounding "natural selective oestrogen receptor modulators," still couldn't stomach tofu.[78] For most Westerners, particularly those interviewed in Jonathan Reynolds informal poll, tofu remained high on the list of the "Most Despised Foods on the Planet."[79] This was the reason that manufactured meat, made of soy protein extracts and dehydrated and compressed defatted soy flour, which did not carry the soybean taste and textures so repugnant to the American eater, became the hot vegetable protein stand-in for new-millennium health seekers. As hot dogs, meatballs, chicken wings, and barbequed ribs, the soy bean was stretched, twisted, molded, and processed into every meat form imaginable.

The most inventive and peculiar of these, such as the Thanksgiving soy proxy, Tofurkey, or seasoned soy slices of fake bologna, were purchased by a very small and stringently vegetarian portion of shoppers. Veggie burgers, on the other hand, made noticeable headway in the mainstream food pool. The Gardenburger and other vegetable patties appeared on the menus of national chain restaurants, including the Hard Rock Café, Red Robin, Texas Burger, Applebees, Subway, and TGI Fridays.[80] According to the Soyfoods Association of North America, in 1998 veggie burgers outsold all other frozen burgers in supermarkets across the nation. Gardenburger inventor and owner, Paul Wenner, played no small part in the vegetarian burger's popularization.

Similar to archetypal nineteenth-century health reformers, such as Sylvester Graham and Harvey Kellogg, Wenner spent a tubercular and asthmatic childhood sheltered from youth's normal enjoyments. At age seventeen, he decided to take control of his biological destiny and entered a health food store to inquire about "whole grain[s]." Thereafter, he swore off milk, meat, and processed foods and was allegedly relieved from his lifelong debilities. "Within three months," Wenner recalled, "I could breathe without effort and had more energy."[81]

This turnaround inspired Wenner to join the Air Force. Miraculously, from his recounting, his entry physical showed no signs of tuberculosis or asthma. After his tour of duty, Wenner settled in the U.S. Northwest and in the 1970s opened a natural foods restaurant. Although quickly closed, Wenner continued to sell his veggie patty, the Gardenburger, from the back of his van. In 1985, he founded a natural foods company, Wholesome and Hearty Food; in 1992 it went public. The original stock value for Wholesome and Hearty shares was high, owing to industry whispers of McDonald's imminent veggie burger. When these rumors proved unfounded, Wholesome and Hearty stocks plummeted from $30 to $3. Eventually, Wenner's company shares, renamed Gardenburger in 1997, leveled off at $12.75. To raise his business's public profile, in 1996 Wenner hired a former Quaker Oats executive, Lyle Hubbard, to refurbish Gardenburger's image. Hubbard suggested that the company invest in an expensive and full-fledged marketing campaign, including a $14 million five-week TV promotional plan with a denouement $1.4 million commercial spot on the May 14, 1998, final episode of *Seinfeld*.[82]

Since the 1960s, most vegetarian and natural foods producers had marketed through traditional print media, coupons, and food store circulars. Gardenburger's television advertising was exceptional. With grand total sales of $57 million in 1997, this small natural foods company decided on a break-the-bank publicity adventure. Gardenburger's advertising consultants had no qualms about the gamble. "It was a no-brainer," commented adman William Marks. "If [the veggie burger] is truly going to be a big category, somebody's got to be there first. This is where we stick our flag in the ground," stated Paul Janus, the company's advertising creative director. While Gardenburger's risk paid off in the short run, with record sales after the Seinfeld ads, by 1999 this comparatively small food producer was posting income losses.[83]

The attempt by Gardenburger to burst out of the health niche into the larger food stream demonstrates both the general acceptance of convenience meat surrogates and the dangers for a small natural foods company competing in the new corporate natural foods market. To cash in on the burgeoning meat-reducing buyer, Gardenburger had to commit to an expensive advertising project, a project that big food producers could effortlessly bankroll. Wenner's little enterprise, on the other hand, had to bet the farm. In the long run, it did not pay off; the company enjoyed a brief upward blip and then a sales decline.

Cognizant that the corporate food producers would eventually create their own health-styled soy products, many small soy foods producers, such as Boca Foods (a Kraft label since 2000) and White Wave soy milk (a Dean Foods product since 1999) resigned to buyouts by food conglomerates. Even the leading mock-meat company and Gardenburger's traditional competitor, Worthington Foods, bowed to financial enticements, handing over its leading meat substitute brand, Morningstar Farms, to Kellogg's in 1999. With a sophisticated marketing, processing, and research team, Kellogg's turned Morningstar Farms into the fastest growing soy meat brand in the nation.

The incorporation of the soy market changed imitation meats dramatically. It made these previously faddish foods more various and more mainstream. As companies with no other purpose than seizing market share and increasing stockholder's dividends, food giants like Kraft, Heinz, Unilever, Conagra, General Mills, Dean Foods, and Kellogg's put their time and monies into extracting the two most profitable features of the soybean—its

FDA-approved health classification and its ability to imitate meat and milk—and discarding everything else. In this highly industrialized-mechanized process, they emptied it of its whole bean core. They reconstituted soy as a neutral medium on which the charms of low cholesterol, low fat, health, and environmentalism could be easily engraved.

Commercially reconstituted, soy became the ultimate postmodern health food—devoid of permanent meaning, detached from its origin—an extracted substance into which myriad health (and animal-/earth-friendly) inflections could be poured. For Terry Hatfield, copresident of a "soy protein isolate supplier," soy's health benefits are all fine, but its real value is its functionality. Soy isolates, he noted, can create "mouthfeel and viscosity" that can make soy beverages "creamy and full bodied." In the not-so-distant future, Hatfield predicted, soy isolates will be added to meat so that "meat products can still meet the [soy protein] health claim."[84] In 2004, Kraft's research and development team strove to erase soy's bean essence, patenting an "ultrafiltration method" that "removes objectionable flavors from soy milk, soy flour, soy protein isolates and other soy derived materials." According to its food scientists, Kraft's mechanism sieves soy until "all flavoring compounds have been removed."[85] While these processing inventions augured well for the future of soy processing, for industry consultant Kathy Wrick, the soybean would not make the big time until agricultural scientists "identify genetics that create these objectionable flavors . . . and minimize or at best eliminate these traits through plant breeding or genetic engineering."[86] No small-scale meat substitute producer could finance such seed-to-table manipulation. Indeed, Wrick noted that, as of 2000, only multinational giants Cargill and ADM & Bunge had done so.

With endless money to throw at stylish commercial campaigns and extensive research teams, food corporations cornered the manufactured soy market. They processed out all of the soybean's "offensive" innate properties and created all-but-the-animal meat and milk replicas with isoflavone health promises and FDA approval intact. Conventional food corporations purchased control of the deep cultural resonances and political history from which the postsixties soy market sprang. They acquired the self-health and anti–medical establishment enmity enclosed in the alternative health movement. And they gained the countercultural vegetarian response to the hyperconsumption of industrially advanced nations. Incongruously, they even captured the antiprocessed, whole foods aesthetic that had drawn many Americans to a natural foods diet since the 1960s.

As Raymond Williams astutely explained, in an advanced capitalist economy, "objects are not enough but must be validated, if only in fantasy, by association with social and personal meanings."[87] Postsixties alternative food consumers bought soy meats—and green tea, whole grain bread, organic vegetables and fruits—to make contact with countercultural values. Indeed, consumers ate "healthful" and "natural" to manage their experience of the postmodern global economy and to believe that, in so doing, they were supporting a different, better, more ecologically sustainable world.

Conagra, Kellogg's, Unilever, and others bought and then sold the chimeras interwoven into these postsixties natural/health foods. They employed genetic engineering to extract soybean's most profitable facets. They created soybean agribusinesses with all their attendant ecological and social justice problems. They entangled producer nations (in South and Central America, Southeast Asia, China, and Africa) in neocolonial agricultural service to "first-world" consumer standards. As they made the organic and natural lifestyle easier and easier for the new-century health seeker, they pushed sound ecological consumption and production further and further away. Of course, even with the natural label's commercial capture and some movement in the conventional system toward healthful, whole, organic foods, access still remained available only to those with economic ability and those trained to the natural market's cues.

Andrew Weil's health advice company assisted (and at times resisted) capitalism's acquisition of natural foods and countercultural codes. Indeed, his celebrity and his integrative health corporation matured synchronously with the emergent social media–consumer complex and as all natural and organic foods, not only soy and green tea, were pulled into the corporate food flow.

INCORPORATING NATURAL FOODS

Recalling his first encounters with "organic products" as an undergraduate at Berkeley in the late 1970s, historian Jeff Charles remembered "disorderly" stores with "floors blocked with 'bulk' barrels filled with scarcely edible grains and 'health foods.'" The poorly lit, dingy hippie markets that housed these goods showed no indication that "these establishments stocked the future of

American food."[88] The unadorned counterinstitutions that sold these then-scarce organic and natural products *were* the parents of a market segment that exploded at the turn of the twenty-first century.

In the 1960s and 1970s, natural foods manufacturers were small in scale, often employed unconventional (sometimes anticapitalist) business methods, and devoted scant time or money to development or marketing. Excited simply to have access to natural goods, faithful consumers asked for little in exchange for their purchases at the local co-op or natural foods stores besides a sense of political rightness and the imputed health assurances of brown rice, organic cucumbers, or wild honey. Reflecting on the early organic movement's inherent commercial weaknesses, Gary Hirshberg, chief executive officer of organic dairy manufacturer Stonyfield Farm, opined, "In the old days, eating organic meant a lot of chewing—producers didn't put quality and taste first. You bought into a value system. But people don't buy just with their brains; they buy with their taste buds."[89] As natural and organic chefs, farmers, store owners, manufacturers (like Hirshberg), and consumers matured, so did the market. Settling into careers, family life, and comparative comfort, many who came into adulthood in the late 1960s and 1970s wanted more from their nonstandard foods. In addition to the health and wellness bottom line, they wanted delight, adventure, and convenience.

In their 1984 sermon on whole grain bread baking, *The Laurel's Kitchen Bread Book*, Laurel Robertson and her coauthors waxed philosophical on the profundity of weekly bread baking, which, they wrote, is "an ideal first step towards a way of life that is more self-reliant, and at the same time consciously interdependent." In their first cooking book, *Laurel's Kitchen*, they warned readers that "breadmaking requires time—and that may mean withdrawing from other activities, doing fewer things better instead of many things superficially."[90] By the 1980s and 1990s, this handcrafted kitchen prototype still struck a chord with many boomers and new generations of culinary idealists. Yet, in the main, natural and organic consumers wanted to spend their leisure enjoying their families and actualizing their own physical, mental, and spiritual capacity, not cloistered in a kitchen kneading bread and watching it rise. Although home production would be reborn in the new century, the majority of natural eaters wanted someone else to bake their whole grain bread. The organic and natural foods market reacted to the elite's lifestyle recalibration by becoming more sophisticated, more nationalized, and more industrial.

Because the word "organic" conjured a suite of environmentally correct production and healthful connotations, organics became the hot spot of the new-century natural foods market. *Prevention* magazine's "Top 10 Reasons to Go Organic" in 2011—including "keep our children and future safe," "preserve agricultural diversity," "reduce pollution and protect water and soil," "avoid chemicals," "support farming directly," and "enjoy better taste"—expressed organics' ideological and promotional expansiveness.[91] The high-mindedness conferred to organic goods attests to what sociologist Deborah Lupton identifies as the emergence in America of a "fully conscious, thinking, reflexive consuming self, a self that buys, prepares, and eats food with a heightened sense of that food's history."[92] Food companies answered, developing newer, fresher, and, in a few cases, cheaper organic merchandise; consumers responded enthusiastically. Between 1989 and 1994, U.S. organic sales increased 20 percent or more yearly. This upswing continued into the twenty-first century.[93]

While commodities typically associated with the organic method, such as fruits and vegetables, constituted approximately 40 percent of organic food sales, processed foods led as the fastest gainer in this sector in the 1990s. In natural foods supermarkets, sales for processed organic meat substitutes, cereals, snacks, and juices rose by 57 percent between 1993 and 1994.[94] On the consumer move toward easy organics, Holly Givens, communications director for the Organic Trade Association, remarked: "These days the great thing is that you don't have to make a huge change in what you eat. You can just choose the organic thing. You don't have to become a vegetarian or cook from scratch."[95] The aesthetic and intellectual seductions of home cooking and artisan fabrication still held, particularly in the top-tier food world. But for the organic ideal to be commercially diffused, the early natural foods movement's antipathy toward convenience and industrialization had to be jettisoned.

Dairy products, particularly milk, were a standout winner. Between 1993 and 1994, organic milk sales doubled to $24 million.[96] This inflation can be attributed to consumer response to the FDA's 1993 approval of a genetically engineered bovine growth hormone, rBGH. A facsimile of a naturally occurring hormone in cows, rBGH increases milk production. By 1994, farmers across America were injecting milk cows with Monsanto's rBGH, Prosilac, despite the fact that Europe and Canada banned the drug because of its possible links to cancer.[97]

As Harvey Levenstein illuminates in *Fear of Food*, since the industrial nineteenth century, parental apprehension about children's proper development made milk a lightning rod for food purity panics and government policy.[98] This long-standing parental vulnerability and the acquisitive protectionism advanced by Weil and other natural health propagators spurred the expansion of the late twentieth-century organic dairy business.

Tapping into fretfulness over children's somatic vulnerability, Horizon Organic's low-fat milk container assured, "Studies have shown that children who eat a predominantly organic diet have far lower levels of pesticide residues in their bodies than children who eat mostly non-organic foods." The Horizon milk package incited environmental nervousness in its target consumers by bringing attention to children's bodily contamination, then calmed these fears with safety guarantees. This strategy converted many ecologically anxious American and European parents into organic milk loyalists. Horizon further tailored its merchandising with a line of child-centered products—such as the first organic infant formula approved by the U.S. Department of Agriculture (USDA) and Whole Milk Baby Yogurt, Horizon Yo-Yos cup yogurt, and Horizon Organic Yogurt Tubes. Utilizing all venues of distribution—club stores, supermarkets, specialty natural grocers—and skillfully appealing to parents' bottomless well of worry, Horizon made itself the largest U.S. purveyor of organic foods.[99]

The development of organic and natural foods industries, such as Horizon, depended both on the preservation discourse of health celebrities, like Dr. Weil, and on government involvement in organic standardization. In 1990, Congress passed the Organic Food Production Act. It then charged a blue-ribbon committee, the National Organic Standards Board (NOSB), to construct guidelines for organic standardization. Comprised of four organic growers, two organic handlers, three public interest advocates, three environmentalists, and a scientist, it took five years for the NOSB to compile recommendations. Congress released its first organic proposal in 1997. Then a real battle began.[100]

Allowing for three agricultural taboos—genetically modified organisms, irradiation to kill bacteria on produce, and sewerage sludge as fertilizer—the USDA stretched organic standards in hopes of satisfying both organic idealists and a developing corporate market segment. Unprecedented citizen and industry activism followed. At the close of the required public comment period, the UDSA had received 220,000 comments. Consumers had united in grassroots organizations, such as Save Organic Standards (SOS), to fight the loopholes in the USDA's preliminary regulations. "This is probably the largest response to a rule in modern history," noted USDA head, Dan Glickman.[101]

In 2000, the USDA submitted its revised organic standards excluding the three most offensive facets of the 1997 rulings. Yet, as Michael Pollan explained in an organic industry exposé, the final organic standards, which went into effect in 2002, favored "big organic" over "little organic."[102] The new regulations allowed operations that used "confined animal feeding operations" or food additives and synthetics to win the USDA seal.[103] Industrial organics beat "movement" organics largely because shoppers' protest, while impressive by late twentieth-century civic involvement norms, was temporary and decentralized. On the whole, organic consumers and producers were abstractly linked through the marketplace, not through advocacy organization membership or electoral affiliation. Their hastily conjoined grassroots retort to USDA standardization was no match for industrial food lobbyists' well-fortified political architecture.

In 1996, prior to the final USDA decisions, the battle between corporate and countercultural organics raged on in public exchanges between NOSB members. In a polemical article, "Can an Organic Twinkie Be Certified?," NOSB member and nutritionist Joan Dye Gussow vociferously argued against the inclusion of what big industry saw as "permissible additives and synthetics." Fellow NOSB member Gene Kahn reflected, "If we had lost on synthetics, we'd be out of business." Kahn, who created the organic produce brokerage Cascadian Farms in the 1970s and who sold the business to General Mills in the 1980s, believed that consumer demand trumped everything. "If the consumer wants an organic Twinkie then we should give it to them. Organic is not your mother," he chided.[104] Mainstream food companies jumped into the natural and organic market because sales figures showed that consumers *did* want convenience organics.

The development of organic industries, backed by natural foods consciousness and health angst, wove natural and organic goods into the corporate web. It turned small-scale farming operations into a nationalized agribusiness. As organic labels established in the countercultural context sold (or offered controlling interest in) their businesses to conventional food companies, the relations established during this period made for strange and, in some organic stalwarts' opinions, compromising bedfellows. In 1997, Mars bought partial ownership of Seeds of Change. This heirloom seed, gardening, and organic food company was created by Kenny Ausubel in the late 1980s to "restore biodiversity and revolutionize the way we think about food."[105] Ten years after Ausubel announced this utopian design, Steve French, Seeds of Change vice president, justified the Mars merger by willfully erasing Ausubel's countercultural mission. "I don't think there are any real difference between Seeds of Change and Mars," French breezily theorized. "Whether it's a Mars product or it's a Seeds of Change product, the product benefits are very, very similar if we're talking about nutrition."[106]

As companies made with ecological and revolutionary objectives combined with industrial food titans and justified such moves as concordant with their original "nutrition" plan, the pace of organic incorporation and industrialization quickened. Between 1996 and 2004, Coca Cola bought the Odwalla natural juice business; Dean Foods purchased White Wave/Silk soy drink and Horizon dairy; Kellogg's bought Kashi natural/organic cereals and Morningstar Farms imitation meats; Phillip Morris/Kraft bought Back to Nature packaged natural foods and Boca Burgers; Europe's Danone Corporation purchased Stonyfield Farm, one of its organic yogurt competitors; General Mills bought organic produce retailer Cascadian Farms. Other food giants created their own organic lines, such as Pepsi with Tostitos Organic Snacks, Campbell's with an organic soup line, and Dole with the Dole Organic label.[107]

Hain natural foods company executed the most successful and sweeping centralization of natural and organic foods. In 2000, Hain owned shares in twelve of the fifteen leading natural foods categories. After merging, in 2000, with tea company Celestial Seasonings, the Hain Celestial Group jointly controlled the majority of the health, organic, and natural foods labels created since the 1960s, including Rice Dreams, Bearitos, Bread Shop Granola, Celestial Seasonings, Garden of Eatin', Terra Chips, Nile Spice, Imagine Foods, Arrowhead Mills, Westbrae Natural and Westsoy, Walnut Acres, Hollywood Cooking Oil, Health Valley, Yves Veggie Cuisine, and more. In 1999 the mainstream food corporation Heinz added another layer of concentration, buying 16.7 percent equity of Hain: by 2000, it had increased control to 19.5 percent.[108]

New-century organic and natural corporate raiders, like Hain's CEO, Irwin Simon, and Celestial Seasonings' chair Mo Siegel, saw no inconsistency between the natural foods market's centralization and the original anticapitalist, anti–mass production critique behind the sixties natural foods uprising. Gary Hirshberg—who sold Danone Corporation 40 percent controlling shares of Stonyfield Farm in 2002—described the mass market as a domain for citizen empowerment: "People don't realize that the supermarket is a voting booth and that corporate America is spending billions to tally those votes. What the consumer needs to understand is that when you buy this conventional stuff, which is filled with additives and so on, you're voting for that. The Bigs are saying, 'They like it—let's give them more.' On the other hand if you vote for products that are made with live, active cultures and are free of genetically modified hormones, and for companies that use low-impact packaging and give a percentage of their profits to improve the planet, then companies like General Mills are going to notice. General Mills doesn't really care *why* you came to organics; they care *that* you came to organics."[109]

Of course, not all natural and organic producers and merchandisers bought into Hirshberg's market populism. Many natural organic labels, such as Amy's Kitchen prepared natural foods, Eden canned natural products, and MaraNatha nut butters, to name just a few, expanded their consumer base without selling control to corporations or completely sacrificing production standards. Yet, these artisan brands were generally carried by mom-and-pop health food stores and did not reach the plurality in the manner that major natural foods chains did. In the new century, larger enterprises, such as countercultural godfathers Whole Foods and Wild Oats, became the retail guardians of a food movement that arose as an ethical and aesthetic retaliation against the postwar supermarket. During the incipient years of the natural and organic foods movement, devoted shoppers had to go out of their way to find nonstandard foodstuffs. A short two to three decades later, the same shoppers, a bit older and a bit richer, along with new natural-organic admirers, could pick up their favorite natural brands at the supermarket.

Even conventional grocery stores invented their own natural product lines. King Kullen, the first supermarket in the United States, took the lead in 1995 by opening a subsidiary supermarket, Wild by Nature, in Huntington, New York. Other national chains not only opened natural groceries but also created organic/natural store brands. In 2003, Kroger's dove headlong into the natural market, showcasing Kroger's Naturally Preferred label.[110] With 2,488 supermarkets in 32 states, this monster grocer's decision to go natural presented a real threat to the fiscal viability of natural supermarkets such as Whole Foods and Wild Oats.[111]

King Kullen, Kroger, and other conventional chains, attempted to replicate the nature and health mythos so precisely embedded into every inch of the first natural supermarket, Whole Foods. The typical new-century "health seeker" could satisfactorily shop in an alternatively styled supermarket owned by a multinational corporation—just as long as it exuded the health experience described by columnist and natural foods shopper Angela Braden: "The moment I step inside I feel at home, basking in the soft glow of chemical-free wholesome goodness. Surrounded by mountains of fresh, organic produce, I breathe in the scent of whole grain bakery treats and fresh spices. A hint of aromatherapy oils wafts my way from the bath and body section. The cares of my day fade in this oasis of purity and well-being—my favorite natural-foods store."[112]

Mass marketing and the global commodification of natural foods at the turn of the twenty-first century allowed any company to create the sensual-spiritual and "medico-populist" ambiance that enticed a great number of Americans.[113] Of course, access to this organic ambiance was circumscribed. In the period when national supermarkets customized floor space and product lines for their economically advantaged suburban customers' organic demands, they were completing their decadelong exodus from black and brown urban neighborhoods and poor white rural locales. Liquor stores, convenience shops, and fast-food restaurants filled the food gap in cities and country outposts, creating what food scholar Nathan McClintock calls "junk food jungles."[114] These infrastructural shifts further segregated turn-of-the-twenty-first-century natural foods consumers and the organic movement from those with less cultural and economic capital.

As an influential promulgater of the self-health culture, Dr. Andrew Weil and his health and nutrition business influenced the incorporation of (and the market segregation of) natural/organic foods and symbols. Weil, like Hain Celestial Group, Horizon Organics, and General Mills, used the media-consumer complex as the distributor of his counternormative health movement. And although he perceived himself to be operating in contradiction to the mainstream corporate world, there was a direct interchange between his conglomerate and others.

Andrew Weil is certainly not responsible for the corporate acquisition of the organic and natural market or the preventive ethos. He, like any other new-century health supplicants, must be troubled by the fact that organic consumption generated an alternative farming system that, according to geographer and historian Julie Guthman, is highly dependent on "sodium nitrates" and "sulfur dust [that] is responsible for more worker injuries than any other farm chemical."[115] Indeed, organic agribusiness is part and parcel of the international consumer dynamo.

A well-read and curious intellectual such as Andrew Weil is likely cognizant of these problems. Yet his daily and weekly webpages, monthly *Self Healing* newsletter, books, CDs, DVDs, and television appearances make no specific references to these issues, nor do they warn consumers away from the most egregiously unecological "natural foods" corporations. Weil Lifestyle, LLC recommends goods made by Weil's "commercial friends." Through endorsements, his corporation advises a particular vision of correct and incorrect consumption. But he and his corporate team do not name names or point blame. They focus on the generalized dangers of industrial food production and agribusiness, not on the actors or on orchestrating a political response.

Perhaps, as Andrew Weil has stated numerous times, market demand will sort it all out. In the meantime, his hands are clean; his best-in-class products are free from direct multinational malfeasance. His interest in and endorsements of Asian foods and dietary preventive health preceded the new-century green tea–soy frenzy. Neither he nor Weil Lifestyle, LLC can take sole credit or blame for the industrialization and commoditization of natural and organic foods. The natural and wellness market is too multilayered and diverse to have one motivator; it is a constant stream with manifold entry points and contributors.

Cultural historian Paul Boyer submits that radicals of the 1960s perceived the "inner world of consciousness and outer world of politics" to be "inextricably connected."[116] Since his countercultural awakening at Harvard, Weil has abided by the tenet that cultural and social change rests on individual psychic reconstitution. This philosophy guided his sixties pro-drug and consciousness campaign, his contributions to the seventies holistic health community, and his new-century, multimedia integrative stardom. Weil's final goal is and always has been self-awareness and self-protection, unhampered by the establishment and status quo thinking. The consumer arena is very amenable to this proposition. Individual shoppers and their insecurities and pleasures are its mainstay. Self-improvement is one of its oldest merchandising gimmicks and resounds meaningfully with middle- and upper-class consumers. Under the conveyance of natural health pundits like Andrew Weil, the multimedia commercial complex has fabricated a realm of personal health and natural well-being that is so sparkling, pure, interesting, safe, and accessible that it has proved, for many, irresistible.

CHAPTER 5

NATURAL FOODS CONSERVATISM
From Hippie Evangelism to Whole Foods

As the story goes, after reaching Yippie acclaim in the 1960s Jerry Rubin cravenly traded in his love beads for a three-piece suit in the 1980s. First, he became a securities broker on Wall Street, then a salesperson for John Muir & Company, and in the 1990s, a marketer for a nutritional drink made from kelp, ginseng, and bee pollen called Wow! In this chameleonlike metamorphoses, Rubin became the representative of the hippie sellout. The media loved this story because it seemed to prove the vapidity of sixties idealism. It also ostensibly attested to the irresistibility of capitalism and unrestrained materialism. In a 1985 article on Jerry Rubin and Abbie Hoffman's "Yippie versus Yuppie" debate tour in the 1980s, *Mother Jones* tagged Rubin as a "born-again capitalist." *Cincinnati Magazine* joined in with a May 1982 feature on Rubin entitled, "Cincinnati's Former Flower Child." Knocking its native son off his hipper-than-thou pedestal, the magazine sniggered that Rubin "unapologetically pursues the almighty dollar like everybody else" these days.[1]

Rubin denied that his transition from cultural outsider to business insider connoted an ethical or ideological declension or that it indicated his generation's revolutionary impotence. Rather, as he often stated, hippie capitalists had not "sold out" but rather were "taking over." In his 1985 *Sun Sentinel* article titled "Yuppie America's Economic Savior," Rubin framed his success as an extension of Yippie insurgency. "The yuppie lifestyle of individual entrepreneurship, self-responsibility, personal growth and enjoyment of life," he claimed, "is changing the world by example."[2] Former hippies, like Rubin's

Yippie partner, Abbie Hoffman, did not share Rubin's yuppie optimism, nor did they believe that the establishment could be undermined from within. Many baby boomers set alight by the political energy of the 1960s continued to take on the system in the feminist, gay rights, abortion rights, and environmental "movement of movements" in the 1970s and after. Rubin rejected the grassroots path to progress that Hoffman, his "cosmic partner," had obeyed until his death in 1989.[3]

Rubin's personal evolution from sixties radical—who famously advised Americans to "use your money as toilet paper"—to eighties free marketeer suggests a generational and national reconceptualization of the marketplace's role in social change.[4] In a nation of corporatized business and bureaucratized social institutions, with an irreparably cleaved congress, the marketplace seemed, for many, the last territory open to citizen impact. Indeed, since the 1960s, food-concerned Americans, from all political backgrounds, have used the alternative foods network for protest and ideological affirmation.

Despite the natural foods movement's philosophical openness, its hippie roots associated it with the political Left and its revolutionary rhetoric. Undoubtedly, the co-op creators, cookbook authors, organic farmers, gardeners, and Rodale publication subscribers, as well as the health pundits who settled natural foods into the American cultural imaginary, were Left leaning. But their offer of self-determination through home and health culture and conscientious consumption had universal appeal. The nonpartisan natural foods movement that burgeoned at the turn of the twenty-first century sometimes fractured as conservatives' libertarianism clashed with liberals' allegiance to governmental defense of socioeconomic equality and environmental protection. Nevertheless, natural foods consumerism became a politico-ethical lingua franca and lifestyle trademark of both the conservative and the progressive elite. It became a cultural and political middle ground.

DON'T TRUST THE GOVERNMENT

In the 1960s, natural foods advocates and other cultural insurgents saw themselves as principled outsiders. The entirety of status quo society, particularly what they saw as America's ossified political system, alienated them. The business world, capitalism, partisan politics, the military, and American culture and politics had become too big, too institutionalized, and undemocratic. Sixties radicals were suspicious of the federal government, and particularly the bureaucracies borne out of the Great Depression, World War II, and the Cold War. Timothy Leary's famous advice—"Don't vote. Don't politic. Don't petition. You can't do anything about America politically"—captures the antipolitical animosity within the counterculture.[5] Regular leftist politics, whether labor or liberal, only "[redesigned] the turrets and towers of the technocratic citadel," counterculture translator Theodore Roszak concluded.[6]

In this same period, a Republican faction constructed its own social movement with antigovernment undertones. Dissatisfied with Eisenhower-era centrism and the seismic cultural and political disruptions of the 1960s, this conservative coalition became the New Right. Barry Goldwater's 1964 presidential campaign's core message of what Van Gosse describes as "anticommunism married to antistatism as a holy cause" refreshed the standing allegiance of Republicans to individualism and small government.[7] President Johnson's advancement of social welfare, civil rights, school desegregation, and urban renewal, funded, in part, by new suburban denizens' tax dollars, birthed a highly motivated, antifederalist, tax-revolting Republican cohort. Washington's institutional expansion, between the 1930s and the 1960s, disturbed both the New Left and the New Right.

Although Goldwater lost overwhelmingly to Johnson in 1964, Ronald Reagan's ascendance in the 1980s attested to the staying power of New Right antistatism. In the forward to James C. Roberts's booster book, *The Conservative Decade: Emerging Leaders of the 1980s*, then California governor and impending presidential candidate, Ronald Reagan, found fault in "liberalism," which he described as "no longer the answer" but rather "the problem." Conservatives envisioned a different direction for the nation, one in which "the excess of big government can be replaced by the inventiveness, creativity, and energy of the individual," Reagan explained.[8] The late twentieth-century cross-party divorce from government undermined electoral participation, causing voter turnout for presidential elections to decline from approximately 63 percent in 1960 to 55 percent in 2012, with a 49 percent all-time low in 1996.[9]

Soaked in this latitudinous antistatism, the natural foods movement refused to wait patiently for the ineffectual government to defend the common good. Instead its food network of environmentally and health conscious producers, consumers, and retailers confronted and solved several social issues, without having to lobby (or linger unsatisfied) for government regulation or legislation. At least that was the plan that fell into place among devoted natural foodists.

The Left and the Right critiques of governmental overreach overlapped with, and perhaps instigated, a postsixties regressive nostalgia. The late 1960s and early 1970s back-to-the-Bible and back-to-the-land movements connoted a broad-based desire to leave the present for a preferred past. Conservative Christians recoiled from the moral decay they associated with the subversive movements of the 1960s. They railed against a secular and "activist" judiciary which took prayer out of school in the 1962 *Engel v. Vitale* case, which undermined Christian schools' tax exemption in the 1971 *Greene v. Connally* case, and which challenged, in their eyes, life's sanctity in the 1973 *Roe v. Wade* abortion rights case.[10] Family, God, and country became their protective shield against the nation's moral relativism and impiety.

Christian evangelist Jerry Falwell, borrowing from countercultural argot, announced a resurrectionary response in a sermon called "The Establishment": "We are in need of a spiritual revolution that will re-establish the establishment. The hippies and yippies have had their day... This is the day of the fundamentalist. We need to re-establish our homes... we need to re-establish our churches. We need to re-establish this nation."[11] For Christian conservatives, traditional gender hierarchies and deference to authority had been the glue that held America together in the past. Without these constants, chaos ensued, they believed.

For the counterculture—responsible for smashing the very sexual and social norms that Falwell grieved as lost—the lure of traditionalism held currency but was defined as the peasant and country past: simple, real, and self-determined. Through farming and self-sufficiency, hippie traditionalists hoped to work authentically and steward the earth like their cultivator forefathers and mothers. The small homesteading publication, *Countryside and Small Stock Journal* (established 1972), listed "reverence for nature and a preference for country life; a desire for maximum personal self-reliance and creative leisure; a concern for family nurture and community cohesion" as foundational back-to-land presumptions.[12] Although presented differently, both the Left and the Right baked traditionalism into their new-order designs.

Postsixties conservatives and the cultural Left also overlapped in consumerist conformance and in their very American regard for the striving entrepreneur. Conservatives had never given up on capitalism and materialism. As Reagan famously quipped at a 1983 news conference, "What I want to see above all is that this remains a country where someone can always get rich."[13] They simply worried that liberal federal interference had weakened the free market's dynamism. In Reagan's 1980s, competitive materialism gave rise to a new Gilded Age.

The sixties cultural Left, on the other hand, always had an uneasy relationship with consumer capitalism. They comprehensively criticized corporate consolidation and the profit motive. When forging alternative societies and associations, such as food co-ops, the counterculture tried not-for-profit, communally owned and operated operations. As historians of countercultural work and business Joshua Davis, Malcolm McLaughlin, and David Farber all describe, hippie entrepreneurs charted their own course within the existing marketplace.[14] In fact, the counterculture's creativity gave American consumerism and capitalism a vital shock of cool energy and hip entrepreneurial ingenuity.

From the late 1960s onward, the natural foods movement simmered in this stew of alienation, antistatism, and cultural traditionalism. In this period that historian Kevin Phillips named the "age of disappointment," the movement answered prevailing political estrangement with a decentralized, regulation-shy, health-preoccupied network of producers and consumers who increasingly identified as libertarian just as easily as they did liberal, and evangelical just as easily as atheist.[15]

TWELVE TRIBES WHOLE FOODS EVANGELISM

As Andrew Weil's biography demonstrates, the counterculture chased spiritual enlightenment through not only drugs but also non-Western religious traditions—such as Buddhism, Taoism, and Hinduism. Nontheistic esoteric sects, which emphasized individual practice and illumination, such as Zen Buddhism, proved particularly compelling to sixties seekers who lived by the "do your own thing" motto. Although a few erudite hippies mined paganism and the Christian Gnostics for illumination, most religious aspirants rejected the Christian church because of its associations with the Western "mindset."[16] In the late 1960s and 1970s, a segment of hippie spiritualists dropped their Christian dyspathy, forming an evangelic and messianic religious group known as the Jesus movement. Cultural historian Grace Hale explains that for the Christian counterculture, Jesus exemplified "the ultimate outsider, a martyr for peace and love and human understanding." They cherished his heroic apostasy.[17]

There is little record of the commingling of natural foods and the Jesus movement. But given that Jesus people came from the hippie habitat, the potential for cross germination was high. The broad precepts that connected the New Left to the New Right and both to natural foods idealism collided in one splinter of the Jesus movement—the communal religious order known over its history as the Vine Street Community Church, the Community, the Northeast Kingdom Community Church, and, finally, the Twelve Tribes.

The story of the Twelve Tribes begins in the late 1960s–early 1970s, when the sect's future founder, Elbert Eugene (Gene) Spriggs, decided to head to California in search of the counterculture. Born in Tennessee, Spriggs's upbringing revolved around the local Methodist church. Like others of his generation, he had bounced from career to career, first as a high school teacher and guidance counselor, later as a tour guide and a carnival employee. Unfulfilled, he hoped that he would find his calling or at least like-minded people in California. When he arrived on the West Coast, the burgeoning Jesus movement reignited his native faithfulness. But he quickly became disillusioned, seeing Jesus freaks as faddish followers rather than the truly committed. Spriggs then set off for Colorado, where he met his future wife, Marsha, a California college dropout who moved to a small ski town in the Rockies to find herself.[18]

In a 1985 letter to Vermont reporter Susan Green, Marsha Spriggs (née Duvall) remembered that as a college student, she felt herself "drowning in the crowded halls of the college campus, rushing passed [sic] hundreds of vacant-looking faces, trying to pass out plastic smiles to the select few. There was much TALK in those days about LOVE but I really wanted to see this talk put into action." Searching for something more genuine, Marsha decided to relocate. In the Rocky Mountains, she discovered kindred spirits who were "trying to 'get back to nature,' to be real, and to really LIVE." Unfortunately this utopian enclave was short lived. It disintegrated when, according to Marsha Spriggs, "Big Business moved in."[19] Marsha met Elbert "Gene" Spriggs during this transition period. She later remembered him as "a man with passion." Gene Spriggs came to Colorado, full of the "good news about the Salvation which he had found in Jesus the Savior of the world," Marsha stated.[20]

In the early 1970s, Gene and Marsha, newly married, moved back to his home state of Tennessee so he could settle some unpaid debts and mend relationships. At first they joined existing churches in their hometown, Chattanooga, but quickly became restless with conventional Christianity's sterile sermons and rituals. One Sunday they went to church and found that service was suspended for the Super Bowl. That was the last straw. That day, they decided to create their own church of sorts, opening their doors to young people in the area, offering family meals every evening, "Rap Sessions" and "Bible Studies" each week, and "Critical Mass" every Sunday.[21]

Many of the teenagers who came to their house were troubled. Some came from dysfunctional families, some were involved in drugs, others, Marsha Spriggs recollected, "didn't have any other place to go."[22] To accommodate their growing brood of needy youth, the Spriggses bought a larger house and at the same time purchased a small building in which they started their first business, the Yellow Deli. Established in 1973, this restaurant provided income for the Spriggses' Vine Street Christian Community. It also furnished them with a public pulpit from which to spread their messianic message. Four to five years after the first Yellow Deli premiered in Chattanooga, "the community" experienced rapid growth, opening seven other Yellow Delis and forming many "clans" (groups of households living near one another) in the surrounding area.

While Christian, at least in its early stages of existence, the Spriggses' sect was an odd mix of Christian and Jewish theology and countercultural notions. Their deity, Yahshua—the purported ancient Hebrew or Aramaic designation for Jesus—illustrates their intermingling of Jewish and Christian concepts. They identify with no church or institution. From their perspective, all formal religions misinterpret the Bible and are secularly tainted. According to religious scholar Susan J. Palmer, although they have not set a date, they believe the Messiah will return once they have restored "the church of the Jewish disciples who surrounded Jesus (Yahshua) as described in the New Testament book of Acts." Their later name, the Twelve Tribes, derives from their supposition that the Messiah's return depends on the resurrection of the Twelve Tribes of Israel. To facilitate this event, they have strived to create religious communities in twelve locations worldwide.[23]

The Tribes' philosophy is a patchwork of religious precepts and countercultural subscripts. In a flowery article, "My Elusive Dream," on the Twelve Tribes webpage, the anonymous authors recount that as "children of the '60s"—whose "Moses was Timothy Leary"—they were "really living" their "dreams" in a "revolution of love." That was until "sensation seeking middle class American tourists . . . swamped the serenity and devoured the distinctiveness of our youthful dream on the Haight." Thereafter, they wandered aimlessly until they found "God" or Yahshua.[24] Despite their hippie disaffection, the Twelve Tribes remain rooted in the counterculture with their long-haired communalism, separatism, and search for authenticity, love, and cultural reinvention. At the same time, Twelve Tribes communities seem equally influenced by conservative Christian standards formulated during the fundamentalist surge of the 1970s.

Postsixties cultural conservatives, particularly Christian conservatives, have exhibited their traditionalism in heteronormative and patriarchal social performance. This is certainly the case with the Twelve Tribes.[25] In a 2012 video interview, one member, Andrew Peter, explained that Tribes women are expected to devote themselves to work in the home, "raising the little ones ... taking care of household chores, cooking lunch and doing laundry."[26] For modesty's sake, they dress plainly in floor-length dresses, full blouses, and long, uncut hair. In a Twelve Tribes website article, titled "Back to the Garden," the anonymous author combined biblical and pseudohistorical justifications for women's uniform hair length: "A hundred years ago women wore long hair, her desire was for her husband, and she allowed him to rule over her. Now woman cuts her hair short, which is a great blow to her conscience for she knows instinctively that her hair should be long. It is natural. It expresses her feminine qualities. It has been the tradition of mankind for thousands and thousands of years." Despite this exaggerated femininity, believer Andrew Peter qualified that women's "intuition and sensitivity" are elicited in the community's council.[27] Thus glorified gender essentialism seems to stand in as the conservative substitute for women's community and social empowerment.

In childrearing, the Twelve Tribes also share mainstream fundamentalists' investment in parental and patriarchal rule, which they see as lost in secular America's moral muddiness and permissiveness. Like other culturally and politically conservative families in the late twentieth century, Tribes children are homeschooled. From the Tribes' perspective, home instruction ensures that children have limited exposure to the "corruption" of mainstream society. It puts their children under the family's control and immerses them in religiously guided living.

The Tribes' childrearing policies—which include "biblically" prescribed physical punishment—and its overall unorthodoxy have caused friction between the order and its neighbors and have entangled it in law enforcement and social service confrontations. The first community, in Chattanooga,

Tennessee, relocated to Island Pond, Vermont, in the early 1980s, because of such conflicts. Once in Vermont, they immediately clashed with local authorities over their childrearing.[28] Since this clash, Twelve Tribes communities around the world have tried to live harmoniously with their neighbors. For transparency's sake, they welcome visitors into their homes and, of course, into their stores and restaurants. The Tribes are convinced that their quotidian activities are as good a demonstration of righteousness as is the word they spread through their *Freepaper*, their web articles, and their various evangelical acts.

Tribes' food production, in its organic farms and in its restaurants, plays a central role in its public relations campaigns and its proselytizing. The decor, the food, and the customer service—from the very first Yellow Deli eatery in Chattanooga to operations in far-flung locales like Katoomba, Australia, and Chilliwack, British Columbia—broadcast the Tribes' syncretic spiritual philosophy. Scripture covers the walls of all Yellow Delis. Customers can learn the message by passively absorbing it or through conversation with employees who are eager to "rap" about their lifeways and beliefs. For uniformity of message, all restaurants look similar, with seventies flower power–style signage. With some local variations, the bill of fare is identical in Twelve Tribes operations around the globe.

While not explicitly organic or "natural foods," the community's first eateries proudly served homemade and whole grain breads and baked goods and dishes made from only fresh and healthful ingredients. In a Twelve Tribes online article, "Our Health," the anonymous author explained, "Many years ago, we departed from the use of processed, boxed and canned food." Indicating its congruence with the natural foods movement's do-it-yourself (DIY) ethos and health protectionism, the contemporary Twelve Tribes strive toward dietary self-sufficiency. "Commercially produced fruits, vegetables, and grains," the article states, "are contaminated with pesticides [and] chemical fertilizers ... for these reasons, our goal is to grow as much food for our diet as possible."[29]

Most of the Twelve Tribes communal households and businesses produce or sell natural/organic goods. In Vista, California, a Twelve Tribes community owns Morning Star Ranch, an organic produce farm. A Twelve Tribes holding established in Buenos Aires in 1997 supports itself through organic gardening, whole wheat bread baking, and developing alternative energies. When Gene and Marsha Spriggs moved to Sus, France, in the 1980s, the

Tribes set up a bakery specializing in whole wheat bread. Marsha Spriggs admitted, in her letter to reporter Susan Green, that the bakery attracted few customers owing to the French taste for white flour baguettes. That did not deter the Tribes' bakers. Replicating secular advocates' whole foods didacticism, Spriggs wrote to Green, "We aren't giving up with our bakery . . . the French people need to learn what REAL bread is all about."[30] Indeed, the Tribes have always shared whole foods idealism and pedantry with secular natural foodists, except that they have couched their dietary justifications in religious terms. Natural foods permeate the order's missionary work, daily life, and ritual practices.

As in the Christian and Judaic traditions, bread plays prominently in Twelve Tribes liturgy, but always whole grain bread. Natural bread has a role in the Tribes' missionary work too. Through their website, their religious journal, the *Freepaper*, a road trip bus (the *Peacemaker*), a ship (the *Peacemaker Marine*), "walkers" (men who walk across America preaching), and public weddings, the Tribes spread their message and seek converts. They travel to fairs, festivals, Christian gatherings, and, with a nod to their countercultural origins, to Grateful Dead concerts.[31] In all these venues they hand out hot cider and whole grain bread as an alternative to "White Bread Jesus." At their weekly Resurrection Celebration, they share a communal meal, which, according to Susan J. Palmer, includes the ritual "breaking and sharing" of, again, whole grain bread, to signify the death and rebirth of Yahshua.[32]

Twelve Tribes food rituals are always inlaid with devotionalism. As they explain in a web article, "What is pleasing to Him is healthy for us. Just as a parent wants to give his child the finest in nutritive care, so too our Heavenly Father is keenly interested in providing his people with the finest foods."[33] Eating, growing, and selling natural foods are acts of faith which reap healthful rewards in the here and now and putative metaphysical rewards in the millennial future. Despite the religious framing of its whole grain allegiances, Twelve Tribes food and nature idealism is in concert with the secular natural foods movement.

The Twelve Tribes is a singular and strange, but illustrative, example of the Left/Right politico-cultural hybridizations that grew out of the flush of seventies countercultural community creation. The Yellow Delis and inventive sacraments verify the fungibility of natural foods and the roominess of the alternative foods movement. In the new century, the leading lights of the next stage of the natural foods crusade—the "food revolution"—also espoused gender conventionality and sylvan retreat as a rejoinder to America's social and dietary decline.[34]

FOOD REVOLUTION ANTIFEMINISM

In the early days of the twenty-first century, a new cohort of food pundits—including Michael Pollan, Mark Bittman, Barbara Kingsolver, James McMillian, Eric Schlosser, Anna Lappé (Frances Moore Lappé's daughter), and others—refreshed and redefined the natural foods movement. These figures, unlike the natural foods hippie instigators, had not been part of the counterculture. They came into adulthood in the 1970s and 1980s, when sixties utopianism and counterinstitutions still existed, but on the outer rings of a society pitching toward social reaction and cultural balkanization. Michael Pollan's *Omnivore's Dilemma* and Eric Schlosser's 2001 exposé *Fast Food Nation: The Dark Side of the American Meal* introduced the reading public (again) to the industrial food critique leveled by hippie farmers and natural food exponents in the late 1960s. While their books, as well as such films as *King Corn* (2007) and *Food, Inc.* (2008), reported the same history of America's dietary and social corruption, the new millennium version faced a much more complex, global corporate food system than that described by Frances Moore Lappé in *Diet for a Small Planet*. Despite this expansion, like their countercultural forerunners, food revolution luminaries evoked the premodern golden age of farming, food, and family as rebuttal and tactic. In so doing, they wove another thread of historical sentimentality and regression into the natural foods imaginary. Remarkably, or not so remarkably, in a period when women's workforce presence seemed settled—with an acceleration from 30.3 million to 72.7 million between 1970 and the 2006—this generation of food muckrakers indirectly implicated professional womanhood in America's alleged unraveling.[35]

Feminism Ruined the Happy Housewife
In the customary food revolution account, midcentury mothers surrendered their handed-down cooking skills for the false glamour of frozen and ready-made gizmos. These articles of historical faith were first dispersed by such hippie food insurgents as Laurel Robertson and earth-mother proponents in the 1960s and 1970s. With little reflexivity, twenty-first-century food revolutionaries revived this critique.

New-century food commentary once again put postwar mothers and the feminist revolt on the chopping block. According to Michael Pollan in *The Omnivore's Dilemma*, America's blind plunge into an industrialized food chain resulted in "our national eating disorder" and women's diminished happiness.[36] In his 2009 *New York Times* article, "Out of the Kitchen, onto the Couch," Pollan elaborated that the combination of processed foods and the influence of second-wave feminists, such as Betty Friedan and her groundbreaking work *The Feminist Mystique*, regretfully "taught millions of women to regard housework, cooking included, as drudgery, indeed as a form of oppression." Before these dual catastrophes, American women, according to this opinion shaper, felt they had "a moral obligation to cook, something they believed to be a parental responsibility on par with child care."[37] In this scenario, cooking proved a mother's love and filled her with pride and position.

Rather than the dowdy peasant cook-mother, pitched by countercultural cookbook authors, Pollan picked Julia Child as his postwar feminine authority. In his depiction, Child's show, *The French Chef*, which premiered in 1963 (the same year *The Feminine Mystique* hit bookstores), gave women viewers a model of cooking craft and pleasure. Her joie de vivre, Pollan recalled, encouraged his mother "not only to cook but to cook the world's most glamorous and intimidating cuisine, and to discover that making foods was a gratifying, even ennobling sort of work, engaging both the mind and the muscle." Without political clangor, Child became a woman of consequence by reconstituting an accepted version of female creativity. French feminist and existential icon Simone de Beauvoir also gained Pollan's approval due to her quintessentially French erudition and gastronomy. De Beauvoir's appreciation that cooking could be "revelation and creation" made her impervious to the housekeeping irreverence of women's libbers. "A bit of wisdom," Pollan remarked, "that some American feminists thoughtlessly trampled in their rush to get women out of the kitchen."[38]

In contrast to Child's culinary élan, well-known early twenty-first-century cooking show hostesses—Paula Deen, Rachael Ray, and Sandra Lee—showed how speed, efficiency, and a working woman's goal to put food on the table had undermined cooking's artistry, according to Michael Pollan. With their "stress on quick results, shortcuts, and superconvenience," these celebrities paled in comparison with Child on *The French Chef*. Even though Deen, Ray, and Lee were all self-made successes, Child was "a more liberated figure," he decided.[39] She had not felt obligated to name the conditions that, for many women, made the kitchen a sinkhole of labor inequity and imprisonment. She simply plunged into the art of French cooking. In this think piece, Pollan never pondered why so many women responded to Friedan's *Feminine Mystique*. He never allowed that some middle-class housewives and mothers may have found in its pages an elucidation of their unhappiness not as a personal defect but as a legitimate response to sex role circumscription.

Barbara Kingsolver, in *Animal, Vegetable, Miracle* (2007), nailed another plank of cultural conservatism into the food revolution. When American women "traded homemaking for careers," she sighed, they threw away the simple satisfactions enjoyed by their (supposedly) more fulfilled foremothers. In a cheeky bastardization of women's movement lingo, Kingsolver wrote, "We have come a long way, baby, into bad eating habits and collaterally impaired family dynamics."[40] To declare their independence from the industrial food maw, Kingsolver, her husband, and their two daughters moved from Arizona to her husband's rural Virginia family home to live and eat locally and naturally. In the year documented in *Animal, Vegetable, Miracle*, Kingsolver cans, kneads, preserves, hoes, husbands, and slaughters herself into erstwhile farmer housewifery—setting a (new and old) high bar for natural foods womanhood.

As an ironic self-studier, Kingsolver admitted the put-on quality of her family's agrarian rank. The true luminaries of *Animal, Vegetable, Miracle* were "real" farmers, specifically her Amish friends, David and Elise. Describing an overnight stay at their homestead, Kingsolver concluded: "[David and Elise] have declined to participate in the modern century's paradigm of agriculture—and family life, for that matter, as they place high-value on nonmaterial things like intergenerational family bonds, natural aesthetics, and the pleasures of shared work."[41] In their unelectrified Ohio home, Kingsolver found the certainties of yeoman self-sufficiency fortified by family and God.

In the farming operations that these food revolutionaries most admired, fathers and husbands ran the household and the business. In her vignette on her favorite Amish agronomists, Kingsolver described the farm as the couple's domain, but it was the husband, David, who was the protagonist. He plucked Kingsolver's admiration with his countrified wisecracks and his gleaner wisdom. Aside from her initial welcome on the Kingsolver family's arrival, David's wife, Elise, disappeared offstage. David was the editor and writer for *Farming Magazine*. He explained the Amish approach to technology; he discussed the problems with the U.S. Department of Agriculture's

National Animal Identification system. Elise and David may have been the object of this author's admiration, but only David was a subject. Away from Kingsolver's observance, Elise may have been a garrulous equal to David. The reader could only guess. In this snapshot of Amish family life, she appeared voiceless. So infatuated with the couple's sturdy premodernity, Kingsolver never pondered David's presence and Elise's absence. She may have recognized that Amish gender conventionality put limits on Elise's possibilities, but she never betrayed this insight. For this appreciative outsider, Elise's feminine modesty and her clan's patriarchal cohesion may have been the just-right rejoinder to the bait and switch of women's "liberation." Interestingly, Kingsolver clearly wanted to follow in David's farmer footsteps, not in Elise's housewifely invisibility.

Michael Pollan's countermeasure to America's off-kilter food system followed similar assumptions. He concluded *The Omnivore's Dilemma* with an atavistic foray into man-the-hunter masculine revivalism. Working from the premise that a truly honest meal must be killed and gathered by the cook, he set out to do it all and to serve his booty in the book's denouement—"The Perfect Meal." In the buildup to this finale, the chapter "Hunting: The Meat" described Pollan's wild pig hunting trips with two Bay Area chefs of European descent, Angelo and Jean Pierre. In their hunting adventure, Pollan's emasculating Long Island suburban upbringing is contrasted with his companions' old-world lineages. They ooze an unselfconscious manliness, at least according to their reverent student. Following a formulaic arc of the blundering intellectual turned virile executioner, at first Pollan blows an opportunity to take down a pig. Later, after teacher Angelo promises that "you are going to kill your first pig today," Pollan taps into his huntsman instinct—offing a beast with a shot to the head. After the pig's on-site gutting and butchering, Pollan and his partners drove home, stopping at a convenience store along the way. In this scene, he proudly observed: "The two of us were exhausted and filthy, the fronts of our jeans stained with blood. We couldn't have smelled terribly fragrant. And under the bright fluorescence of the 7-Eleven, in the mirror behind the cigarette rack behind the cashier, I caught a glimpse of the grungy pair of self-satisfied animal killers and noted the wide berth the other customers in line were only happy to grant them. Us."[42] Pollan's metamorphosis was complete.

The "Hunting" chapter ends with the author later contemplating a photo of himself and his slaughtered prey while entertaining the spiritual completeness of food procured through ancient methods. "Here in this single picture you could actually observe this food chain in its totality," he rhapsodized, "the entire circuit of energy and matter that had created the pig we were turning into meat for our meal ... Sun-soil-oak-pig-human: There it was, one of the food chains that have sustained life on earth for a million years made visible in a single frame, one uncluttered and most beautiful example of what is."[43] Through their own sex-role regeneration, Pollan and Kingsolver hoped to exhibit legitimate interaction with food and the earth. Otherwise liberal and secular in outlook, they, like conservative Christians, recommend an individual and national return to gender and familial certitudes to abate postmodern dissolution.

Traditionalism, so fundamental to natural foods deliberations since the 1960s, proved a powerful enticement for consumers and a bottomless marketing maneuver for producers. Captains of the organic and whole foods industry, John Mackey and Michael Potter, built their very successful businesses selling goods that fetishized this prevalent disposition. With culture and commerce as their stage and their technique, Mackey, Potter, other retailers, and dedicated consumers helped the natural foods movement cast off its anticapitalist and anarchist associations. In so doing, the natural foods league made room for political conservatives.

NATURAL FOODS LIBERTARIANISM: JOHN MACKEY

In 2009, Whole Foods CEO, John Mackey, wrote a scathing review of the Affordable Care Act (ACA) in the *Wall Street Journal*, entitled "The Whole Foods Alternative to ObamaCare." Revealing his abiding antistatism, Mackey opined that "Obamacare" would eventuate in "billions of dollars of new unfunded deficits and move us much closer to a government takeover of our health care system." Mackey went on to refute the idea that health care was a "right." A quick scan of America's founding documents—the Declaration of Independence and the Constitution—would "not reveal," he surmised, "an intrinsic right to healthcare, food, or shelter."[44] Rather than a government-sponsored system, Mackey proposed market competition and individual responsibility. Marching out the crisis report of America's rising obesity and dietary disease, he asserted that most illness was "self-inflicted." With a passing reference to "recent scientific and medical evidence," he alleged that most people could live "largely disease free lives ... into [their]

90s or even past 100 years of age," if they would simply become vegetarian. "We are all responsible for our own lives and our own health," Mackey concluded in true libertarian fashion.[45]

Whole Foods devotees, according to Nick Gillespie and Matt Welch in the libertarian journal *Reason*, "went ballistic." A Facebook page dedicated to boycotting Whole Foods quickly gained 34,000 members. Discussion of Mackey's "betrayal" spread among Whole Foods shoppers like wildfire. How could the founder of the largest natural foods grocery chain take such positions, his largely "urban, upscale and left of center" customer base wondered?[46] From Mackey's perspective, "left-wing McCarthyism" triggered the social media kerfuffle that followed his critical editorial.[47]

John Mackey's rugged individualist approach to health care certainly seemed out of sync with many natural foods consumer's endorsement of federal social support. It was an article of faith that Mackey, who had lived in a vegetarian collective in Austin in the early 1970s, who was an environmental advocate, and who had built a business around whole, organic, "real" food must be ideologically squared with his patrons. Mackey, himself, remembered that as a young man "alienated from society," he was drawn into "the counterculture movement."[48] Yet, for him, there was no inconsistency. The ideal of unfettered personal ingenuity, clear of governmental and social interference, undergirded the counterculture of his late sixties and seventies early adulthood and the free market libertarianism of his new-century middle age.

Shortly after he opened the first Whole Foods store in Austin in 1980, Mackey says he recognized that anticapitalism "no longer adequately explained how the world really worked." Instead, in those first years as a natural foods grocer, he concluded that "business wasn't based on exploitation or coercion at all [but on] voluntary cooperation." In search of a more suitable philosophy, he "stumbled" on the works of acclaimed libertarians and free market proponents Ayn Rand, Friedrich von Hayek, Ludwig von Mises, and Milton Friedman. These thinkers lit Mackey's imagination. Thereafter, he voted "strictly Libertarian." Free market business, Mackey proclaimed, was "possibly the greatest force for good on the planet today."[49] Whole Foods' success—with 431 stores in the United States, Canada, and the United Kingdom, 91,000 employees, and net sales of $15.4 billion in 2015—verified Mackey's reverence for capitalism.

This truth did not resonate with his leftist customers. Yet, Mackey never retreated. He remained unabashedly vocal about his political biases. It was just that most of his clientele had not been paying attention. Or they had intentionally avoided pondering the discord between their worldview and that of their favorite grocery store's CEO. Mackey summarily dismissed his critics, stating that the progressive intelligentsia "have always disdained commerce ... have always sided with aristocrats to maintain a society where business people were kept down."[50] Despite this fact, capitalism needed to combat its "bad brand," Mackey conceded. The business world must take some responsibility for the public's and particularly the Left's mistrust.[51]

Stitching together his economic libertarianism to progressive social uplift and environmentalism, John Mackey became a natural foods luminary and postsixties booster for capitalism. He became, as *New Yorker* columnist Nick Paumgarten describes, an "auteur CEO" whose business is "built on his personality."[52] On his Whole Foods blog, in his 2014 book *Conscious Capitalism*, in interviews, and as a regular speaker at the libertarian gathering "Freedom Fest," he labored to rebrand business. Of course, he routinely promoted Whole Foods as the prototype of reformed capitalism.

In a 2004 speech titled "Winning the Battle for Freedom and Prosperity," Mackey claimed that he had "created a business of heart." From his perspective, a heart-driven business sold products that (according to the store's mission) "improve the health and well-being of everyone on the planet through higher-quality foods and better nutrition."[53] A heart-centered business pursued profit while cultivating enlightened management and corporate conscientiousness—weighing the well-being and satisfaction of employees, customers, stockholders, and the world equally. To this end, Whole Foods employees were called "team members," took part in forming store policy and, purportedly, collaborated with supervisors to settle workplace conflict.[54] In accord with leftist judgments of imbalanced corporate pay scales, the salaries of Whole Foods' top executives could not surpass nineteen times the average worker's wages. Mackey, himself, only collected one dollar in yearly compensation, although he owned $30 million in company stock.[55] "I am a very wealthy man; that's no big deal," Mackey blandly remarked in 2016.[56]

In its Whole Planet, Whole Kids, and Whole Cities programs, Whole Foods endorsed typical "good deeds" philanthropy. Whole Planet sponsored and financed small-scale entrepreneurs across the globe. The Whole Kids and Whole Cities programs aligned with early twenty-first-century food reformism that presumed that the poor health status of America's underprivileged derived primarily from lack of access to and lack of knowledge about *real* food. Dietary revivalism was embedded in Whole Foods' core mission.[57] When asked by columnist Nick Paumgarten to choose between seeing his business "flourish" or seeing the Whole Foods dietary health mission realized, Mackey chose the latter.[58]

Mackey's countercultural and libertarian immersions informed his dedication both to liberty and to self-determination. In turn, those dicta shaped his characterizations of disease and wellness as matters of will, rather than physiological chance or socioeconomic status. Whole Foods could provide a healthy context, but finally, Mackey's libertarian outlook made the individual his/her own health keeper. As he stated in his anti-Obamacare piece, America's weight-related illnesses were "self-inflicted." Governmental intervention was misspent because "every adult American is responsible for his or her own health."[59] Personal upkeep was open to all, he confidently insisted.

By making individual regulation of the mind and the body the key to achieving optimal living, Mackey and other preventive pundits imagined a meritocracy of health. This popular bootstraps theory of wellness supposed that proper diet, exercise, and limited excess ensured rightly deserved health. Neglect resulted in unfortunate but self-induced suffering. Food sociologists Josee Johnston, Michelle Szabo, and Alexandra Rodney persuasively argue that while "presented as classless," this turn-of-the-twenty-first-century dietary health regime was drenched in signs of social distinction and status. Through "talk of food quality and healthfulness," they argue, "white middle class families" have drawn "boundaries between themselves as 'good' eaters and others as 'bad' eaters."[60] Of course, Mackey was not the inventor of these class conceits. From the late 1970s forward, the fit, thin, healthy body became *the* emblem of self-discipline and personal achievement for all Americans.[61] Beholden to this dominant cultural script, many Whole Foods loyalists probably nodded in agreement with Mackey's "personal responsibility" health ethos. They likely found his ideas about "conscious capitalism" intriguing. They may have praised him for his philanthropic generosity. His antiunionism, on the other hand, created cognitive dissonance between their Whole Foods expectations and those of Mackey.

"Beyond Unions" at Whole Foods

In the early 1980s, Mackey infamously quipped to a reporter, "The union is like having herpes. It doesn't kill you, but it's unpleasant and inconvenient and it stops a lot of people from becoming your lover."[62] Meant to be playful,

Mackey's comment, nevertheless, connoted his unbending disdain for organized labor. In the highly unionized grocery industry, at the start of the twenty-first century Whole Foods was the second largest union-free retailer: Walmart was the first. Mackey's disregard for worker collectivity was regularly demonstrated in his company's battles against employee unionization. In 1998, *Forbes* columnist Seth Lubove reported that when Whole Foods' unionized employees struck in Brentwood, California, Mackey made managers "unfurl giant banners [across the storefront] exposing picketers as union hires who've never even worked at Whole Foods."[63] In another example, Whole Foods staff in Madison, Wisconsin, brought in the United Food and Commercial Workers Union. Employees approved the union and hammered out a new contract that included "equitable raise distributions, grievance procedures and arbitrary firing protections." Whole Foods' lawyer dragged his feet during the contract negotiations, while management hired antiunion workers and fired the union organizers. Taking cues from Industrial Age union busting, Madison's store manager accused union organizers of being plants and out-of-towners. In this same period, a leaked Whole Foods memo indicated a company-wide goal to become "100% union free" by 2013.[64]

In the late 1990s, Mackey penned a nineteen-page treatise, "Beyond Unions," to explicate, in New Age lingo, how Whole Foods employees could rise above the unthinking worker-masses. His employees' attraction to unionization, Mackey argued, demonstrated unevolved consciousness, being "stuck in an old paradigm." Unions, he charged, perpetuated thinking that "all employees were weak and powerless (childlike?), and that all employers are greedy and exploitive." But finally it was "competition for labor not unions and their Marxist socialist rhetoric" that would ensure solid wages and work standards. Whole Foods did not need unions because his stores' work conditions, pay, and benefits far surpassed those of unionized competitors. "Unions," Mackey stated simply, "are not part of the solution at Whole Foods Market."[65] For some employees and labor organizers, Mackey's "Beyond Unions" polemic seemed a whole lot of smoke and mirrors, connoting what critic Kim Fellner called Whole Foods' "benevolent paternalism."[66]

As both a supporter of worker autonomy and a union antagonist, a critic of crony capitalism and a corporate raider, an environmentalist and a climate change skeptic, an alternative dietary health advocate and a personal health scold, John Mackey seems to be a study in contradictions. But, in fact, he embodies what Andrew Kirk describes as the "left-right fusion of free minds and free markets" that developed in the DIY-entrepreneurial wing of the counterculture.[67] This political cloudiness infuriated and perplexed Whole Foods' leftist shoppers and workers. On one hand, Whole Foods' advertising and branding, broadcast with self-congratulatory alacrity by its CEO, seemed to affirm postsixties progressivism. On the other hand, Mackey's barefaced rejection of the ACA and unionization, as well as his 2017 decision to sell his business to online behemoth Amazon, forced Whole Foods shoppers and employees to confront the fact that, although the natural foods movement emanated from the sixties Left, no political party or ideology owned the natural foods marketplace or the natural foods philosophy. Eden Foods' March 2013 suit against the U.S. Department of Health and Human Services (HHS), for an exemption from the ACA's birth control mandate, further corroborated this truth.

EDEN FOODS FREE ENTERPRISE

Natural foods pioneer Michael Potter followed a similar route to a natural foods career as had John Mackey. In Ann Arbor, Michigan, in the late 1960s, Potter and his friend started Eden food co-op. This operation eventually became a natural foods store specializing in macrobiotic merchandise. Originally, Eden co-op relied on such California suppliers as Erewhon and Chico-San and, later, on local resources. By 1979, Eden had its own warehouse, which employed 100 people and supplied 500 natural foods stores and restaurants, with annual sales of $5 million. Less than a decade later, Eden Foods had become one of the most well-known and popular natural and organic foods producers and retailers in the United States. It was particularly associated with dried and canned beans, whole grain pastas, soy milk, and macrobiotic supplies such as miso, mocha, and sea vegetables. The enlargement of Eden Foods' Michigan warehouse to 70,000 square feet in 2006 indicated Potter's dominance of the natural foods sector.[68]

Until 2013, Michael Potter confined public political statements to food issues. In the early 1990s, Potter and Eden Foods had been at the forefront of campaigns against genetically modified organisms (GMOs) and GMO labeling campaigns. To ensure the purity of its own products, Eden Foods instituted a GMO inspection process. This in-house regulation was publically vetted in 1997 when the *New York Times* investigated and tested eleven soy milk brands for GMOs. Only Potter's Edensoy passed muster.[69]

An advocate of government regulation and GMO labeling, Potter became a board member of the "non-GMO project." Eden Foods also led the way in BPA-free (Bisphenal-A) can lining. Debra Stark, owner of another natural foods industry giant, Debra's Natural Gourmet, admired Eden for this standard-setting posture. "It cost them hundreds of thousands of dollars. They didn't brag about it. They just did it," she remarked in a *Natural Foods Merchandiser* article.[70]

Potter's birth control pronouncements took the company far outside food safety and consumption politics, making its CEO's Catholic and libertarian leanings public. For his suit against HHS, Potter hired lawyers from the Thomas More Law Center. Thomas More is, according to its mission statement, a "public interest law firm [created to] . . . preserve America's Judeo-Christian heritage."[71] More's pro bono lawyers argued that Potter's obligation to pay for contraception, through the ACA, interfered with both his First Amendment rights and his religious autonomy as articulated in the Religious Freedom and Restoration Act instituted in 1993.[72] But in a series of interviews with *Salon* columnist Irin Carmon, Potter seemed more enraged by "government overreach" than by the religio-ethical, right-to-life principles associated with contraception. As he inartfully stated in an April 2013 interview: "I don't care if the federal government is telling me to buy my employees Jack Daniels or birth control. What gives them the right to tell me what to do?"[73] Potter's ACA rebellion also displayed his agreement with a generalized antichemical and antipharmaceutical naturalism typical among postsixties traditionalists.

Before the ACA came into effect, the Eden Foods employee insurance plan included prescription drug opt-in and opt-out prerogatives. According to Eden's public letter to the Independent Natural Foods Retailers Association, under the company's self-styled insurance coverage, 63 percent of employees opted out. This unusual insurance design originated from Potter's censure of anything synthetic. "Eden Foods," he reasoned in the letter to the association, "frowns on myopic pharmaceutical medicine and toxic chemical dependent agriculture."[74] Contraception, which his lawsuit described as "procedures [that] almost always involve immoral and unnatural practices," fell into this pile of modern poisons. Announcing her support for Potter's right to follow his "freedom-of-religion thing," Debra Stark articulated the antiestablishment convictions that informed her own company's reluctant compliance with the ACA: "Our staff have heard me grousing that our store is forced by law to pay for health insurance that many of us in the store don't believe in or use. I, for one, don't do the meds, yet am required to pay for that kind of insurance even while I pay out of pocket for dietary supplements and herbs that keep me out of the doctor's office."[75] Echoing John Mackey's arch libertarianism, Potter and Stark felt the federal government was a weak resister of big pharma's, big food's, and big farming's dictates. Consequently, it could not be trusted to construct a right-thinking natural health plan.

As part of the natural foods tribe, Debra Stark could not let her support of women's reproductive autonomy supersede loyalty to Potter and his natural foods leadership. She clarified that she wasn't on board with Potter's anticontraception "politics." In fact, she hoped he lost "his court case in spectacular fashion." Nonetheless, she would not be boycotting Eden Foods. It was a business, she wrote, that did "the right thing, not because it's good publicity, or a tax write-off, but because it would be unthinkable for them not to."[76] Debra Stark's political compartmentalization was replicated in the lively public debate over Potter's legal action.

Potter's original suit, filed with the federal appeals court in 2013, was dismissed. The court decided that "a secular non-profit corporation cannot establish that it can exercise religion." Yet, after the Supreme Court ruled in favor of the Hobby Lobby chain, which filed a similar religious freedom case in June 2014, Potter's lawyers resubmitted his complaint to the U.S. Court of Appeals, Sixth Circuit.[77] Shortly thereafter, the aroused natural foods community took to the internet with two online petitions and a "Boycott Eden" Facebook page. As historical leaders in retail protest, food co-ops participated in heated member interchanges over their institutions' response to Potter's suit. As in the past, boycott discussions only accentuated members' contrary and antagonistic designs for their co-ops. In the Wild West of internet discussion boards, co-op members, under the shadow of anonymity, viciously swarmed on one another without mercy or concern for their fragile common structure.

When members of the Ypsi Food Co-op, in Ypsilanti, Michigan, proposed an Eden Foods boycott, the community divided into warring fronts in online discussions. Some members implored their co-op to defend quality-of-life principles—the pursuit of "beauty, health, and permanence"—that had allied the food-concerned citizenry since the late 1960s.[78] In this vein, one commenter warned that an Eden boycott would interfere with his access to products with high organic and food grade marks. "There are no equal quality for their products and people who are allergic to life-killing chemicals will suffer. It is no one else's right to restrict my access to high quality foods. Please stop trying to remove them from my Co-op!!!" this indignant member yelled. In the name of women's rights and equal treatment, another Ypsi member countered that communal self-government was the co-op's primary mission. "That is what it means to have a membership controlled coop. The membership has control!" posted Lynne in response.[79] Dan Gillotte, general manager of Wheatsville co-op in Austin, Texas, chimed in, wondering how any particular political or ethical interest could represent the membership as a whole: "This is the difficult position that ethical food stores are in—for some GMOs are most important to avoid, for others local food is most important, for some the treatment of workers is more critical, still others care if the food is vegan or gluten free or paleo or meets some other specific dietary need... our co-ops lose when we try too hard to be food cops. Have some basic guidelines of what you most support and care about and leave the rest up to your owners and shoppers telling you [what] they want through their purchases."[80]

Gillotte's ponderings pointed to a truism: conscientious consumption, actualized through boycotts or product/producer loyalty, was an uncertain vehicle for ideological and political influence and citizen unification. Historian David Steigerwald warns that, after all, "the act of consumption... has no larger social meaning beyond the subjective impulse of the individual."[81] Nonetheless, swayed by new-century marketplace idolatry, shoppers suffered soul-searching self-examination with each retail interaction. Granular decisions, such as which canned bean to purchase, symbolically (and practically) seemed to determine the world's decline or its redemption and the shopper's hand in both. In this inflated environment, consumers carried infinite and competing narratives in their minds and their shopping carts.

One Ypsi Co-op discussant, writing under the handle "Toxic Hormones," resolved this noise by asserting a simple rule of the road: "I don't need to have the same ethical beliefs as the companies that make my food. I need to have the same FOOD beliefs."[82] Healthful, ecologically produced food surpassed all else: axiomatic clarity. If that end could be achieved through cloudy means or by producers with unpalatable politics, so be it.

Eden Foods' ecological branding signaled "progressive" to its left-leaning customers. Potter's lawsuit pulled back the curtain, revealing a CEO who balanced environmentalism with social conservatism—a seemingly contradictory mix. In the internet town square, his vocal and faceless customer-critics spewed venom and slung mud. Eden Foods took these attacks personally. A statement on the Eden Foods website brooded over the "grotesque mischaracterizations and fallacious arguments ... maliciousness and corruption" that followed the assertion of its "religious freedom."[83] On environmental protection and sustainable farming, as well as food purity, natural foods executives and their customers naturally aligned. But on the relation between the individual and the state, Potter's and Mackey's libertarian capitalist adulation clashed with progressive shoppers' wish for government-enforced civil rights and social welfare.

The disconnect between Mackey and Potter and their patrons underscored what John Wilkinson defines as the "permanent tension" that exists between "markets and social movements in the case of transactions heavily laden with values."[84] Although some loyalists supposed otherwise, capitalist ventures—even politically styled ones such as Whole Foods and Eden Foods—were weak machinery for civic intervention. When natural foods followers traded partisan citizenship for pocketbook politics, natural foods CEOs became the objects of both popular frustration and admiration. Yet shoppers' assumption of ideological consensus with their natural foods idols was a category mistake. Potter and Mackey were not politicians or movement activists, they were businessmen—and free market stalwarts at that.

That being said, many natural foodists still believed that the expansion of the quality foods marketplace implied concurrent development of an environmentally and socially responsible production system. As conservative journalist, Rod Dreher, assessed, "Taking care of little things can become the first steps to creating a big solution."[85] Shopping at Whole Foods may seem like a "little thing." But it was a first step that, converging with other antiestablishment individual and familial decisions, might tip the cultural balance. Dreher's confidence in the political gravity of individual acts was a bedrock assumption of the natural foods movement and the sixties gestalt from which it arose. Yet the fact that this trope came out of the mouth of a right-wing Catholic social commentator meant that countercultural conservatism had arrived.

CRUNCHY CONS: THE RISE OF COUNTERCULTURAL CONSERVATISM

In 2002, Rod Dreher, in a spirited piece in the *National Review* titled "Birkenstocked Burkeans," confessed that he and his wife's style of living surprisingly correlated these two abiding Catholics with the hippie counterculture.

Dreher's 2006 *Crunchy Cons: The New Conservative Counterculture and Its Return to Roots* explained in full the conservative bohemianism sketched out in the "Birkenstocked" article. Entering the media stream in the same year as Michael Pollan's *Omnivore's Dilemma*, *Crunchy Cons* indicted that the natural foods movement's core constituency had swelled well beyond its original political-cultural borders.

Dreher's proposals coordinated more with Twelve Tribes religious separatism and Pollanesque gastronomy than with the social-economic libertarianism of John Mackey and Potter. His "crunchy con" future did not entail conscious capitalism spreading organic and natural commerce and the progress ethic worldwide. As Dreher worried, "Free-market, technology-driven capitalism, for its benefits, tends to pull families and communities apart by encouraging individualism." Instead, he advised readers to resist materialism's siren song and return to "the way of traditionalism." This traditionalism would be actualized in culture, not politics. And it would be rooted in what Dreher's conservative idol, Russell Kirk, called "the Permanent Things"—family, God, and community—that gave life meaning and moral grounding.[86]

Dreher's Christian pro-life friend, Frederica Mathewes-Green, had explained to him that "authenticity [and] the distrust of mass-produced sentiments and materials" was the bridge that joined emergent "granola conservatives" to the natural foods Left.[87] In pursuit of this authenticity, Rod and Julia Dreher departed from the mainstream in every way possible. In their architecturally original Dallas bungalow, with their homeschooled sons, stay-at-home mom, and organic, local meals, the Drehers made family and home their sanctuary and their bully pulpit. As Dreher opined, "It can't be denied that we show what we believe not by what we say but by what we do."[88] In a conservative homage to sixties self-invention, they made their lives their revolution.

Predictably, the figures of Rod Dreher's greatest esteem were off-the-grid farmers—food producers of unimpeachable sovereignty. Like Kingsolver and Pollan, Dreher coveted the straightforward purposefulness of the farming life, particularly Christian family operations. Because of their piety in an overwhelmingly secular world, Dreher judged the fundamentalist farming families that he encountered as equal to, if not more countercultural than, Haight-Ashbury hippies. Robert Hutchins, an organic livestock producer from Greenville, Texas, confirmed this perception for the author.

As Dreher recounted, for most of his life Hutchins had been an ambitious young Republican, first as a naval officer and then as a defense industry executive. In 2000, he got off the hamster wheel after twenty years as a well-compensated, high-ranking professional. "God convinced me," Hutchins told Dreher, "that this kind of life was not what he wanted for me." Divinely directed, Hutchins, his wife, Nancy, and their twelve children began to raise free-range and organic chicken, beef, and pork, which they sold at farmer's markets under the label "Texas Supernatural Meats." It wasn't only Hutchins's professional departure that convinced Dreher of his creditable nonconformity. In the mid-1980s, well before Robert traded a lucrative profession for the uncertainties of self-employment, the Hutchinses pulled their growing brood out of the public system to begin homeschooling. This decision made them take stock of the whole of their lives. "Once we started seeing things in our children that led us to choose homeschooling," Hutchins explained to Dreher, "we started wondering if our eating habits were really lined up with God's best, and whether or not my occupation was lined up with what God really wanted for us."[89] These fundamentalist Christians had "turned on, tuned in, and dropped out."

Hutchins informed Dreher that although most small farmers came to sustainable agriculture from a "pantheistic, kind of earth-worshiping basis," his fundamentalism did not make him an outsider. "It's okay to be a Christian in in our community," he reflected. "It's almost like there's more acceptance for diverse viewpoints within this community than there is from people looking in from the outside."[90] In their parallel and alternative marketplace, mistrust of the established foods industry, and the cultural and political systems that fortified it, knitted together small food producers of different religious and philosophical backgrounds.

Notably, as in Kingsolver's exchanges with the Amish farming couple, Robert Hutchins, rather than his wife, Nancy, reviewed the family's history. He, not she, was the participant in the sustainable farming community. He explained the problems with the "industrial meat infrastructure" and with the Republican Party's acceptance of "globalization." He, not his wife, expressed the immeasurable good of "living the life of homeschooling agrarians."[91] Nancy Hutchins made one appearance during Dreher's visit to the family's ranch, when she called both men in for a noontime bowl of Texas chili. Again, because the author did not solicit Nancy's thoughts, we are left to make our own decisions about her role and power within the family and the business.

The Dreher and Hutchins families' religious and political convictions seemed to require conventionally patriarchal gender arrangements. For Dreher, a dual-income household did not make good economic sense, once child-care costs were taken into account. More important, on the level of taste and style, a working father and the tender care of an at-home mother and wife outweighed the monetary perks of a dual-career partnership. "It is hard to convey the gratitude and satisfaction I feel when I come home after a long day at the office to a delicious home-cooked dinner, and the security the boys and I have in knowing that Julie is always there, making our house a home," Dreher dreamily related.[92] Dreher's admiration for "real" families, "real" farming, and "real" food of a, supposedly, more real past connected this conservative Catholic to the liberal Michael Pollan and Barbara Kingsolver and the countercultural and evangelical Twelve Tribes. In the new-century food movement, previously conflicting political perspectives blended in the verities of cultural conservationism.

Near the end of *Crunchy Cons'* "Food" chapter, Dreher recalls a visit to libertarian-evangelical, livestock farmer Joel Salatin's Polyface Farm. Salatin's critique of industrialized food production, in provocatively titled books such as *Everything I Want to Do Is Illegal: War Stories from the Local Food Front* (2007) and *Folks, This Ain't Normal: A Farmer's Advice for Happier Hens, Healthier People, and a Better World* (2011), made him a hero of the twenty-first-century crunchy Left and Right. His tirades against USDA regulations affirmed a pervasive big government enmity. As Dreher explained, for contemporary conservatives "distrust of big government is in [our] DNA." Salatin was certain that his local, artisanal intervention in the meat chain was far superior to warfare with food regulatory agencies that claim to "protect the general welfare" but really just safeguarded "big agribusiness from rural independent competition."[93] Don't trust the government, Salatin and Dreher resolved. No "true" conservative, Dreher clarified, would suppose that the government could reanimate core American values and cultural ways, not even a Republican administration.

Sounding like an altered states apostle or a mystical supplicant from sixties bohemia, Salatin concluded that the cultural Right must raise its consciousness. Conservatives, who dismissed his farming ideology as antiprogress, did not see the innate worth of ethically crafted food because, as Salatin explained to Dreher, they "tend to be very Western in [their] thinking." They suffered from "Greco-Roman-linear-segmented-compartmentalized thinking ... as opposed to the Eastern mind-set, which thinks more holistically," Salatin concluded.[94] For many in the postsixties Left and Right, public politics could never facilitate profound renovations. Only islands of conscientious familial, neighborly, and commercial self-reliance, rooted in traditionalism and nature, could do that work.

The natural foods movement that came to life in the early 1970s subscribed to the radical premises of the sixties movement. It saw itself as the home front and storefront scaffolds of the revolution. The naturalist nostalgia that attracted Christian traditionalists, such as the Twelve Tribes, and the gender and cultural conventionalism that later brought "granola conservatives" into the fold had always been tucked in the movement, as was the consumer individualism that Whole Foods CEO, John Mackey, glorified. Conservatives' presence in this hippie-left movement surprised and disturbed natural foods proponents with countercultural biographies and affinities. It should not have. Cultural preservation, pastoral sentimentality, and moralistic consumerism—the movement's fundamentals—were always there, ready for conservative adaptation.

CONCLUSION

THE FUTURE OF COUNTERCULTURAL FOOD POLITICS

I n the early days of the first Obama administration—when many Americans believed that this historic election denoted a monumental national evolution—Michael Pollan made a spirited appeal to the new president in a *New York Times Magazine* piece titled "Farmer in Chief." Drawing from his research into postwar agricultural history, with urgency and passion he pitched wide-ranging reform to the rookie chief executive. The climate, public health, foreign policy, and trade, the very vitality of the economy and society, relied on a sustainable food system. Evoking a green future, Pollan argued for a "sun-food" agenda that would "wring the oil out of the system." Specifically, Pollan asked the president to change reigning agricultural practice by "resolarizing the American farm," "reregionalizing the food system," and "rebuilding American food culture." "Your sun-food agenda promises to win support across the aisle," this food writer assured the president.[1] Concluding, he suggested that the first family should demonstrate its pledge to healthful food and farming by eating and growing organic vegetables. Michelle Obama seemed persuaded by these recommendations, when, a year after Pollan's article, she established the organic White House Kitchen Garden on the South Lawn and when she hired organic food champion, Sam Kass, as the White House's assistant chef.[2]

Pollan's foray into policy counsel augured a more classically political posture for a natural foods movement with a historically antistatist countenance. Yet, because Pollan made the president the steward of agricultural change, after reading his persuasion piece, food-concerned Americans could only wait expectantly for their newly elected leader to take on America's most powerful industries. Pollan had not named a role or responsibility for average citizens in this battle. Nevertheless, at the turn of the twenty-first century, food system critiques by Pollan and his acolytes had galvanized a renaissance in natural/organic allegiance and enterprise.

Eight years later, in the twilight of the Obama White House, Pollan returned to the *New York Times* to review the outcome of his "sun-food" proposition. In the ominously titled piece "Big Food Strikes Back," this significant shaper of food ideas gave the administration a failing grade. Big Food won, Pollan judged. The "$1.5 trillion industry that grows, slaughters, processes, imports, packages and retails most of the food America eats" had blocked all attempts to reorganize the nation's agriculture and diet.[3] At every turn, from Secretary of Agriculture Thomas Vilsack's investigations into anticompetition in agriculture to Michelle Obama's pressure on processed food corporations to adopt nutritional ingredients, Big Food outmaneuvered the Obama administration's determined attempts.

As the most influential food pundit in America, what political pressure had Pollan wielded to mobilize Obama and the nation to sustainable food production? What exactly had Pollan been up to between his 2008 Farmer in Chief cri de coeur and his 2016 Big Food dirge? With some exceptions, his writing, lecturing, and campaigning remained squarely aimed at local, healthful, and delight-filled eating and cooking. In his 2008 book *In Defense of Food: An Eater's Manifesto*, Pollan backpedaled from the sweeping structural remonstrations of the "Farmer in Chief" letter to self-protective, self-affirming, and private acts of consumption. To navigate the postmodern food morass, Pollan offered a simple maxim: "Eat food. Not too much. Mostly Plants."[4] In the follow-up user's guide, *Food Rules: An Eater's Manual*, he compiled sixty-four rules for right eating, sent, at his request, from admiring fans. "Today," he wrote, "the challenge of eating well comes down to choosing real food and avoiding . . . industrial novelties." As a folksy counselor, he dispensed nutritional sentimentalities—"Don't eat anything your great-great-grandmother wouldn't recognize"—and debatable dietary tropes, such as "Avoid products that contain more than five listed ingredients" and "It's not food if it arrives through the window of your car." *Food Rules* tutored readers in dodging the mass food behemoth, not in orchestrating civic resistance to that system. Nor did *Food Rules* address unequal access to the food marketplace (the farmer's markets, community-supported agriculture [CSA], organic grocery stores) that he insisted readers frequent. "Not everyone can afford to eat well in America, which is a literal shame, but most of us can," Pollan stated rather indifferently.[5] The desire for tasty food, healthfulness, and humane capitalism were certainly not exclusive to Pollan's white, middle- and upper-class constituency. Yet, as geographer Rachel Slocum describes, the "objectives, tendencies, strategies, the emphases and absences, the things overlooked in [the natural foods movement] make them so."[6] Pollan's judgment that those who "could afford it" *must* "eat well" exemplifies how his "emphases and absences" included some and inadvertently excluded others.

In addition to doling out salutary axioms to foodies, during the age of Obama, Pollan returned to his true love: the culinary arts. In 2013 he showed "those who could afford it" how to cook and eat deliberately in a sumptuously crafted documentary series, *Cooked*, based on his book of the same name. Echoing Carol Flinders's gastropolitical posts from her seventies countercultural kitchen, the show and the book submitted that cooking was a quintessentially human activity and could be, in his words, "the most important thing an ordinary person can do to help reform the food system."[7] As narrator and lead character in this cable series, Pollan tracked methods of cooking, fermenting, cheese making, brewing, and baking from their indigenous beginning to contemporary manifestations.

Described by *New York Times* columnist Frank Bruni as the "designated repository of the nation's food conscience," and by the website thestranger.com as "the food God-man," Pollan did not become politically stimulated by his own revolutionary call.[8] He and many of his adherents had not found a way to refute the conventional system or to support the "sun-food" strategy beyond shopping, cooking, and eating local and natural. Pollan occasionally used his journalist bully pulpit to draw attention to the president's and the U.S. Department of Agriculture's (USDA) acquiescence to agribusiness lobbyists. But, on the whole, after sending the president a convincing exposition on the corporate food system's dangers, he had returned to his Northern California "real food" idyll of kitchen, family, and natural producers.

Before he sat down to chastise the Obama administration, Michael Pollan might have checked more precisely what the USDA had done between 2008 and 2016. If he had, he would have found that this federal agency had listened to and then served the loudest food-preoccupied faction. Supporting organic farming's augmentation with a "streamlined certification process," the USDA had provided $11.5 million in aid for the certification of farms converting to organic. Between 2009 and 2014, it invested $1 billion in 40,000 local and regional food businesses. In 2015, the department premiered an Organic Integrity Database—included in the 2014 Farm Bill—which regularly updated information about changes on organic farms and the addition of newly certified operations. This database gave consumers constant access to the organic credentials of local and national businesses. Organic businesses, in turn, used it as a marketing tool.[9]

Department of Agriculture backing and consumer demand assisted the enlargement of natural and organic foods. National Organic Program data noted a 12 percent increase in certified organic operations between 2015 and 2016. According to the USDA, this one-year burst was the greatest growth since 2008 and a "nearly 300%" inflation since 2002. Local food sales also rose from $5 billion in 2008 to $12 billion in 2014.[10] Farmer's markets, treasured by the food revolution, increased from 1,755 in 1994 to 8,144 in 2013.[11] The USDA had energetically responded to popular opinion, putting money, resources, and its power into the location where most food movement partisans gravitated: the alternative marketplace.

With some investigation, Pollan also would have found that in the invigorated food revolution atmosphere, advocacy organizations, such as Friends of Farmworkers (established in 1975) and the Food Trust (established in 1992), were welcoming a swell of volunteerism, donations, and public notice. He would also have seen a fresh racially and economically diverse set of actors farming, organizing, and tackling what Natasha Bowen, founder of the multicultural "Color of Food" project, described as America's "broken food system."[12] He would have found that "food justice" thinkers and activists, like their "food for people" sixties movement ancestors, were grappling with the economic and racial tangle behind America's long-standing nutritional and health disparities. He would have found that, although his natural gastronomy was clearly the lead story, the battle lines between good/healthy food and food justice, laid down in countercultural co-ops and other food fora in the late 1960s and early 1970s, were being redrawn by new-century food activists.

As an agribusiness critic and provocateur, Pollan was under no obligation to spearhead citizen influence or to catalogue activist organizations. But it is not surprising that the twenty-first-century intellectual patriarch of a movement with a historically tenuous relationship to, if not outright disdain for, traditional politics did not jump into the gritty and boring business of electoral and grassroots coordination.

Toward the end of the "Big Food" essay, Pollan related an exchange between Dan Barber, one of the first farm-to-table restauranteurs, and President Obama. The night before his first inauguration, Obama challenged Barber to "show me a movement." An apt command, considering that to call the "collection of disparate groups . . . which still barely exists as a political force in Washington" a fully-fledged movement was "an act of generosity and hope," Pollan conceded. Given this truth, Pollan instructed his faithful followers that "our future food politics, may lie in grassroots campaigns targeted not at politicians in Washington, but directly at Big Food and its consumers, taking aim at its Achilles heel: those precious brands."[13] Echoing a similar circumspection, conservative counterculturalist Rod Dreher had warned, "Politics and economics will not save us. If we are to be saved at all it will be through living faithfully to the Permanent Things, preserving these ancient truths in the choices we make in everyday life."[14] In fact, Pollan and other food revolution defenders *had* reared a substantive movement that had, from food scholar Maria Fonte's perspective, commoditized and marketized "ethical values."[15] That movement, bound to countercultural concepts and enhanced by USDA outlays, thrived in farm-to-table eateries, Whole Foods, CSAs, and urban and school gardens. Its cultural traditionalism, antistatism, and aesthetics of authenticity charmed a pool of adherents who moved about in whole foods channels, creating a healthy lifestyle standard which influenced new-century food, body, and diet ideals. For a natural foods movement that was doubtful of citizen leverage, underpracticed in multiracial and cross-class partnerships, and operating in a neoliberal world, this was (almost) an inevitable conclusion.

Although the original countercultural adversaries of the dominant food system had minimal regard for corporate capitalism, they saw promise in the marketplace and in the authority of critical consumption. Consequently, they built an outsider food world to both evade and compete with supermarkets and agribusiness—farming organically, circumventing the supermarket by selling natural goods in hippie stores, and buying beyond the "system." This plan succeeded. Hippies made a robust customized food network, initially just for other hippies and later for a more dispersed, but still primarily middle- and upper-class consumer base.

With much of their energy bound to the surrogate food structure, natural foods advocates left the conventional food system and food and farming legislators and regulators to march on largely unchallenged. Indeed, from the 1960s forward, the conventional food and agricultural systems grew in size, scope, and depth. The alternative food system grew too, but comparatively less. Individuals who might have previously spearheaded progressive agricultural and food policy or civic service had their hands full making and maintaining their dissident businesses and associations. Citizens who were not becoming organic/natural foods entrepreneurs put their political clout and economic stock into buying and supporting the parallel food structure. Together, natural foods producers and consumers made, in Julie Guthman's words, "food positive activity... part of a national zeitgeist."[16]

In every stage of the natural foods movement's maturation, the bedeviling shortcomings of using moralistic eating, farming, and shopping as weapons in the war against consumer capitalism persisted. Many food rights and eco-gastronomic actors pronounced their dissatisfaction through public interest lobbying, as well as traditional grassroots labor. But the marketplace is where the natural foods movement found its momentum and its voice, and it was in the marketplace that individuals staked their natural foods politics and identity.

CODA: FOOD POLITICS AFTER TRUMP

Donald Trump's election in November 2016, along with his opening strike on immigration, health care subsidies, school lunch nutrition, and other liberal protections and policies, acted as a wake-up call for politically detached progressives. Politics seemed to urgently matter, not just movement politics, but electoral, Washington-establishment politics.

Before Donald Trump's inauguration, good food leaders Michael Pollan and Mark Bittman issued a casus belli in an article titled "Food and More: Expanding the Movement for the Trump Era." With equal measures of desperation and determination, Pollan and Bittman—along with Olivier De Schutter, U.N. food rights advocate, and Union of Concerned Scientists Food and Environment Program director, Ricardo Salvador—opined that the food movement must awaken to the crisis. It must direct its energy not just towards environmental and nutritional reform, but also to "a more immediate cause: protecting the disadvantaged and defending democracy." Eating consciously, supporting local and sustainable producers, even campaigning for farm and food legislation—the previous thrust of Bittman's and Pollan's advisement—would not save America. Instead, they warned, citizens must think and act comprehensively: "Parochial food issues, such as the labeling of GMOs or the formulation of national nutritional standards, are bound to be overshadowed as the larger fight for social justice becomes more urgent." Activists needed to coordinate: "Demonstrators for reproductive rights [should] join Food Chain Alliance activists . . . members of the Young Farmers Coalition [should turn] out to support Black Lives Matter," they commanded.[17]

In November 2017, Michael Pollan stood on the Capitol Hill steps in Washington endorsing an alternative farm and food bill, proposed by Oregon representative Earl Blumenauer. "I'm hoping to be more engaged," Pollan told the cluster of reporters.[18] If Pollan's example roused the millions of organic and natural foods loyalists to leverage their well-demonstrated cultural and political power, not only for good food, but also for the health, well-being, equality, and pleasure of all, they would be a force to be reckoned with.

NOTES

PREFACE

1. Gregory Calvert, "White America: Radical Consciousness and Social Change," in *The New Left: A Documentary History*, ed. Massimo Teodori (New York: Bobbs-Merrill, 1969), 412–18.

INTRODUCTION: THE GATHERING STORM

1. Laurel Robertson, Carol Flinders, and Bronwen Godfrey, *Laurel's Kitchen: A Handbook for Vegetarian Cookery and Nutrition* (Petaluma, CA: Nilgiri Press, 1976), 20–21.
2. Robertson, Flinders, and Godfrey, *Laurel's Kitchen*, 12, 23. According to Sherrie Inness, *Laurel's Kitchen* sold eighty thousand copies in its first two years and was one of the most popular natural foods cookbooks in the 1970s. See *Secret Ingredients: Race, Gender, and Class at the Dinner Table* (New York: Palgrave, 2006), 98–99.
3. Robertson, Flinders, and Godfrey, *Laurel's Kitchen*, 41, 12, 53.
4. Charles A. Reich, *The Greening of America* (New York: Bantam, 1970), cover.
5. Alice Echols smartly describes the cultural and political Left's propensity in the 1960s toward personal politics in "Nothing Distant about It: Women's Liberation and Sixties Radicalism," in *The Sixties: From Memory to History*, ed. David Farber (Chapel Hill: University of North Carolina Press, 1994), 149–74.
6. Robertson, Flinders, and Godfrey, *Laurel's Kitchen*, 57.
7. Many historians, including Gerry Schremp, Harvey Levenstein, and Sylvia Whitman, to name just a few, have covered food modernization. My article, "Back to the Kitchen," *Ms.* 23, no. 1 (Winter 2013): 42–45, also presents an overview of ready-made cooking and food history.
8. Laura Shapiro, *Something from the Oven: Reinventing Dinner in 1950s America* (New York: Penguin Books, 2004), 12.
9. Shapiro, *Something from the Oven*, 15.
10. Ginger Ale Salad-Lime Jell-O package, circa 1953; Spaghetti Oven Dinner in *Better Homes and Garden New Cook Book* (New York: Meredith Publishing: 1953), 179.

11. Most fifties food histories rely on cookbooks, women's magazines, and materials which unreflectively repeat the harried housewife trope pedaled by convenience marketers. In a genre-defining article, "Populux: The Suburban Cuisine of the 1950s," *Journal of American Culture* 15, no. 3 (Fall 1992): 73–78, Joshua Gitleson used cookbooks, product label recipes, and food advertisements to claim that a suburban ethos of "Speed, Modernity, and Progress" (73) infused fifties food. Karal Ann Marling uses *Betty Crocker's Picture Book*, a General Mills creation, to show women's adoption of cake mixes in *As Seen on TV: The Visual Culture of Every Day Life in the 1950s* (Cambridge, MA: Harvard University Press, 1994), 203–32. Cookbooks, product labels, and ads are aspirational texts. Countercultural critics, who may have overclaimed the demise of cooking from scratch, added to the confusion between cultural hype and actual cooking and eating in the 1950s and 1960s.
12. Robertson, Flinders, and Godfrey, *Laurel's Kitchen*, 24.
13. My hope is that this book will add to the rich foundation Belasco laid in *Appetite for Change: How the Counterculture Took on the Food Industry, 1966–1988* (New York: Random House, 1989). First published in 1989, Belasco reflects back on the natural foods movement in a very different moment. In the Reagan 1980s, natural foods institutions were growing but under attack. At that point, Belasco could not have predicted the surge of natural consumerism that washed over the twenty-first-century United States. I take the natural foods narrative beyond Belasco's elegiac conclusion.
14. Maurice Isserman, in "The Not So Dark and Bloody Ground: New Works on the 1960s," *American Historical Review* 94, no. 4 (October 1989): 990–1010, rightly questions whether Students for a Democratic Society (SDS) participants, such as Todd Gitlin, James Miller, and Ronald Fraser, overdraw the importance of themselves and their organization to the period's character. Counterculture histories settle for San Francisco and Greenwich Village and naming Ken Kesey, the Diggers, Timothy Leary, and occasionally Janis Joplin as the scene's locale and protagonists. I challenge these narratives by finding countercultural sensibilities and activities across America.
15. "Andrew Weil, M.D.," *Academy of Achievement*, May 22, 1998, http://www.achievement.org/achiever/andrew-weil-m-d.
16. Allen Matusow, *The Unraveling of America: A History of Liberalism in the 1960s* (New York: Harper Torchbooks, 1986), 290.
17. Andrew Weil, *The Natural Mind: An Investigation of Drugs and the Higher Consciousness* (New York: Houghton Mifflin, 1972), 73.
18. Overviews that influenced my analysis of sixties politics and culture include Stewart Burns, *Social Movements of the 1960s: Searching for Democracy* (New York: Twayne Publishers, 1990); Milton Voirst, *Fire in the Streets: America in the 1960's* (New York: Touchstone, 1981); Todd Gitlin, *The Sixties: Years of Hope, Days of Rage* (New York: Bantam, 1987); David Steigerwald, *The Sixties and the End of Modern America* (New York: St. Martin's Press, 1995); Arthur Marwick, *The Sixties: Cultural Revolution in Britain, France, Italy, and the United States, c. 1958–c. 1974* (Oxford: Oxford University Press, 1998); Nick Bromell, *Tomorrow Never Knows: Rock and Psychedelics in the 1960s* (Chicago: University of Chicago Press, 2000); James J. Farrell, *The Spirit of the Sixties: Making Postwar Radicalism* (New York: Routledge, 1997); Jeremy Varon, Michael S. Foley, and John McMillian, "Time Is an Ocean: The Past and Future of the Sixties," *Sixties: A Journal of History, Politics and Culture, Culture and History* 1, no. 1 (June 2008): 1–7; M. J. Heale, "The Sixties as History: A Review of the Political

Historiography," *Reviews in American History* 33 (2005): 133–52; Jeremi Suri, "The Rise and Fall of an International Counterculture," *American Historical Review* 114, no. 1 (2009): 45–68.

19. Russell Rickford's "'We Can't Grow Food on All This Concrete': The Land Question, Agrarianism, and Black Nationalist Thought in the Late 1960s and 1970s," provides insight into black agrarianism and its particular relevance in the Black Power era. See *Journal of American History* 103, no. 4 (March 2017): 956–80.

20. For an interesting review of rural and farming utopianism, see Brent Cunningham, "Pastoral Romance," *Lampham's Quarterly*, June 10, 2011, https://www.laphamsquarterly.org/food/pastoral-romance.

21. Roland Marchand, *Advertising the American Dream: Making Way for Modernity, 1920–1940* (Berkeley: University of California Press, 1985), xxi.

22. "A Young $10 Billion Power: The US Teen-age Consumer Has Become a Major Factor in the Nation's Economy," *Life*, August 31, 1959, 78–84.

23. For a discussion of food's cultural freight, see Warren Belasco and Philip Scranton, eds., *Food Nations: Selling Taste in Consumer Societies* (New York: Routledge, 2002), chap. 1; Pierre Bourdieu, *Distinction: A Social Critique of the Judgement of Taste* (Cambridge, MA: Harvard University Press, 1984), 1–6, 177–96.

24. For this interpretation, see Christopher Lasch, *Culture of Narcissism: American Life in an Age of Diminishing Expectations* (New York: Norton, 1979); Ulrich Beck, *The Reinvention of Politics: Rethinking Modernity in a Global Social World* (Cambridge: Polity Press, 1996); Peter Clecak, *America's Quest for the Ideal Self: Dissent and Fulfillment in the 60s and 70s* (New York: Oxford University Press, 1983); Carl Boggs, *The End of Politics: Corporate Power and the Decline of the Public Sphere* (New York: Guilford Press, 2000).

25. Raymond Mungo, "Searches for a New Age at Total Loss Farm, 1970," in *Major Problems in American History since 1945*, ed. Robert Griffith and Paula Baker (New York: Houghton Mifflin, 2001), 332.

26. For perspicacious analyses of class and food consumerism, see Marjorie Devault, *Feeding the Family: Caring as Gendered Work* (Chicago: University of Chicago Press, 1992), 201. Also see Mike Featherstone, *Consumer Culture and Postmodernism* (London: Sage, 1991), and Josee Johnston, Michelle Szabo, and Alexandra Rodney, "Good Food, Good People: Understanding the Cultural Repertoire of Ethical Eating," *Journal of Popular Culture* 11, no. 3 (2011): 293–318.

27. E. Melanie Dupuis, "Angels and Vegetables: A Brief History of Food Advice in America," *Gastronomica: The Journal of Food and Culture* 7, no. 3 (Summer 2007): 34.

28. Charlotte Biltekoff, *Eating Right in America: The Cultural Politics of Food and Health* (Durham, NC: Duke University Press, 2013), 4.

29. Norman Mailer, "Superman Comes to the Supermarket," *Esquire*, November 1960, http://www.esquire.com/news-politics/a3858/superman-supermarket/.

30. Allen Ginsberg, "A Supermarket in California," in *American Literature: Tradition and Innovation 4: Henry Adams to the Present*, ed. Harrison T. Meserole, Walter Sutton, and Brom Weber (Lexington, MA: D. C. Heath, 1974), 3676.

31. One survey, conducted for a 1958 home economics dissertation, asked 210 families in Pennsylvania whether women had enough time to cook. Three-quarters of the respondents replied that they did. Another survey undermined the assumption that working women relied on convenience foods, finding that they used ready-made

ingredients at the same rates as did stay-at-home moms. For these very informative surveys, see Shapiro, *Something from the Oven*, 46–48.

32. *Moosewood Cookbook* (Berkeley: Ten Speed Press, 1993), vi; Robertson, Flinders, and Godfrey, *Laurel's Kitchen*, 23–24; Anna Thomas, *The Vegetarian Epicure* (New York: Vintage, 1972), 7, 4, 195.

33. E. Melanie Dupuis and David Goodman, "Should We Go 'Home' to Eat? Towards a Reflexive Politics of Localism," *Journal of Rural Studies* 21 (2005): 361, for this problem in the twenty-first-century food movement.

34. Alice Waters, *Coming to My Senses: The Making of a Countercultural Cook* (New York: Clarkson Potter Publishers, 2017), 148–49.

35. Andrew G. Kirk, *Counterculture Green: The "Whole Earth Catalog" and American Environmentalism* (Lawrence: University Press of Kansas, 2007), 206.

36. Joshua Clark Davis, "Activist Businesses: The New Left's Surprising Critique of Postwar Consumer Culture," *American Historian* 12 (May 2017): 24–29. Clark qualifies that most counterinstitutions did not survive long; those that did often perpetuated radical rhetoric more than radical action.

37. Fred Turner, *From Counterculture to Cyberculture: Stewart Brand, the Whole Earth Network, and the Rise of Digital Utopianism* (Chicago: University of Chicago Press, 2006), 97.

38. Julie Guthman provocatively discusses the chase for meaningful work by a new generation of middle-class, college-educated Americans as volunteer organic and alternative farmer-hands in "Willing (White) Workers on Organic Farms? Reflections on Volunteer Farm Labor and the Politics of Precarity," *Gastronomica: The Journal of Critical Food Studies* 17, no. 1 (2017): 15–19.

39. Coverage of the "obesity epidemic'" is too vast and repetitive to cite meaningfully. For an interesting debate on the subject, see Paul Campos, Abigail Saguy, Paul Ernsberger, Eric Oliver, and Glenn Gaesser, "The Epidemiology of Overweight and Obesity: Public Health Crisis or Moral Panic," *International Journal of Epidemiology* 35 (2006): 55–60.

40. Nathan McClintock explains that from 1978 to 1982, six hundred markets closed in poorer locales nationwide. Liquor stores often took over food retail in the void left by the urban retreat of grocery stores, turning poor city neighborhoods into junk food jungles. See his excellent case study "From Industrial Garden to Food Desert: Demarcated Devaluation in the Flatlands of Oakland, California," in *Cultivating Food Justice: Race, Class, and Sustainability*, ed. Alison Hope Alkon and Julian Agyeman (Cambridge, MA: MIT Press, 2011), 89–120.

41. In Jackson Lears's article "A Matter of Taste: Corporate Cultural Hegemony in a Mass Consumption Society," in *Recasting America: Culture and Politics in the Age of Cold War*, ed. Lary May (Chicago: University of Chicago Press, 1989): 38–57, he describes this process among fifties intellectuals (William Whyte, C. Wright Mills, Herbert Marcuse) who named conformity, commercialization, and bureaucratization, issues that they were confronting as a class, as the era's problems.

42. Lears, "A Matter of Taste," 50.

43. See Belasco, *Appetite for Change*, chaps. 6 and 7, for the mass media and corporate attacks on natural foods.

44. Alice Waters quoted in Reed McManus, "'I Call It a Delicious Revolution': A Famous Restaurateur Promotes Reading, Writing, and Arugula," *Sierra*, November/December 2004, 29. https://vault.sierraclub.org/sierra/200411/interview.asp.

45. Susan Friedberg, *French Beans and Food Scares: Culture and Commerce in an Anxious Age* (Oxford: Oxford University Press, 2004), 5.

CHAPTER 1: "MORE THAN JUST CHEAP CHEESE"

1. For more on "right livelihood," see David Farber, "Building the Counterculture, Creating Right Livelihoods: The Counterculture Goes to Work, *Sixties* 6, no. 1 (2013): 1–24, and "Self-Invention in the Realm of Production: Craft, Beauty, and Community in the American Counterculture, 1964–1978," *Pacific Historical Review* 85, no. 3 (August 2016): 408–42; Timothy Miller, *The Hippies and American Values* (Knoxville: University of Tennessee Press, 2011), 122.
2. Anne Enke, *Finding the Movement: Sexuality, Contested Space, and Feminist Activism* (Durham, NC: Duke University Press, 2007), is a keynote source on lesbian business collectivity; Anne Valk, *Radical Sisters: Second-Wave Feminism and Black Liberation in Washington, D.C.* (Champaign: University of Illinois Press, 2008).
3. Anthony P. Sager, "Radical Law: Three Collectives in Cambridge," in *Co-ops, Communes and Collectives: Experiments in Social Change in the 1960s and 1970s*, ed. John Case and Rosemary C. Taylor (New York: Pantheon, 1979), 137.
4. Daniel Zwerdling, "The Uncertain Revival of Food Cooperatives," in Case and Taylor, *Co-ops, Communes and Collectives*, 90. This figure includes small groups, known as "buying clubs," that gathered to buy foods not easily found in the 1970s or to save money through bulk purchasing.
5. Case and Taylor, *Co-ops, Communes and Collectives*, 1–2.
6. Tracey Deutsch presents a thoughtful counter to the declension history of chain stores overtaking local food markets. She suggests that supermarkets liberated women from clerk control of merchandise and the suffocating gossip endemic to tight-knit urban ethnic enclaves that corner grocers served, in "Untangling Alliances: Social Tensions surrounding Independent Grocery Stores and the Rise of Mass Retailing," in *Food Nations: Selling Taste in Consumer Societies*, ed. Warren Belasco and Philip Scranton (New York: Routledge, 2002), 156–74.
7. Gerry Schremp, *Kitchen Culture: Fifty Years of Food Fads* (New York: Pharos Books, 1991), 54–55; Harvey Levenstein, *Paradox of Plenty: A Social History of Eating in Modern America* (New York: Oxford University Press: 1993), 113.
8. Schremp, *Kitchen Culture*, 54–55.
9. Levenstein, *Paradox of Plenty*, 114–15.
10. Levenstein, 114.
11. "The People's Food Co-op: Statement of Purpose," 1971, FC2P419 P419, Bentley Historical Library, University of Michigan, Ann Arbor, MI (hereafter BHL).
12. Sirotkin quoted in Stephanie McKinnon, "It Began on a Cold Day on State Street," *People's Food Co-op Connection*, September/October 1995, 1, BHL.
13. Winfield quoted in Michael Bodden, "People's History: A History of the Mifflin Street Community Co-op," September 3, 2001, 4, 9, http://www.sit.wisc.edu/~mifflin/history.htm, site discontinued.
14. Jules Timerman, "Weavers Way General Membership Meeting Minutes," May 22, 1974, 2, Weavers Way Papers, used with the permission of Weavers Way Co-op (hereafter WW Papers). Originally accessed in Weavers Way office storage, currently available through Weavers Way Co-op Records, SRC 208, Special Collections Research Center (hereafter SCRC), Temple University Libraries, Philadelphia, Pennsylvania.

15. Zwerdling, "Uncertain Revival of Food Cooperatives," 105.
16. Coughlin quoted in William Ronco, *Food Co-ops: An Alternative to Shopping in Supermarkets* (Boston: Beacon Press, 1974), 96–97
17. Thomas Frank argues this in *Conquest of Cool: Business Culture, Counterculture, and the Rise of Hip Consumerism* (Chicago: University of Chicago Press, 1998).
18. Ronco, *Food Co-ops*, 104.
19. Ronco, 23.
20. Zwerdling, "Uncertain Revival," 109.
21. Norman Weiss quoting Pieri, interview by author, July 19, 2003.
22. Joseph G. Knapp, *The Rise of American Cooperative Enterprise: 1620–1920* (Danville, IL: Interstate Printers & Publishers, 1969), 39, 8.
23. Lizbeth Cohen, "The New Deal State and the Making of Citizen Consumers," in *Getting and Spending: European and American Consumer Societies in the Twentieth Century*, ed. Susan Straser, Charles McGovern, and Matthais Judt (Cambridge: Cambridge University Press, 1998), 111.
24. Kathleen Donahue, "From Cooperative Commonwealth to Cooperative Democracy: The American Cooperative Ideal, 1880–1940," in *Consumers against Capitalism? Consumer Cooperation in Europe, North America, and Japan, 1840–1990*, ed. Ellen Furlough and Carl Strikwerda (New York: Rowman and Littlefield, 1999), 116–25.
25. Producer cooperatives had a much easier time in the teens and the twenties as they modeled their organizations after corporations. Marketing and distribution co-ops, for example, the California Fruit Growers Exchange, were supported by such federal policies as the Capper-Volstead Act of 1922, which exempted co-ops from antitrust prosecution; the Agricultural Credits Act of 1923, which provided short-term government credit to marketing co-ops; and the Cooperative Marketing Act of 1926, which exempted co-ops from federal business taxes. For more on producer co-ops in the early twentieth century, see Steve Leikin, "The Citizen Producer: The Rise and Fall of Working-Class Cooperatives in the United States," in *Consumers against Capitalism?*, 93–113.
26. Jacob Baker, "Helping Cooperative to Be Self-Sustaining," *New York Times*, May 27, 1934, XX12.
27. Cohen, "The New Deal State," 124.
28. Thomas F. Conroy, "Consumer 'Co-ops' Show Steady Rise," *New York Times*, April 7, 1935, F9; "Cooperatives Gain Here," *New York Times*, August 5, 1929, 39.
29. John Curl, "The Rise and Fall of the Berkeley Co-op," n.d., http://red-coral.net/BerkCoop.html, site discontinued.
30. Curl, "Rise and Fall," 5.
31. Curl, 5.
32. Curl, 5.
33. The Co-op Handbook Collective, *The Food Co-op Handbook: How to Bypass Supermarkets to Control the Quality and Price of the Food You Eat* (Boston: Houghton Mifflin, 1975), 29.
34. What caused the demise of Berkeley's co-op was a subject of much discussion and concern in co-op circles. Some believed that the CCB overextended itself, opening too many branches. Others, like the CCB's first manager, Bob Neptune, argued that politics killed the co-op by alienating members who just wanted cheap food and not boycotts that interfered with their shopping experience. Others argued that the CCB

became too preoccupied with the bottom line. The major co-op trade magazine, *The Cooperative Grocer*, devoted numerous articles to the cooperative's downfall. For more, see *The Cooperative Grocer*, no. 18, 19, 38, https://www.grocer.coop/articles/development-directions; https://www.grocer.coop/articles/development-directions-part-2; https://www.grocer.coop/articles/berkeley-lessons-co-op-leaders.

35. Arthur Miller quoted in Alice Echols, "Nothing Distant about It: Women's Liberation and Sixties Radicalism," in *The Sixties: From History to Memory*, ed. David Farber (Chapel Hill: University of North Carolina Press, 1994), 156.
36. Mort Brooks, "Special Flyer," July 15, 1986, WW Papers.
37. Dorothy Guy, interview by author, July 16, 2003.
38. Jack Smyth, "Mold Was Broken to Give Mt. Airy Special Flavor," *Philadelphia Evening Bulletin*, October 31, 1977, 9.
39. John H. Gordy, "Mt. Airy Group Drafts Code of Ethics for Home Sales," *Philadelphia Evening Bulletin*, February 18, 1959, 4b.
40. "29 Realty Firms Agree to Anti-Bias Code," *Philadelphia Evening Bulletin*, February 10, 1966, 29.
41. John Corr, "Mt. Airy Braggarts, not Bigots," *Philadelphia Inquirer*, July 7, 1974, B2.
42. Norman Weiss, interview by author, September 19, 2003; Guy interview.
43. The namesake of the newsletter was the weaver's shuttle, referencing the originators of cooperation, the nineteenth-century flannel weavers of Rochdale, England.
44. Greg Moore, "Feast or Famine," *Shuttle*, n.d. (estimated prior to first board election January 1974), 1, WW Papers.
45. Co-op Handbook Collective, *Food Co-op Handbook*, 141, 137, 148.
46. For more on this pattern, see Joseph Heath and Andrew Potter, *Nation of Rebels: Why Counterculture Became Consumer Culture* (New York: HarperCollins, 2004), 9.
47. Lyn Davis, "Responding to Greg Moore's Editorial, 'Feast or Famine,'" *Shuttle*, February 1974, 1, WW Papers.
48. Maggie Heineman, "Development of the Board: Authority and Responsibility," *Weavers Way Handbook for Board of Directors*, June 20, 1978, WW Papers.
49. Jules Timerman, "Manager's Report," *Weavers Way General Membership Meeting Minutes*, May 22, 1974, WW Papers.
50. Guy interview.
51. Weiss interview.
52. Jules Timerman, "Open Letter: Why I Am Resigning as Manager of the Weavers Co-op," September 23, 1974, WW Papers.
53. "The People's Food Co-op Stages a Comeback," *Ann Arbor Observer*, December 1985, 20.
54. "A Brief History of People's Food Co-op," 3, n.d., store records at People's Food Co-op, Ann Arbor, Michigan, used with the permission of the People's Food Co-op.
55. "Brief History," 5.
56. Chapman quoted in McKinnon, "It Began on a Cold Day," 7.
57. Chapman quoted in McKinnon, 7.
58. Slaughter quoted in Karis Crawford, "People's Food Co-op in the 'Old Days': Remembrances from Two Longtime Members," *People's Food Co-op Connection*, May 1989, 4, BHL.
59. "Brief History," 6.
60. "Food Co-op Stages a Comeback," 21.

61. Bob Sechler coined the phrase "opulent hipness" to describe the Whole Foods retail spectacle in "Whole Foods Picks Up the Pace of Its Expansion," *Wall Street Journal*, September 29, 2004, B2E.
62. Guy interview.
63. "Get to Know Your Candidates," *Shuttle*, n.d., 3, WW Papers.
64. Weiss interview.
65. Weiss interview. Weiss is correct in assuming that education and not necessarily income is the determinant in natural foods market demography. See Kitty Shea, "Titans of Tofu," *Minneapolis St. Paul*, June 1998, 2.
66. Shea, "Titans of Tofu," 2.
67. Co-op Handbook Collective, *Food Co-op Handbook*, 84.
68. "Special Issue of the Flexible Flyer," n.d., WW Papers.
69. "New Food Product and Product Line Selection Process and Criteria," August 1978, WW Papers.
70. "Food Co-op Stages a Comeback," 21.
71. Mark Braskie, "Setting Up the New Meat Department," *Cooperative Grocer*, no. 37, November–December 1991, https://www.grocer.coop/articles/setting-new-meat-department.
72. Braskie, "Setting Up," 5.
73. Weiss interview.
74. "Policy Statement on 'Politics,'" *Weavers Way Board of Directors Handbook*, August 11, 1976, WW Papers.
75. Joe Restifo quoted in "Member Meeting Minutes," June 3, 1987, WW Papers.
76. Although such historians as Van Gosse reject the designation "identity politics" for the social causes that arose in the late 1960s and early 1970s, I believe this term identifies the axes around which leftist mobilization revolved in this period. The names of the social movements signify identity's importance. See Van Gosse, *Rethinking the New Left: An Interpretive History* (New York: Palgrave, 2005), and *The World the Sixties Made: Politics and Culture in Recent America* (Philadelphia, PA: Temple University Press, 2003).
77. Students for a Democratic Society, *The Port Huron Statement* (Chicago: Charles H. Kerr Publishing, 2004), 30.
78. Todd Gitlin, *The Sixties: Years of Hope, Days of Rage* (New York: Bantam, 1987), 2.
79. "A Movement of Many Voices," *ERAP-SDS Document*, Fall 1963, BHL.
80. At the end of the decade, as the antiwar movement faced its own ineffectuality, SDS splintered into numerous factions following irreconcilable political philosophies. See Gitlin, *The Sixties*, for analysis of this period in SDS history.
81. Gosse, *Rethinking the New Left*, 189; Lewis V. Baldwin, *Towards the Beloved Community: Martin Luther King Jr. and South Africa* (Cleveland: Pilgrim Press, 1995), 2–3.
82. Notable SDSer Tom Hayden moved to Berkeley after the Chicago 1968 Democratic Convention and became part of a commune called the Red Family. Gitlin, *The Sixties*, 353.
83. Sara Evans, *Personal Politics: The Roots of Women's Liberation in the Civil Rights Movement and the New Left* (New York: Vintage, 1979), 127.
84. Gitlin, *The Sixties*, 7.
85. Mrs. Johnson, "For Expansion Now!," *Shuttle*, January 1978, 2, WW Papers.
86. Bud Cook, "For Affirmative Action," *Shuttle*, May 1978, 7–8, WW Papers.

87. Cook, "Affirmative Action," 6–7.
88. Cook, 6–7.
89. Jack Zucker and Anne Zucker, letter to the editor, *Shuttle*, May 1978, 5, WW Papers.
90. "Special Membership Meeting Minutes," January 17, 1979, WW Papers; Guy interview.
91. Linda Schatz quoted in "Letters in Response to Co-op Flyers, 'Should We Move?,'" January 5, 1986, WW Papers.
92. Chuck Barbieri, letter to the editor, *People's Food Co-op Connection*, July/August 1986, 6, BHL.
93. David Rhode, "Food Co-op Bitter to the Core," *New York Times*, January 26, 1997, CY8.
94. Freeman quoted in Connie Vail Green, "Brattleboro Food Co-op: Coming of Age," *Cooperative Grocer*, no. 24, September–October 1989, 6, https://www.grocer.coop/articles/brattleboro-food-co-op-coming-age.
95. Richard A. Kaye, "Tie-Dyed Food," *New York Times*, April 21, 2002, 3.
96. Guy interview.
97. Ed McGann, "Manager's Corner," *Shuttle*, January 2003, 1, WW Papers.
98. "Weavers Way Accountability Committee Report," June 30, 2003, 7, WW Papers.
99. "Accountability Committee Report," 7, WW Papers.
100. Faith Quintavell, "Members Hear the Bad Financial News at December 8 Emergency Membership Meeting," *Shuttle*, January 2003, 2, WW Papers.
101. Noble quoted in "Membership Meeting Minutes," February 10, 2003, WW Papers.
102. Melissa Dribben, "Special Membership Meeting Addresses Weavers Way's Financial Crisis," *Shuttle*, February 2003, 4, WW Papers.
103. "Mission Statement and Goals," series 1, box 1, folder 7, SCRC, Temple University Libraries, Philadelphia, Pennsylvania.
104. Maanvi Singh, "Why a Philadelphia Grocery Chain Is Thriving in Food Deserts," *NPR: The Salt: What's on Your Plate*, May 14, 2015, http://www.npr.org/sections/thesalt/2015/05/14/406476968/why-one-grocery-chain-is-thriving-in-philadelphias-food-deserts.
105. Glenn Bergman, "Ends Report, 2009–2010," 15, box 1, folder 26, Temple University Libraries, SCRC, Philadelphia, PA.
106. Bergman, "Ends Report," 15.
107. Ruth Heigis, "Fixing Fresh Food: Greater Philly's Co-ops Find Their Way," August 16, 2011, http://www.flyingkitemedia.com/features/phillyfoodcoops0823.aspx.
108. Michael Pollan, *The Omnivore's Dilemma: A Natural History of Four Meals* (New York: Penguin, 2006), 243.
109. In fact, for West Oak Lane shoppers, the Shoprite supermarket near the Ogontz Weavers and its lower prices may have trumped Weavers' aesthetic and intellectual lures.
110. Lawrence Geller, letter to the editor, "Ogontz Store Should Go," *Shuttle* 40, no. 2, February 2011, 20.
111. "Readers Respond to 'Ogontz Store Should Go' Letter in February *Shuttle*," letters to the editor, *Shuttle* 40, no. 3, March 2011, 23.
112. Josee Johnston, Michelle Szabo, and Alexandra Rodney, "Good Food, Good People: Understanding the Cultural Repertoire of Ethical Eating," *Journal of Consumer Culture* 11, no. 3 (November 2011): 293–318.

113. For instances, see Alana Joblin Ain, "Flunking Out at the Co-op," *New York Times*, October 23, 2009.
114. Reeves quoted in Thomas B. Edsall, "How the Other Half Lives," *New York Times*, April 27, 2016.
115. Bodden, "People's History," 9.
116. Karen Heller, "Weavers Way Co-op Gets a Ritzy Rebirth," September 12, 2012, http://www.philly.com/philly/columnists/karen_heller/20120912_Karen_Heller__Weavers_Way_Co-op_gets_a_ritzy_rebirth.html.

CHAPTER 2: RECIPES FOR A NEW WORLD

1. Frances Moore Lappé, *Diet for a Small Planet* (New York: Ballantine Books, 1971), xiv.
2. Lappé, *Diet for a Small Planet*, xiv.
3. Lappé, inside cover, *Diet for a Small Planet*.
4. For sales figures on each book, see the front cover of *Diet for a Small Planet* (New York: Ballantine Books, 1975); Thom Leonard, "Inside *Laurel's Kitchen*," *EastWest Journal* (January 1986): 48; Barbara Stacy, "Tassajara Cooking," *EastWest Journal* (April 1986): 33; Alex Witchel, "Breakfast as the New Cure-All," *New York Times*, October 9, 2002, F10; "Books," Vegetarian Epicure Website, July 27, 2003, http://www.vegetarianepicure.com, webpage discontinued.
5. Jean Hewitt, dedication, *New York Times Natural Foods Cookbook* (New York: Quadrangle Books, 1971).
6. Mary Drake McFeely, *Can She Bake a Cherry Pie?: American Women and the Kitchen in the Twentieth Century* (Amherst, MA: University of Massachusetts Press, 2000), 3.
7. McFeely, *Can She Bake a Cherry Pie?*, 68, 60–63.
8. My explanation of WW II foodways relies on Harvey Levenstein, *Paradox of Plenty: A Social History of Eating in Modern America* (New York: Oxford University Press, 1993), particularly chap. 6; Sherrie Inness, *Dinner Roles: American Women and Culinary Culture* (Iowa City: University of Iowa Press, 2001), and *Secret Ingredients: Race, Gender, and Class at the Dinner Table* (New York: Palgrave, 2006); and Richard Pillsbury, *No Foreign Food: The American Diet in Time and Place* (Boulder, CO: Westview Press, 1998): 186–208.
9. *Better Homes and Gardens New Cook Book* (New York: Meredith, 1953), 246.
10. See Jessamyn Neuhaus, "Is Meatloaf for Men? Gender and Meatloaf Recipes," in *Cooking Lessons: The Politics of Gender and Food*, ed. Sherrie A. Inness (Lanham, MD: Rowman & Littlefield, 2001), 87–109.
11. Gerry Schremp, *Kitchen Culture: Fifty Years of Food Fads* (New York: Pharos Books, 1991), 43.
12. *New Cook Book*, 322, 327.
13. Schremp, *Kitchen Culture*, 54, 50. In 1947, yellow margarine was illegal in twenty-two states. In 1967, Wisconsin was the first state to legalize yellow margarine sales.
14. *New Cook Book*, 372.
15. *New Cook Book*, 236, 173.
16. Levenstein, *Paradox of Plenty*, 124.
17. Ruth Berolzheimer, ed., *The Culinary Arts Encyclopedic Cookbook* (Chicago: Book Production Industries, 1950), 82.
18. Francis Bello, "How Good Is Mr. Hurley's Diet?," *Fortune*, December 1959, 130.

19. Allan M. Winkler, *Life under a Cloud: American Anxiety about the Atom* (New York: Oxford University Press, 1993), 102.
20. Laura Shapiro, in *Perfection Salad: Women and Cooking at the Turn of the Century* (New York: Farrar, Strauss, and Giroux, 1986), 41, discusses the politicization of the kitchen and middle-class women's cooking by nineteen- and early twentieth-century progressives.
21. Laurel Robertson, Carol Flinders, and Bronwen Godfrey, *Laurel's Kitchen: A Handbook for Vegetarian Cookery and Nutrition* (Petaluma, CA: Nilgiri Press, 1976), 22.
22. Robertson, Flinders, and Godfrey, *Laurel's Kitchen*, 24.
23. Robertson, Flinders, and Godfrey, 24.
24. Robertson, Flinders, and Godfrey, 24, 26, 29.
25. Robertson, Flinders, and Godfrey, 29.
26. Robertson, Flinders, and Godfrey, 30.
27. Robertson, Flinders, and Godfrey, 27–28.
28. Robertson, Flinders, and Godfrey, 48.
29. Robertson, Flinders, and Godfrey, 48.
30. Robertson, Flinders, and Godfrey, 32.
31. Lewis Mumford, "The Human Prospect" (1962), in *Interpretations and Forecasts: 1922–1972* (New York: Harcourt Brace, 1979), 463.
32. Dragonwagon quoted in Stephanie Hartman, "The Political Palate: Reading Commune Cookbooks," *Gastronomica* 3, no. 2 (Spring 2003): 36–27.
33. Robertson, Flinders, and Godfrey, *Laurel's Kitchen*, 34.
34. Robertson, Flinders, and Godfrey, 243, 286.
35. Laurel Robertson, Carol Flinders, and Bronwen Godfrey, *The Laurel's Kitchen Bread Book: A Guide to Whole-Grain Breadmaking* (New York: Random House, 1984), 19, 17.
36. Robertson, Flinders, and Godfrey, *Laurel's Kitchen Bread Book*, 19.
37. Robertson, Flinders, and Godfrey, 73.
38. Robertson, Flinders, and Godfrey, 23, 24.
39. Robertson, Flinders, and Godfrey, 23–24.
40. Robin Morgan's "Goodbye to All That," in *Going Too Far: The Personal Chronicle of a Feminist* (New York: Random House, 1977), 121–30, written in the heat of the movement in 1970, famously called the sixties Left out for its misogyny. In 1979, Sara Evans, in *Personal Politics: The Roots of Women's Liberation in the Civil Rights Movement and the New Left* (New York: Knopf, 1979), gave scholarly support to Morgan's critique.
41. Gretchen Lemke-Santangelo, in *Daughter of Aquarius: Women of the Sixties Counterculture* (Lawrence: University Press of Kansas, 2009), argues that countercultural women configured their own feminism based on women's essential difference from men. Yet, as I explain in chapter 5, natural foods movement traditionalism has often made working womanhood the source for America's social and dietary woes.
42. Robertson, Flinders, and Godfrey, *Laurel's Kitchen Bread Book*, 26.
43. Robertson, Flinders, and Godfrey, 95, 245, 117, 62.
44. Noel Furie interview with Kristin Baxivanos, August 25, 2009, Bloodroot Collective Records (MS 1955), Manuscripts and Archives, Yale University Library, New Haven, CT.

45. The Bloodroot Collective, *The Second Seasonal Political Palate: A Feminist Vegetarian Cookbook* (Bridgeport, CT: Sanguinaria Publishing, 1984), xxii.
46. The Bloodroot Collective, *The Political Palate* (Bridgeport, CT: Sanguinaria Publishing, 1981), 61, 114, 91.
47. The Bloodroot Collective, *The Political Palate*, xvii.
48. The Bloodroot Collective, 17, 123, 224.
49. The Bloodroot Collective, 21, xii, 36.
50. Adams quoted in the Bloodroot Collective, *The Second Seasonal Political Palate*, vii.
51. The Bloodroot Collective, vii–viii.
52. The Bloodroot Collective, i.
53. Furie, interview with Baxivanos.
54. The Bloodroot Collective, *The Second Seasonal Political Palate*, viii.
55. The Bloodroot Collective, ix.
56. The Bloodroot Collective, *The Political Palate*, xviii.
57. The Bloodroot Collective, xii.
58. The Bloodroot Collective, *The Second Seasonal Political Palate*, xix.
59. Laura Butterbaugh, "One-Stop Shopping: Food and Feminism at Bloodroot," *Off Our Backs* 23, no. 11 (November 30, 1993): 19.
60. Mollie Katzen, *The Enchanted Broccoli Forest: And Other Timeless Delicacies* (Berkeley, CA: Ten Speed Press, 1982), 290.
61. Katzen's sales with Ten Speed Press and Hyperion total over six million.
62. Alex Witchel, "Breakfast as the New Cure-All," *New York Times*, October 9, 2002, F10.
63. Katzen, *Enchanted Broccoli Forest*, 283.
64. Katzen, 170, 126.
65. Katzen, 188, 194–95, 198.
66. Katzen, *Moosewood*, 2nd ed. (Berkeley, CA: Ten Speed Press, 1992), vi.
67. Katzen, *Enchanted Broccoli Forest*, 85.
68. Laura B. Weiss, "The 'Moosewood Cookbook' Turns 40," *Publishers Weekly*, Nov. 14, 2014, https://www.publishersweekly.com/pw/by-topic/industry-news/cooking/article/64746-the-moosewood-cookbook-turns-40.html.
69. Anna Thomas, *The Vegetarian Epicure* (New York: Vintage Books, 1972), 4.
70. Robert Ebert, "Confessions (with Recipes) of the Vegetarian Epicure," *Chicago Sun Times*, July 24, 1996, 2.
71. Thomas, *Vegetarian Epicure*, 8.
72. Thomas, 211, 195, 228.
73. Thomas, 4.
74. Anna Thomas, *The Vegetarian Epicure Book Two* (New York: Knopf, 1978), 262.
75. Thomas, *Vegetarian Epicure Book Two*, 237.
76. Thomas, 280.
77. Thomas, *Vegetarian Epicure*, 251.
78. Thomas, 195.
79. Alice Waters, *Coming to My Senses: The Making of a Countercultural Cook* (New York: Clarkson Potter, 2017), 148. See David Kamp, *The United States of Arugula: How We Became a Gourmet Nation* (New York: Broadway Books, 2006), for an overview of late twentieth-century American gastronomy.
80. Thomas, *Vegetarian Epicure Book Two*, 128, 130, 223.
81. Edward Espe Brown, *Tassajara Cooking* (Berkeley: Shambhala Publications, 1973), 1, 3.

82. Brown, *Tassajara Cooking*, 242.
83. Edward Espe Brown, *The Tassajara Bread Book* (Berkeley: Shambhala Publications, 1970), unnumbered page before the Table of Contents.
84. Peg Streep, *Spiritual Gardening: Creating Sacred Space Outdoors* (New York: Time Life, 1999), 107.
85. Brown, *Tassajara Cooking*, 49.
86. Brown, *Tassajara Bread Book*, 1, 45.
87. Brown, *Tassajara Cooking*, 85, and *Tassajara Bread Book*, 6.
88. Brown, *Tassajara Bread Book*, 6, 11.
89. For more on the Buddhist Middle Path, see Walpola Rahula, *What the Buddha Taught* (New York: Grove Press, 1959), 45.
90. Edward Espe Brown, *Tomato Blessings and Radish Teachings: Recipes and Reflections* (New York: Riverhead Books, 1997), xxiii.
91. Brown, *Tassajara Bread Book*, 141.
92. Josee Johnston and Shyon Baumann, *Foodies: Democracy and Distinction in the Gourmet Foodscape* (New York: Routledge, 2010), 43.
93. "The Use of Complementary and Alternative Medicine in the United States," NIH National Center for Complementary and Alternative Medicine States, http://nccih.nih.gov/research/statistics/2007/camsurvey_fs1.htm.
94. Larissa Lee, "Home-Centered Life and Contemporary Feminism," *New Beginnings* 16, no. 5 (September–October 1999), 163, http://llli.net/nb/nbsepoct99p163.html.
95. Selma Miriam, "Why Bloodroot Is Vegan/Vegetarian," April 5, 2012, http://selmaslist.blogspot.com/2012/04/why-bloodroot-is-veganvegetarian.html.
96. Carolanne Curry, Miriam's partner, emphasized this distinction, stating, in a March 13, 2003 email exchange with the author, "[Bloodroot] is not viewed as a natural food source, but as a vegetarian source ... vegan source with an emphasis on organic ingredients."
97. Anna Thomas, *The New Vegetarian Epicure* (New York: Knopf, 1996), xxi.
98. Thomas, *New Vegetarian Epicure*, xxii.
99. Thomas, *Vegetarian Epicure*, 3.
100. Anna Thomas, "Lunch with Julia," *Vegetarian Epicure*, April 2003, 1, http://www.vegetarianepicure.com/newsletter/apr03.html, webpage discontinued.
101. Thomas, *Vegetarian Epicure*, 3.
102. Alice Waters, *Chez Panisse Menu Cookbook* (New York: Random House, 1982), x.
103. See Schremp, *Kitchen Culture*, 104–6, and Levenstein, *Paradox of Plenty*, 220–26.
104. See Donald Altman, *Art of the Inner: Eating as Spiritual Path* (San Francisco: Harper, 1999), and Sue Bender, *Plain and Simple: A Woman's Journey to the Amish* (New York: HarperCollins, 1989).
105. Earthbound Farm News, "Zen and the Art of Doing Good Works: Earthbound Farm Helps Zen Center One Scenic Step at a Time," http://www.earthboundfarm.com/news/ebf/ed-brown.html, webpage discontinued.
106. "What Folks Are Saying about Mollie Katzen," *Mollie Katzen Website*, June 2, 2003, http://www.MollieKatzen.com.presskit, webpage discontinued.
107. Mollie Katzen. "The Heart of the Plate," Talks at Google, December 27, 2013, https://youtu.be/5QMSE0Vte-0.
108. See Warren J. Belasco, *Appetite for Change: How the Counterculture Took on the Food Industry, 1966–1988* (New York: Random House, 1989), chaps. 8, 9, and 10.

109. "Organic Market Overview," USDA, http://www.ers.usda.gov/topics/natural-resources-environment/organic-agriculture/organic-market-overview.aspx.
110. Michele Lamont, *Money, Morals, and Manners: The Culture of the French and American Upper-Middle Class* (Chicago: University of Chicago Press, 1992), 13.

CHAPTER 3: "ORGANIC STYLE"

1. David E. Sumner, *The Magazine Century: American Magazines since 1900* (New York: Peter Lang Publishing, 2010), 104.
2. Wade Greene, "Guru of the Organic Food Cult," *New York Times*, June 6, 1971, 30.
3. Capp quoted in Allan M. Winkler, *Life under a Cloud: American Anxiety about the Atom* (New York: Oxford University Press, 1998), 84.
4. Robert Crawford, "A Cultural Account of 'Health': Control, Release, and the Social Body," in *Issues in the Political Economy of Health Care*, ed. John B. McKinlay (New York: Tavistock Publications, 1994), 74.
5. Norman Mailer, "The White Negro: Superficial Reflections on the Hipster," *Dissent* 4 (1957): 276–77.
6. J. I. Rodale, *Autobiography* (Emmaus, PA: Rodale Press, 1965), 33.
7. Sir Albert Howard, *An Agricultural Testament* (Oxford: Oxford University Press, 1943), 112.
8. J. I. Rodale, "The History of My Colds: Part I," *Prevention*, April 1954, 8.
9. Rodale, *Autobiography*, 41.
10. Seizures from spray residues were common enough to warrant the FDA to compile seizure statistics from sprayed produce between 1933 and 1940. See James Whorton, *Before "Silent Spring": Pesticides and Public Health in the Pre-DDT America* (Princeton, NJ: Princeton University Press, 1974), 243.
11. Whorton, *Before "Silent Spring,"* 249.
12. Gypsy moth eradication included a Long Island program that incited a 1958 class-action suit by residents of Nassau and Suffolk Counties. Edmund Russell, *War and Nature: Fighting Humans and Insects with Chemicals from World War I to "Silent Spring"* (Cambridge: Cambridge University Press, 2001), 211–12.
13. For a discussion of trace radioactivity in 1950s' milk supplies, see Winkler, *Life under a Cloud*, 101–3.
14. Wallace quoted in Russell, *War and Nature*, 18, 31.
15. Gerry Schremp, *Kitchen Culture: Fifty Years of Food Fads* (New York: Pharos Books, 1991), 82.
16. Adelle Davis's books, *Let's Eat Right to Keep Fit* (1954), *Let's Get Well* (1965), *Let's Cook it Right* (1947), and *Let's Have Healthy Children* (1951), together sold seven million copies.
17. Schremp, *Kitchen Culture*, 54, 64.
18. American Medical Association, "Council on Food and Nutrition," 1971, quoted in Michael S. Goldstein, *The Health Movement: Promoting Fitness in America* (New York: Twayne Publishers, 1992), 64.
19. For pre–*Silent Spring* environmental consciousness, see Thomas Judt, *Greening the Red, White, and Blue: The Bomb, Big Business, and Consumer Resistance in Postwar America* (Oxford: Oxford University Press, 2014).
20. President's Science Advisory Committee, "The Use of Pesticides," May 15, 1963, in

Dorothy McLaughlin, "Silent Spring Revisted," *Frontline*, https://www.pbs.org/wgbh/pages/frontline/shows/nature/disrupt/sspring.html.
21. "Nature Is for the Birds," *Chemical Week*, July 28, 1962, 5.
22. Rodale, *Autobiography*, 5. For more on the USDA's defense of chemical farming, see Harvey Levenstein, *Paradox of Plenty: A Social History of Eating in Modern America* (New York: Oxford University Press, 1993).
23. Analyses on postwar conformity include Herbert Marcuse, *The One-Dimensional Man: Studies in the Ideology of Advanced Industrial Society* (Boston: Beacon, 1964); David Reisman, *The Lonely Crowd* (New Haven, CT: Yale University Press, 1950); William H. Whyte, *The Organization Man* (New York: Simon and Schuster,1950); C. Wright Mills, *White Collar: The American Middle Class* (Oxford: Oxford University Press, 1951); and Paul Goodman, *Growing Up Absurd* (New York: Random House, 1960).
24. *Prevention* 4, no. 2, February 1952, cover.
25. Early circulation figures come from Joe Dobrow, *Natural Prophets: From Health Food to Whole Foods—How the Pioneers of the Industry Changed the Way We Eat and Reshaped American Business* (New York: Rodale Books, 2014), 18.
26. J. I. Rodale, "Does Gardening Prevent Cancer?," *Prevention*, October 1955, 16.
27. J. I. Rodale, *The Organic Front* (Emmaus, PA: Rodale Press, 1949), 15.
28. Rodale, *Organic Front*, 87.
29. J. I. Rodale, ed., with Ruth Adams, *The Health Finder: An Encyclopedia of Health Information from the Preventive Point-of-View* (Emmaus, PA: Rodale Books, 1954), 206.
30. Frances Bello, "The Murderous Riddle of Coronary Disease," *Fortune*, September 1958, 143.
31. J. I. Rodale, *Happy People Rarely Get Cancer* (Emmaus, PA: Rodale Press, 1970), 17.
32. J. I. Rodale, "When Having a Baby Was Part of a Busy Day," *Prevention*, November 1958, 65.
33. Rodale, *Happy People Rarely Get Cancer*, 6.
34. Jack Kerouac, *On the Road* (New York: Penguin, 1955), 180.
35. J. I. Rodale, *Autobiography*, 50.
36. Rodale, "History of My Colds," 8.
37. J. I. Rodale, "Walk, Do Not Run to the Doctor," *Prevention*, January 1973, 211.
38. In the 1960s, countercultural organic converts regularly visited the Rodale farm. J. I. disdained these hippie visitors, calling them social misfits raised on diets of white sugar and "artificial 'ready' foods." See Rodale, *Natural Health, Sugar, and the Criminal Mind* (Emmaus, PA: Prevention/Pyramid Books, 1968), 137–40.
39. "The Perils of Eating, American Style," *Time*, December 18, 1973, 65.
40. Anne Colamosca, "Health Foods Prosper Despite High Prices," *New York Times*, November 17, 1974, 205.
41. Robert Rodale, "The Leisure Fiasco," *Fitness for Living*, July/August 1970, 52.
42. Robert Rodale, "How to Strengthen Your Organic Family," *Organic Gardening and Farming*, December 1971, 33, 37.
43. Joni Mitchell, "Woodstock," *Ladies of the Canyon*, Reprise Records, 1970.
44. Roy Reed, "Back-to-Land Movement Seeks Self-Sufficiency," *New York Times*, June 9, 1975, 19, col. 1.

45. Tom Monte, "The Test Kitchens of Betty Crocker and Robert Rodale," *Nutrition Action* 7, no. 1, January 1980, 13.
46. Berry quoted in James J. Farrell, *The Spirit of the Sixties: Making Postwar Radicalism* (New York: Routledge, 1997), 241.
47. Robert Rodale, "It's Time for a New Declaration of Independence," *Organic Gardening and Farming*, September 1976, 49.
48. On Carter's oil policies, see Jennifer D. Keene, Saul Cornell, and Edward O'Donnell, *Visions of America: A History of the United States* (Boston: Pearson, 2013), 853–54.
49. Rodale quoted in "Building a Way to Cope with Today's Troubles," *Philadelphia Inquirer*, March 16, 1980, 2L.
50. Bob Wittman, "Robert Rodale Helped Define Today's Issues," *Morning Call*, January 1, 2000, S.03.
51. Berry quoted in Farrell, *Spirit of the Sixties*, 240.
52. Robert Rodale quoted in "Rodale Urges 'Regeneration' to Improve Quality of Life," *Morning Call*, October 21, 1984, B10.
53. Robert Rodale, "Let (Health) Freedom Ring!," *Prevention*, January 1983, 12.
54. Robert Rodale, *The Best Health Ideas I Know: Including My Personal Plan for Living* (Emmaus, PA: Rodale, Press, 1974), 37.
55. Cowan quoted in "Are We in the Middle of the 'Second American Revolution'?," *New York Times*, May 17, 1970.
56. Others marched forward, securing the consumer and activist base for their alternative foods co-ops, organic farms, health food companies, and environmental organizations.
57. Peter Clecak, *America's Quest for the Ideal Self: Dissent and Fulfillment in the 60s and 70s* (New York: Oxford University Press, 1983), 148.
58. Albin Wagner, "Drop City: A Total Living Environment," in *Notes from the New Underground*, ed. Jesse Kornbluth (New York: Viking, 1968), 232.
59. "Bob Rodale: Man behind It All," *Morning Call*, June 25, 1978, C-10.
60. Dr. George Sheehan, *Running and Being: The Total Experience* (New York: Simon and Schuster, 1978), 245.
61. Christopher Lasch, *The Culture of Narcissism: American Life in the Age of Diminishing Expectations* (New York: Norton, 1979), 103–22.
62. Sheehan quoted in James C. Whorton, *Crusaders for Fitness: The History of American Health Reformers* (Princeton, NJ: Princeton University Press, 1982), 348.
63. "What PREVENTION Advertising Means to You," *Prevention*, April 1976, 21.
64. Geoff Gehman, "Rodale Tests Its Place in a Changing Reader Market," *Morning Call*, February 22, 1986, S22.
65. Scott Bieber, "Rodale Gives a Facelift to *Organic Gardening*," *Morning Call*, March 23, 1988, B12.
66. As of 2018, the Rodale Institute Farming System stands as the longest organic farming experiment.
67. "Organic Farmers See Solution to Food Crisis," *New York Times*, August 24, 1981, A13.
68. "84% Want Organic Fruits and Vegetables; Almost Half Would Pay More for It," Gallup survey for Rodale Press. See Environmental Protection Agency website, National Service Center for Environmental Publications, "Assessing the Environmental Consumer Market," April 1991, A-3, pdf file, https://nepis.epa.gov.

69. Pete Leffler, "Food Pesticide Plan Gets Backing," *Morning Call*, October 27, 1989, A04.
70. Howard Kohn, "Fields of Dreams: Old Farm Is New Again," *Rolling Stone*, October 5, 1989, 41–42.
71. Julie Guthman, *Agrarian Dreams: The Paradox of Organic Farming in California* (Berkeley: University of California Press, 2010), 110–16.
72. Rita Ciolli, "Men's Health Is Magazine Success Story of the '90s," *Morning Call*, April 4, 1994, D01.
73. "Prevention Prepares for Managed Care," *Advertising Age*, March 11, 1996, S4; "Magazines Slumping on Newsstands," *Advertising Age*, March 3, 1997, 68.
74. "Rodale's *The Doctors Book of Home Remedies* Successful because of TV Campaign," *Morning Call*, March 1, 1994, D.01.
75. *Organic Gardening*, March 1996, 45.
76. Alec Foege, "The New Country Sophisticates," *Mediaweek*, July 16, 2001, 22. Rodale's financial records are not available to the public.
77. Gregory Karp, "Family Reasserts Control," *Morning Call*, July 14, 2002, 11.
78. Karp, "Family Reasserts Control," 9.
79. Tom Lowry, "How Rodale Takes Care of Its Health," *BusinessWeek*, July 23, 2001, 79; Jim Milliot, "Rodale Promotes Murphy," *Publishers Weekly*, January 21, 2002, 14.
80. Foege, "New Country Sophisticates," 22.
81. "Taste of Place," *Organic Gardening*, January/February 1999, table of contents.
82. "Breaking New Ground," *Organic Gardening*, January/February 1999, 4.
83. Maria Rodale, "The Best of Times," *OG*, May/June 1999, 3.
84. "Letters," *OG*, July/August 1999, 7.
85. Ruth La Ferla, "Fashionistas, Ecofriendly and All-Natural," *New York Times*, July 15, 2001, ST1.
86. La Ferla, "Fashionistas," ST1.
87. Due to failing subscription rates, *Organic Life* went all digital in 2017. For a promotional piece on this change, see Chris O'Shea, "Rodale's Organic Life Goes Digital-Only," *Adweek*, January 17, 2017, https://www.adweek.com/digital/rodales-organic-life-goes-digital-only.
88. Alec Foege, "Emmaus on the Hudson," *MediaWeek*, July 16, 2001.
89. Wade Greene, "Guru of the Organic Food Cult," *New York Times Magazine*, June 6, 1971, 70.
90. Maria Rodale, "Welcome to Our World," *Organic Style*, Preview Issue, 2.
91. Rebecca Barry, "Nora Pouillon's Elegant Rebellion," *Organic Style*, Preview Issue, 62.
92. Seo quoted in La Ferla, "Fashionistas," ST2.
93. Foege, "Emmaus on the Hudson," 2.
94. Maria Rodale, "Changing Brews," *Organic Style*, May/June 2002, 20.
95. Robinson quoted in Tessa DeCarlo, "The Better Beef Guide," *Organic Style*, March 2004, 108.
96. Robert Rodale, "Finding Your Island of Purity," *Prevention*, January 1981, 22.
97. Rodale, "Finding Your Island," 24.
98. Gayle Forman, "Leap of Faith," *Organic Style*, November/December 2003, 92.
99. Diane Di Costanzo, "Is Your Child's School Toxic?," *Organic Style*, March 2004, 95.
100. Ulrich Beck, *The Reinvention of Politics: Rethinking Politics in a Global Social Order* (Cambridge, UK: Polity Press, 1996), 94–98.

101. Thomas Frank, *One Market under God: Extreme Capitalism, Market Populism, and the End of Economic Democracy* (New York: Doubleday, 2000), xv.
102. Greg Dool, "Hearst's Acquisition of Rodale Brings Sweeping Changes to Several Titles," *Folio*, January 9, 2018, https://www.foliomag.com/hearsts-acquisition-rodale-brings-sweeping-changes-several-titles/.

CHAPTER 4: DR. ANDREW WEIL AND THE POSTSIXTIES PROMISES OF FOOD

1. David J. Lipke, "Good for Whom? Health Benefits of Organic Food," *American Demographics*, January 2001, 1.
2. Angela Braden, "Going Natural: The Reshaping of America's Food Industry," *Vibrant Life*, May–June 2004, 1.
3. Lipke, "Good for Whom?," 1.
4. For further information on shoppers' intentions, see David Pearson, Joanna Henryks, and Hannah Jones, "Organic Food: What We Know (and Do Not Know) about Consumers," *Renewable Agriculture and Food Systems* 26, no. 2 (2011): 171–77, doi:10.1017/S1742170510000499; Renee Shaw Hughner, Pierre McDonagh, Andrea Prothero, Clifford J. Shultz, and Julie Stanton, "Who Are Organic Food Consumers? A Compilation and Review of Why People Purchase Organic Food," *Journal of Consumer Behaviour* 6 (May 21, 2006): 94–110; "Global Trends in Healthy Eating," August 30, 2010, Neilson Website, https://www.nielsen.com/us/en/insights/news/2010/global-trends-in-healthy-eating.html.
5. Richard Alpert never forgave Weil for these articles that led to his dismissal. For more on the Alpert-Weil alienation, see Don Lattin, *The Harvard Psychedelic Club* (New York: HarperCollins, 2011).
6. Theodore Roszak, *The Making of a Counter Culture: Reflections of the Technocratic Society and Its Youthful Opposition* (Garden City, NY: Anchor Books, 1969), 168.
7. Stephen Lyng, *Holistic Health and Biomedical Medicine* (Albany: State University of New York, 1990), 73.
8. Lyng, *Holistic Health and Biomedical Medicine*, 104.
9. Andrew Weil, *Health and Healing*, 3rd ed. (Boston: Houghton Mifflin, 1998), 273.
10. Peter N. Carroll, *It Seemed Like Nothing Happened* (New York: Holt, Rinehart, and Winston, 1982), 308–9.
11. For sources on holistic healing and the New Age, see Robert Basil, ed., *Not Necessarily the New Age: Critical Essays* (Buffalo, NY: Prometheus Books, 1988); Rosalind Coward, *The Whole Truth: The Myth of Alternative Health* (London: Faber and Faber, 1989); Scott Montgomery, "Illness and Image in Holistic Discourse: How Alternative Is 'Alternative'?," *Cultural Critique* 25 (1993): 65–89; James C. Whorton, *Nature Cures: The History of Alternative Medicine in America* (Oxford: Oxford University Press, 2002); Douglas Stalker and Clark Glymour, eds., *Examining Holistic Health* (Buffalo, NY: Prometheus Books, 1985); Wayne B. Jonas, "Alternative Medicine—Learning from the Past, Examining the Present, Advancing the Future," *Journal of American Medicine* 280, no. 18 (1998): 1616–18; Steven Sutcliffe and Marion Bowman, eds., *Beyond New Age: Exploring Alternative Spirituality* (Edinburgh, UK: Edinburgh University Press, 2000); Meredith McGuire, "Health and Spirituality as Contemporary Concerns," *Annals of the American Academy of Political and Social Science* 527 (1993): 144–54; and Fred M. Frohock, *Healing Powers: Alternative Medicine, Spiritual Communities, and the State* (Chicago: University of Chicago Press, 1992). Works that

connect the new age to broader cultural and social trends are Richard G. Kyle, *The New Age Movement in American Culture* (Lanham, MD: University Press of America, 1995); Paul Heelas, *The New Age Movement: The Celebration of the Self and the Sacrilization of Modernity* (Oxford: Blackwell Press, 1996); and Mark Satin, *New Age Politics* (New York: Dell, 1978).

12. Robert Crawford, "A Cultural Account of 'Health': Control, Release and the Social Body," in *Issues in the Political Economy of Health Care*, ed. John McKinley (New York: Tavistock, 1984), 60–103, and "Healthism and Medicalization of Everyday Life," *International Journal of Health Services* 10 (1980): 365–88.
13. Jeffrey Kluger, "Mr. Natural," *Time*, May 12, 1997, 71.
14. Andrew Weil, *The Natural Mind* (New York: Houghton Mifflin, 1972), 84.
15. Weil, *Natural Mind*, 168.
16. Weil, 196, 201.
17. Andrew Weil, *The Marriage of the Sun and the Moon* (New York: Houghton Mifflin, 1980), 2.
18. Weil, *Marriage*, 107–17.
19. Weil, 157.
20. Weil, 165.
21. Weil, 3.
22. Kathryn Levy Felman, "M.D. at Q.V.C: Andrew Weil Sells a Message of Healing," *Inside*, June 30, 1998, 37.
23. "Andrew Weil, M.D.," *Academy of Achievement*, May 22, 1998, http://www.achievement.org/achiever/andrew-weil-m-d/#interview.
24. Larissa MacFarquhar, "Andrew Weil, Shaman, M.D," *New York Times*, April 24, 1997, 628, https://www.nytimes.com/1997/08/24/magazine/andrew-weil-shaman-md.html.
25. MacFarquhar, "Andrew Weil," 628.
26. MacFarquhar, 628.
27. Mike Tanner, "Time Inc. Acquires Dr. Weil Site," May 9, 1997, https://www.wired.com/1997/05/time-inc-acquires-dr-weil-site/.
28. In 2001, Weil's corporation severed ties with Time Inc.
29. Ronald E. Rice, "Influences, Usage, and Outcomes of Internet Health Information Searching: Multivariate Results from the Pew Surveys," *International Journal of Medical Infromatics* 75 (2006): 8–28, https://www.sciencedirect.com/science/article/pii/S1386505605001462.
30. On the counterculture's contradictory anticonsumerism, see Thomas Frank, *The Conquest of Cool* (Chicago: University of Chicago Press, 1997), and Joseph Heath and Andrew Potter, *Nation of Rebels: Why Counterculture Became Consumer Culture* (New York: HarperBusiness, 2004).
31. "About Weil Lifestyle, LLC," https://www.drweil.com/about/about-weil-lifestyle/.
32. "Weil Lifestyle, LLC Forms Licensee Agreements with Best-In-Class Corporate Partners," October 12, 2004, https://www.newhope.com/supply-news-amp-analysis/weil-lifestyle-llc-forms-licensee-agreements-best-class-corporate-partners.
33. Andrew S. Relman critically interrogates Weil's holistic claims in "A Trip to Stonesville," *New Republic Online*, December 13, 1998, https://newrepublic.com/article/118224/arnold-relman-reviews-andrew-weil-alternative-medicine.
34. Andrew Weil, "Some Interesting Sound Effects," *Self Healing*, September 2004, 6.

35. James B. Twitchell, *Adcult USA: The Triumph of Advertising in America* (New York: Columbia University Press, 1997), 31.
36. "Weil, M.D.," interview.
37. MacFarquhar, "Andrew Weil," 628.
38. "Weil M.D.," interview.
39. MacFarquhar, "Andrew Weil," 628.
40. Kathryn Levy Feldman, "M.D. at QVC: Andrew Weil Sells Message of Healing," *Inside*, June 30, 1998, 37.
41. Howard Brick, *Age of Contradiction: American Thought and Culture in the 1960s* (Ithaca, NY: Cornell University Press, 2000), 116.
42. Andrew Weil, *Eating Well for Optimum Health* (New York: Quill, 2001), 23.
43. Weil, 63.
44. Andrew Weil, *Eight Weeks to Optimum Health* (New York: Fawcett Columbine, 1997), 72.
45. Kim Lau, *New Age Capitalism* (Philadelphia: University of Pennsylvania Press, 2000), 91.
46. "Green Tea and Reducing Your Risk for Prostate Cancer," *Self Healing*, December 2003, 3; "Controlling Elevated Cholesterol and Triglycerides," *Self Healing*, December 2002, 4; "Tip: Treat Your Bones to a Cup of Tea," *Good Morning from Dr.Weil.com*, October 15, 2002; "More Good News about Tea," *Dr. Andrew Weil's Weekly Wellness Bulletin*, September 16, 2003.
47. Crawford, "Healthism," 10. Also see Ivan Illich, *Medical Nemesis: The Expropriation of Health* (New York: Pantheon, 1975); Susan Sontag, *Illness as Metaphor* (New York: Doubleday, 1989); and Peter Stearns, *Battleground of Desire: The Struggle for Self-Control in Modern America* (New York: New York University Press, 1999).
48. Jessica Mudry, "Counting on Dinner: Discourses of Science and the Refiguration of Food in USDA Nutrition Guides," *Environmental Communication* 4, no. 3 (2010): 341.
49. For a consideration of microconceptualizations of the body and health, see Donna Haraway, "The Promises of Monsters: A Regenerative Politics for Inappropriate/d Others," in *Cultural Studies*, ed. Lawrence Grossberg, Cary Nelson, and Paula Treichler (New York: Routledge, 1992), 295–337.
50. Crawford, "A Cultural Account of 'Health,'" 74.
51. Two excellent analyses of the microscopic approach to eating and nutrition are Gyorgy Scrinis, "On the Ideology of Nutritionism," *Gastronomica: The Journal of Critical Food Studies* 8, no. 1 (Winter 2008): 39–48, and Mudry, "Counting on Dinner."
52. Alison Stein Wellner, "Eat, Drink, and Be Healed," *American Demographics*, March 1998, 2.
53. Brian Keating, "U.S. Tea Industry: Heating Up and Getting Hotter," October 1, 2004, 3, Sage Group International, LLC, https://www.nutraceuticalsworld.com/issues/2004-10/view_features/u-s-tea-industry-heating-up-amp-getting-hotter; Florence Fabricant, "Evolution of Tea Drinking: Now It's Hip," *New York Times*, March 30, 1994, C1.
54. Mark Bittman, "As a Fish Needs Green Tea," *New York Times*, April 25, 2001, F3.
55. Keating, "U.S. Tea Industry," 2.
56. Jane Pettigrew, "Tea Drinkers Go Green," *The Free Library*, https://www.thefreelibrary.com/Tea+Drinkers+Go+Green.-a076668025, accessed November 18, 2018.

57. Stephanie Thomas, "Lipton Line Goes on a Health-Tea Kick," *AdAge*, March 28, 2005, https://adage.com/article/news/lipton-line-a-health-tea-kick/102682/. Lipton's health claims were legally challenged in a class action suit in 2008 and warranted an FDA warning in 2010. Lipton eventually removed the antioxidant signs on its packaging and website. See Manatt Phelps and Phillips LLP, "FDA Warns Companies about Green Tea Claims," *USA*, September 21, 2010, https://www.lexology.com/library/detail.aspx?g=083c2695-3a9c-4242-ac66-bcc9aadfbeac.
58. Salada was issued an FDA warning, in 2010, for its health claim; see Daniel J. Demoon, "FDA: Labels Misleading on Major Food Brands," March 3, 2010, https://www.webmd.com/food-recipes/news/20100303/fda-labels-misleading-on-major-food-brands#1. By 2018, the Salada website contained no medicinal green tea assertions, but Asian references remained; Salada website, https://salada.com/guide-to-green-tea.
59. Weil, *Eating Well*, 118.
60. Andrew Weil, "Feeling Timid about Tofu," *Self Healing*, September 2003, 6; "Preventing Lung Cancer in Women," *Self Healing*, January 2005, 1; "The Latest News about Prostate Cancer," *Self Healing*, December 2003, 3; and "Tip: Ovarian Cancer Awareness Month: Part I," *Good Morning from Dr. Weil*, September 2003, 1; Andrew Weil, "Tip: Eating to Eliminate Menstrual Problems," *Good Morning from Dr. Weil*, October 2003, 1.
61. Gary Taubes's encyclopedic book, *Good Calories, Bad Calories: Fats, Carbs, and the Controversial Science of Diet and Health* (New York: Anchor, 2007), challenges this correlation. Taubes critiqued the fat–cardiac health connection yet employed dietary reductionism, making sugar, rather than fat, the source of myriad chronic diseases in *The Case against Sugar: Why We Get Fat* (New York: Knopf, 2016).
62. Frances Moore Lappé, *Diet for a Small Planet* (New York: Ballantine Books, 1971), Surgeon General's report quoted in Michelle Stacey, *Consumed: Why Americans Love, Hate, and Fear Food* (New York: Touchstone, 1994), 158–59.
63. Nancy Chapman, "Where Is the Soyfood Market Headed?," *Third Annual Soyfoods Symposium Proceedings*, 1998, 4.
64. Andrew Weil, "Three New Food Trends," *Self Healing*, May 8, 2005.
65. Mark Tatge, "Vegetarian Sales Get Meaty," *Forbes*, September 15, 2004, https://www.forbes.com/2004/09/15/cz_mt_0915organic.html.
66. Richard Corliss, "Should We All Be Vegetarians?," *Time*, July 15, 2002, 52.
67. Kathy Wrick, "The U.S. Soy Market: An Update and Outlook," *Nutraceuticals World*, January–February 2003, 3, http://www.newhope.com/supply-news-amp-analysis/us-soy-market-update-outlook.
68. John Henkel, "Soy: Health Claims for Soy Protein, Questions about Other Components," *U.S. F.D.A. Consumer Magazine*, May–June 2000, 2, https://www.ncbi.nlm.nih.gov/pubmed/11521249; Wrick, "The U.S. Soy Market"; "Soyfoods Sales Reach 4.5 Billion," *Today's Dietician*, n.d., https://www.todaysdietitian.com/news/exclusive0714.shtml.
69. "Supermarkets Embrace Soyfoods to Become the Leading Outlet," *Publication of Packaged Facts*, November 1, 2000, www.packagedfacts.com/pub/143480.html.
70. Henkel, "Soy," 1.
71. Wrick, "The U.S. Soy Market," 4

72. Andrew Weil, *Natural Health, Natural Medicine: A Comprehensive Manual for Wellness and Self-Care* (Boston: Houghton Mifflin, 1998), 34–35.
73. John Urquart, "A Health Food Hits Big Time: Taste Makeover Moves Soymilk into Mainstream," *Wall Street Journal*, August 3, 1999, B1.
74. Golbitz quoted in Joy Powell, "The Rapid Rise of Soy," *Star Tribune*, October 15, 2003, 1.
75. Henkel, "Soy," 4.
76. Nancy Clark, "Jumping for Soy," *Nutrition Advisor*, April 23, 1998, 111.
77. Jonathan Reynolds, "Do You Tofu? Soybean Curd Isn't Just for Health-Food Nuts Anymore," *New York Times*, November 5, 2000, SM181.
78. Radd S. Setchell, "Soy and Other Legumes: 'Bean' Around a Long Time, but Are They the 'Superfoods' of the Millennium and What Are the Safety Issues for Their Constituent Phytoestrogens?," *Asia Pacific Journal of Clinical Nutrition* 9 (September 2000): S13–S22.
79. Reynolds, "Do You Tofu?," SM181.
80. Jack Challem, "Today's Natural Foods Taste Great," 2, www.nutritionreporter.com, site discontinued due to author's death; Chapman, "Where Is the Soyfood Market Headed?"
81. Challem, "Today's Natural Foods," 2.
82. Bill Richards, "Gardenburger Bets the (Soybean) Farm on the Last Seinfeld," *Wall Street Journal*, April 13, 1998, A10.
83. "Non-Meat Gardenburger Sales Down," *Meat Industry: Internet News Service*, July 24, 1999; Marks and Janus quoted in Richards, "Gardenburger Bets the (Soybean) Farm," A10.
84. Hatfield quoted in Linda Milo Ohr, "A Magic Bean Sprouts," *Prepared Foods* 69, no. 2 (February 2000): 60.
85. "Wiping Out 'Off Flavors' from Soy Foods," *Membrane and Separation Technology News*, October 2004.
86. Wrick, "The U.S. Soy Market," 8.
87. Raymond Williams, "Advertising: The Magic System," in *The Cultural Studies Reader*, ed. Simon During, 2nd ed. (London: Routledge, 1999), 422.
88. Jeff Charles, review of *Agrarian Dreams: The Paradox of Organic Farming in California* by Julie Guthman, *H-Net Reviews*, November 2004, https://networks.h-net.org/node/9249/reviews/10760/charles-guthman-agrarian-dreams-parodox-organic-farming-california.
89. Hirshberg quoted in Joe Dolce, "Power Yogurt," *Organic Style*, May–June 2002, 59.
90. Laurel Robertson, Carol Flinders, and Bronwen Godfrey, *The Laurel's Kitchen Bread Book: A Guide to Whole-Grain Breadmaking* (New York: Random House, 1984), 29; Laurel Robertson, Carol Flinders, and Bronwen Godfrey, *Laurel's Kitchen: A Handbook for Vegetarian Cookery and Nutrition* (Petaluma, CA: Nilgiri Press, 1976), 308.
91. Renee Loux, "Top 10 Reasons to Go Organic," *Prevention*, November 3, 2011, https://www.prevention.com/food-nutrition/healthy-eating/a20453119/top-reasons-to-choose-organic-foods/.
92. Deborah Lupton, *Food, the Body, and the Self* (London: Sage Publications, 1996), 87.
93. Julie Anton Dunn, "Organic Foods Find Opportunity in the Natural Food Industry," *Food Review*, September–December 1995, 1; "USDA Reports Record Growth in U.S.

Organic Producers," April 4, 2016, http://www.usda.gov/wps/portal/usda/usda mobile?contentid=2016/04/0084.xml&contentidonly=true.
94. Dunn, "Organic Foods Find Opportunity," 4, 5.
95. Givens quoted in Heather McIver, "Organic Hip," *Better Nutrition*, February 2004, 58.
96. Dunn, "Organic Foods Find Opportunity," 5.
97. Ronnie Cummins, "Monsanto's Genetically Engineered Bovine Growth Hormone Poses Significant Risks for Consumers," *Organic Consumer Association*, January 24, 2008, https://www.organicconsumers.org/essays/ronnie-cummins-monsantos-genetically-engineered-bovine-growth-hormone-poses-significant-risks.
98. For illuminating histories of milk and popular health consciousness, see Harvey Levenstein, *Fear of Food: A History of Why We Worry about What We Eat* (Chicago: University of Chicago Press, 2013), chap. 2, and E. Melanie Dupuis, *Nature's Perfect Food: How Milk Became America's Drink* (New York: New York University Press, 2002).
99. "Horizon Organic Reaches $200 Million Sales Milestone," *PR Newswire*, June 18, 2003, 1; Michael Pollan, "How Organic Became a Marketing Niche and a Multibillion Dollar Industry. Naturally," *New York Times Magazine*, May 13, 2001, 30–37.
100. Susan D. Haas, "A Real Organic Food Supply," *Morning Call*, April 19, 1998, A21.
101. Glickman quoted in Ben Lilliston and Ronnie Cummins, "Organic vs. 'Organic': The Corruption of a Label," *Ecologist*, July/August 1998, http://www.orpheusweb.co.uk/john.rose/orglab.html.
102. Pollan, "How Organic Became a Marketing Niche," 134.
103. Rich Heffern, "The Ethic of Eating," *National Catholic Reporter Online*, May 24, 2002, 3, http://natcath.org/NCR_Online/archives2/2002b/052402/052402a.htm.
104. Kahn quoted in Pollan, "How Organic Became a Marketing Niche," 134.
105. Ken Ausubel, *Seeds of Change: The Living Treasure: The Passionate Story of the Growing Movement to Restore Biodiversity and Revolutionize the Way We Think about Food* (San Francisco, CA: Harper San Francisco, 1994).
106. French quoted in Paul Glover, "What We Need to Know about the Corporate Takeover of the 'Organic' Food Market," *Organic Consumers Association*, June 2003.
107. Phil Howard, "Organic Industry Structure," *Journal of New Media Caucus* 5, no. 3 (Winter 2009), http://median.newmediacaucus.org/winter-2009-v-05-n-03-agriart-companion-planting-for-social-and-biological-systems-organic-industry-structure/.
108. Glover, "What We Need to Know"; Howard, "Organic Industry Structure."
109. Joe Dolce, "Power Yogurt," *Organic Style*, May–June 2002, 61.
110. "Kroger Goes Organic," *Drug Store News*, May 19, 2003, 6.
111. "Kroger's Launches 'Naturally Preferred' Brand of Premium Natural and Organic Products Nationwide," *PR Newswires*, April 28, 2003.
112. Braden, "Going Natural," 1.
113. Peter Clecak, *America's Quest for the Ideal Self* (New York: Oxford University Press, 1983), 364n59.
114. Nathan McClintock, "From Industrial Garden to Food Desert," in *Cultivating Food Justice: Race, Class, and Sustainability*, ed. Alison Hope Alkon and Julian Agyeman (Cambridge, MA: MIT Press, 2011), 89–120.
115. Guthman quoted in Jeff Charles, review of Julie Guthman, *Agrarian Dreams: The*

Paradox of Organic Farming in California, H-California, *H-Net Reviews*, November 2004.
116. Paul Boyer, *Promises to Keep: The United States since World War II* (Boston: Houghton Mifflin, 1999), 267.

CHAPTER 5: NATURAL FOODS CONSERVATISM

1. Dennis Wilken, "Cincinnati's Former Flower Child," *Cincinnati Magazine*, May 1982, 57.
2. Jerry Rubin, "The Yuppie America's Economic Savior: Former Anti-war Activist Jerry Rubin Now Preaches the Gospel of Yuppiedom, Claiming That Yuppies Are Responsible for America's Current Good Economy," *South Florida Sun Sentinel*, October 19, 1985.
3. David Gate, "He Didn't Need a Weatherman," *Newsweek*, December 11, 1994, https://www.newsweek.com/he-didnt-need-weatherman-185448.
4. Jerry Rubin, "Rubin Raps: Money's to Burn," *Berkley Barb*, January 19–26, 1968.
5. Leary quoted in Martin A. Lee and Bruce Shlain, *Acid Dreams: The CIA, LSD and the Sixties Rebellion* (New York: Grove Press, 1985), 166.
6. Theodore Roszak, *The Making of the Counterculture: Reflections on the Technocratic Society and Its Youthful Opposition* (New York: Anchor, 1969), 5.
7. Van Gosse and Richard Moser, eds., *The World the Sixties Made* (Philadelphia: Temple University Press, 2003), 20. Also see Meg Jacobs, William J. Novak, and Julian E. Zelizer, eds., *The Democratic Experiment: New Directions in American Political History* (Princeton: Princeton University Press, 2009), chap. 1.
8. Reagan, forward to James C. Roberts, *The Conservative Decade: Emerging Leaders of the 1980s* (Westport, CT: Arlington House Publishers, 1980), 2.
9. Voter Turnout in Presidential Elections, *The American Presidency Project*, https://www.presidency.ucsb.edu/statistics/data/voter-turnout-in-presidential-elections; Morris P. Fiorina, "Parties, Participation, and Representation in America: Old Theories Face New Realities" (paper presented at Political Science Association Conference, Washington, D.C., August 31–September 3, 2000), http://web.stanford.edu/~mfiorina/Fiorina%20Web%20Files/Fiorina%20SOD.pdf.
10. For coverage of the rise of postwar conservatism, see Julian E. Zelizer, "Reflections: Rethinking the History of American Conservatism," *Reviews in American History* 38, no. 2 (2010): 367–92; Robert Norvell, "Modern Conservatism and the Consequences of Its Ideas," *Reviews in American History* 36 (2008): 456–67; Michael Kazan, "The Grassroots Right: New History of U.S. Conservatism in the Twentieth Century," *American Historical Review* 97, no. 1 (February 1992): 136–55; Lisa McGirr, "Piety and Property: Conservatism and Right-Wing Movements in the Twentieth Century," in *Perspectives on Modern America: Making Sense of the Twentieth Century*, ed. Harvard Sitkoff (New York: Oxford University Press, 2001), 33–54; Leo Ribuffo, "Why Is There So Much Conservatism and Why Do So Few Historians Know Anything about It?," *American Historical Review* 99, no. 2 (April 1994): 438–49; Eric Foner, "The Contested History of American Freedom," *Pennsylvania Magazine of History and Biography* 137, no. 1 (January 2013): 12–31.
11. Falwell quoted in Grace E. Hale, *A Nation of Outsiders: How the White Middle Class Fell in Love with Rebellion in Postwar America* (Oxford: Oxford University Press, 2011), 256.

12. *Countryside and Small Stock Journal* quoted in Robin O'Sullivan, *American Organic: A Cultural History of Farming, Gardening, Shopping, and Eating* (Lawrence: University Press of Kansas, 2015), 106.
13. Ronald Reagan, June 28, 1983, https://www.presidency.ucsb.edu/documents/the-presidents-news-conference-940.
14. Joshua Clark Davis, "The Business of Getting High: Head Shops, Countercultural Capitalism, and the Marijuana Legalization Movement," *The Sixties: A Journal of History, Politics and Culture* 8, no. 1 (2015): 27–49, https://doi.org/10.1080/17541328.2015.1058480; Malcolm McLaughlin, "Storefront Revolutionary: Martin Sostre's Afro-Asian Bookshop, Black Liberation, Culture, and the New Left, 1964–75," *The Sixties: A Journal of History, Politics and Culture* 7, no. 1 (2014): 1–27, https://doi.org/10.1080/17541328.2014.930265; David Farber, "Self-Invention in the Realm of Production: Craft, Beauty, and Community in the American Counterculture, 1964–1978," *Pacific Historical Review* 85, no. 3 (August 2016): 408–42.
15. Bill Moyers interview with Kevin Phillips, *Bill Moyers Journal*, PBS, November 7, 2008, https://billmoyers.com/content/kevin-phillips-on-americas-financial-crisis/.
16. Robert Wuthnow, *After Heaven: Spirituality in America since the 1950s* (Berkeley: University of California Press, 1998); Wade Clark Roof, *Spiritual Marketplace: Baby Boomers and the Remaking of American Religion* (Princeton, NJ: Princeton University Press, 1999); Don Lattin, *Following Our Bliss: How the Spiritual Ideals of the Sixties Shape Our Lives Today* (New York: Harper Collins, 2003).
17. Hale, *Nation of Outsiders*, 239; also Carl Boggs, *The End of Politics: Corporate Power and the Decline of the Public Sphere* (New York: Guilford Press, 2000), 179.
18. Parts of my account of the life of Gene Spriggs are derived from Marsha Spriggs's letter to Vermont journalist Susan Green, dated February 8, 1985, in the possession of and used with the permission of Neil Favreau.
19. Spriggs letter to Green, 3.
20. Spriggs letter to Green, 3.
21. Gene Spriggs, "In the Vine House Days," *The Twelve Tribes*, https://twelvetribes.org/articles/vine-house-days.
22. Spriggs letter to Green, 7.
23. Susan J. Palmer, "The Twelve Tribes: Preparing the Bride for Yahshua's Return," *Nova Religio: The Journal of Alternative and Emergent Religions* 13, no. 3 (2010): 59.
24. "My Elusive Dream," *The Twelve Tribes*, http://twelvetribes.org/articles/elusive-dream.
25. Neil Favreau, "Considering the Stone Kingdom: Ethnography and Symbol Analysis in a Religious Commune" (master's thesis, University of Wyoming, 1995), 35.
26. Andrew Peter quoted in Cooper Nelson, Gabby Vargas, Chris Jonke, and Steve Fitzpatrick, "The Yellow Deli People: Twelve Tribes Oneonta," video, 7:43, August 2012, https://youtu.be/XFPXOFXKLGc.
27. "Back to the Garden," *The Twelve Tribes*, n.d., http://twelvetribes.org/articles/got-get-ourselves-back-garden; Andrew Peter quoted in "The Yellow Deli People."
28. On June 22, 1984, Vermont state trooper and the Department of Social and Rehabilitation Services (SRS) removed all children under 18 from the Island Pond Twelve Tribes Community, owing to child abuse allegations. The SRS investigations found no evidence of abuse and the children were returned.
29. "Our Health," *Twelve Tribes*, http://twelvetribes.org/articles/our-health.

30. Spriggs letter to Green, 13.
31. The Tribes believe that "Dead Heads" are misdirected spiritual searchers. See Favreau, "Considering the Stone Kingdom," 26–27.
32. Palmer, "The Twelve Tribes," 71.
33. "Our Health," *Twelve Tribes*.
34. The origin of the term "food revolution" should probably be attributed to Jamie Oliver and the American television series *Jamie Oliver's Food Revolution*, which first aired in March 2010. After the series ended in June 2011, the term "food revolution" was applied to the new natural foods movement.
35. Mehroz Baig, "Women in the Workforce: What Changes Have We Made?," *Huffington Post*, December 12, 2013, http://www.huffingtonpost.com/mehroz-baig/women-in-the-workforce-wh_b_4462455.html.
36. Michael Pollan, *The Omnivore's Dilemma: A Natural History of Four Meals* (New York: Penguin, 2006), 1–8.
37. Michael Pollan, "Out of the Kitchen, onto the Couch," *New York Times*, August 2, 2009, 5, 13.
38. Pollan, "Out of the Kitchen," 4–5.
39. Pollan, 4–5.
40. Barbara Kingsolver, *Animal, Vegetable, Miracle: A Year of Food Life* (New York: Harper Perennial, 2007), 126–27.
41. Kingsolver, *Animal, Vegetable, Miracle*, 169.
42. Pollan, *Omnivore's Dilemma*, 340, 337.
43. Pollan, 362–63.
44. John Mackey, "The Whole Foods Alternative to ObamaCare: Eight Things We Can Do to Improve Health Care without Adding to the Deficit," *Wall Street Journal*, August 11, 2009, http://www.wsj.com/articles/SB10001424052970204251404574342170072865070.
45. Mackey, "The Whole Foods Alternative."
46. Nick Gillespie and Matt Welch, "Whole Foods Health Care," *Reason* 41, no. 8 (2010): 36–43.
47. Nick Paumgarten, "Food Fighter: Does Whole Foods' C.E.O. Know What's Best for You?," *New Yorker*, January 4, 2010, http://www.newyorker.com/magazine/2010/01/04/food-fighter.
48. John Mackey, "The Accidental Grocer," *The Whole Story: A Marketplace of Ideas*, September/October 1989, 7.
49. John Mackey, "Winning the Battle for Freedom and Prosperity" (keynote address, Freedom Fest, May 2004), posted February 27, 2006, https://www.wholefoodsmarket.com/blog/john-mackeys-blog/winning-battle-freedom-and%C2%A0prosperity.
50. Mackey quoted in Nick Gillespie, "Why Intellectuals Hate Capitalism," *Reason* 47, no. 6 (November 2015), https://reason.com/r/137C.
51. Jaquetta White, "Whole Foods CEO Says the Corporate World Has a 'Bad Brand'" *New Orleans Times-Picayune*, October 16, 2009, http://www.nola.com/business/index.ssf/2009/10/whole_foods_ceo_says_the_corpo.html.
52. Paumgarten, "Food Fighter."
53. Mackey, "Winning the Battle for Freedom and Prosperity."
54. In a meeting, surreptitiously videotaped by an employee, Whole Foods's stated rule of worker-supervisor conflict resolution is shown to be less definite than given in

store policy. This video is not absolute proof of the falsity of Whole Foods's conflict policy statements, but it does show simmering management-worker discord. "Use Your Voice: Whole Foods Anti-union Meeting," April 30, 2015, by Joe Mte, https://youtu.be/2mvIzlVeP9U.
55. Paumgarten, "Food Fighter."
56. Harold Skousen, "Libertarian CEO Debate Freedom Fest 2016," YouTube video, July 29, 2016, https://www.youtube.com/watch?v=4FtQxRU3ICU, site discontinued.
57. "Whole Foods Market Mission and Values," http://www.wholefoodsmarket.com/mission-values/core-values/declaration-interdependence.
58. Paumgarten, "Food Fighter."
59. Mackey, "The Whole Foods Alternative."
60. Josee Johnston, Michelle Szabo, and Alexandra Rodney, "Good Food, Good People: Understanding the Cultural Repertoire of Ethical Eating," *Journal of Consumer Culture* 11 (2011): 306.
61. Michal S. Goldstein, *The Health Movement: Promoting Fitness in America* (New York: Twayne Publishers, 1992); Marc Stern, "The Fitness Movement and the Fitness Center Industry, 1960–2000," *Business and Economic History On-Line* 6 (January 2008).
62. Emma G. Keller, "Whole Foods CEO John Mackey Calling Obamacare Fascist Is Tip of the Iceberg," *Guardian*, January 18, 2013, https://www.theguardian.com/business/us-news-blog/2013/jan/18/whole-foods-john-mackey-fascist.
63. Seth Lubove, "New Age Capitalist," *Forbes*, April 6, 1998, http://www.forbes.com/global/1998/0406/0101049a.html.
64. Whole Foods memo quoted in Josh Harkinson, "Are Starbucks and Whole Foods Union Busting? Inside the Secret Anti-union Meetings, and How the Companies Plan to Rewrite the Labor-Friendly Employee Free Choice Act," *Mother Jones*, April 6, 2009, http://www.motherjones.com/politics/2009/04/are-starbucks-and-whole-foods-union-busting.
65. Mackey quoted in Lubove, "New Age Capitalist."
66. Fellner quoted in Harkinson, "Are Starbucks and Whole Foods Union Busting?"
67. Andrew G. Kirk, *Counterculture Green: The "Whole Earth Catalog" and American Environmentalism* (Lawrence: University Press of Kansas, 2007), 183.
68. "About Us," Eden Foods, http://www.edenfoods.com/about/.
69. Marian Burros, "Eating Well," *New York Times*, May 21, 1997.
70. Debra Stark, "Why We're Not Boycotting Eden Foods," *Natural Foods Merchandiser*, July 30, 2014, http://www.newhope.com/merchandising/why-were-not-boycotting-eden-foods.
71. Thomas More Law Center, https://www.thomasmore.org/.
72. Ian Millhiser, "How a Right-Wing CEO's Big Mouth Could Kill His Attack on Birth Control," *Think Progress*, April 15, 2013, https://thinkprogress.org/how-a-right-wing-ceos-big-mouth-could-kill-his-attack-on-birth-control-f94ee9179678#.ly33gylpv.
73. Irin Carmon, "Eden Foods Doubles Down in Birth Control Flap," *Salon*, April 15, 2013, http://www.salon.com/2013/04/15/eden_foods_ceo_digs_himself_deeper_in_birth_control_outrage/.
74. Clare O'Connor, "Eden Food to Grocers: Stick with Us Despite Birth Control 'Attack,'" *Forbes*, July 22, 2014, https://www.forbes.com/sites/clareoconnor/2014

/07/22/eden-foods-to-grocers-stick-with-usdespite-birth-control-attack/#3c0a2f50 3de8; "Eden Foods Public Statement," Eden Foods website, July 21, 2014, https://www.edenfoods.com/articles/view.php?articles_id=232.
75. Stark, "Why We're Not Boycotting."
76. Stark, "Why We're Not Boycotting."
77. Clare O'Connor, "Whole Foods: Shoppers Can 'Vote with Their Dollars' on Pro-Life Eden Foods," *Forbes*, July 14, 2014, http://www.forbes.com/sites/clareoconnor/2014/07/14/whole-foods-shoppers-can-vote-with-their-dollars-on-pro-life-eden-foods/#2d8d6bb5287e.
78. Samuel P. Hays discusses the ascendance of quality-of-life issues in postwar America in *Beauty, Health, and Permanence: Environmental Politics in the United States, 1955–1985* (Cambridge: Cambridge University Press, 1987).
79. Mark Maynard, "The Campaign to Get Eden Foods Products Off Our Local Co-op Shelves," March 14, 2015, http://markmaynard.com/2015/03/the-campaign-to-get-eden-foods-products-off-our-local-co-op-shelves/.
80. Dan Gillotte, in comments section to Maynard, "The Campaign to Get Eden Foods."
81. David Steigerwald, "All Hail the Republic of Choice: Consumer History as Contemporary Thought," *Journal of American History* 93, no. 2 (September 2006): 399.
82. "Toxic Hormones," in comments section to Maynard, "The Campaign to Get Eden Foods."
83. "HHS Update: Media Release," Eden Foods, July 3, 2014, https://www.edenfoods.com/articles/view.php?articles_id=229.
84. John Wilkinson, "The Quality Turn (around)—from Niche to Mainstream: The New Qualification of Global Commodity Markets—the Case of Soy" (paper presented to the Workshop on the New Frontiers of Consumption, Warwick, Warwick University, May 2009), 20.
85. Rod Dreher, *Crunchy Cons: The New Conservative Counterculture and Its Return to Roots* (New York: Random House, 2006), 179.
86. Dreher, *Crunchy Cons*, 41, 1.
87. Mathewes-Green quoted in Dreher, "Birkenstocked Burkeans," *National Review*, July 12, 2002, http://www.nationalreview.com/article/223546/birkenstocked-burkeans-rod-dreher.
88. Dreher, *Crunchy Cons*, 61.
89. Dreher, 71.
90. Dreher, 72.
91. Dreher, 74–75.
92. Dreher, 50.
93. Dreher, 65.
94. Salatin quoted in Dreher, 83.

CONCLUSION: THE FUTURE OF COUNTERCULTURAL FOOD POLITICS

1. Michael Pollan, "Farmer in Chief," *New York Times Magazine*, October 9, 2008, http://www.nytimes.com/2008/10/12/magazine/12policy-t.html.
2. For a discussion of Michelle Obama's organic garden, see Emily Baumgaertner, "Fans of White House Garden Hope New Tenants Keep It Green," *New York Times*, July 2, 2017, https://www.nytimes.com/2017/07/02/us/politics/white-house-garden

-michelle-obama.html. A profile of Sam Kass can be found on the White House website, https://obamawhitehouse.archives.gov/blog/author/sam-kass.
3. Michael Pollan, "Big Food Strikes Back," *New York Times Magazine*, October 9, 2016, 44.
4. Michael Pollan, *In Defense of Food: An Eater's Manifesto* (New York: Penguin, 2008), 1.
5. Michael Pollan, *Food Rules: An Eater's Manual* (New York: Penguin, 2009), 5, 7, 15, 20, 99.
6. Rachel Slocum, "Whiteness, Space, and Alternative Food Practice," *Geoforum* 38 (2007): 526, http://sites.middlebury.edu/gsfswhitepeople/files/2016/09/slocum.pdf.
7. Michael Pollan, *Cooked: A Natural History of Transformation* (New York: Penguin, 2013), 1.
8. Frank Bruni, "In Defense of Decadence," *New York Times*, February 6, 2008, F11, https://www.nytimes.com/2008/02/06/dining/reviews/06rest.html; https://www.thestranger.com/events/15895436/an-evening-with-michael-pollan.
9. "USDA Reports Record Growth in U.S. Organic Producers," April 4, 2016, https://www.usda.gov/media/press-releases/2016/04/04/usda-reports-record-growth-us-organic-producers.
10. "USDA Reports Record Growth."
11. "USDA Organic Market Overview," last updated April 4, 2017, https://www.ers.usda.gov/topics/natural-resources-environment/organic-agriculture/organic-market-overview.aspx.
12. Natasha Bowen, "The Color of Food: America's Invisible Farmers," May 14, 2015, https://civileats.com/2015/04/14/the-color-of-food-an-introduction/.
13. Pollan, "Big Food," 81, 83.
14. Ron Dreher, *Crunchy Cons: The New Conservative Counterculture and Its Return to Roots* (New York: Random House, 2006), 2.
15. Maria Fonte, "Reflexive Localism: Toward a Theoretical Foundation of an Integrative Food Politics," *International Journal of Sociology of Agriculture and Food* 20, no. 3 (2013): 397.
16. Julie Guthman, *Weighing In: Obesity, Food Justice, and the Limits of Capitalism* (Berkeley: University of California Press, 2011), 159.
17. Mark Bittman, Michael Pollan, Olivier De Schutter, and Ricardo Salvador, "Food and More: Expanding the Movement for the Trump Era," *Civil Eats*, January 16, 2017, https://civileats.com/2017/01/16/food-and-more-expanding-the-movement-for-the-trump-era/.
18. John Lauinger, "Michael Pollan Sees a Farm Bill Opening," *Politico*, November 17, 2017, https://www.politico.com/newsletters/morning-agriculture/2017/11/17/michael-pollan-sees-a-farm-bill-opening-026748.

INDEX

Page numbers in italics indicate illustrations.

Adams, Carol, 69
additives: Delaney Amendment, 99; "generally regarded as safe" list and, 99; J. I. Rodale and, 103–4, 111, 130; Johnson's FDA review of, 106; organic standards and, 163, 165
Agrarian Dreams (Guthman), 118–19
Agricultural Testament, An (Howard), 98
agriculture: alternative and, 6, 19, 95, 106, 193; conventional, 9; DDT and, 99; history of organic, 5; after World War II, 96, 100, 105; before World War II, 98–99
Alpert, Richard, 134. *See also* Ram Dass, Baba
American Medical Association (AMA): J. I. Rodale and, 100–101; natural foods critique of, 100
Animal, Vegetable, Miracle (Kingsolver), 180–81
Appetite for Change (Belasco), 4, 204n13
atomic anxiety, 59, 96
Ausubel, Kenny, 163–64

baby boomers, 3, 6, 169; childhood food and, 55; Cold War and, 3; consumerism of, 6–7, 140, 142; globalism of, 110; health ideals of, 140, 143–44; Peace Corps and, 110; vegetarianism and, 153
back-to-the-land movement, 108, 111–12, 117, 171
Barber, Dan, 200
black nationalism, 5, 37, 100
Beats, 8, 101, 104, 138, 147
Becker, Marion Rombauer, 58–59
Be Here Now (Ram Dass), 27
Belasco, Warren, 4, 93, 204n13
Berkeley, California, 1, 2, 94
Berry, Wendell, 109, 110–11
Better Homes and Gardens New Cook Book, 56–58
Biltekoff, Charlotte, 7
Bittman, Mark, 178, 201
Black Panthers, 37, 110
Bloodroot Collective, 15, 54, 71; ethnic cultures and, 68; health fads and, 70; radical feminism of, 63, 67–71, 88; seasonal cooking and, 68–69; vegetarianism and, 68–70, 88–89; work ideals of, 68, 70
Bloodroot Restaurant, 67–68
Brattleboro Food Co-op, 36, 43
Brown, Edward Espe, 5, 54, 82; commercialization and, 85, 91–92; New Age spirituality and, 91; political agnosticism of, 84; Zen cooking of, 81–85
brown rice, 10, 17, 35, 77, 126, 160

California cuisine, 12; Bay Area and, 85; Brown and, 12, 85, 91; Thomas and, 89; Waters and, 9, 90–91. *See also* New American cuisine
capitalism: *Laurel's Kitchen* and, 66; "market populism" and, 56, 129, 131, 165, 168; *Organic Style* and, 131
Carson, Rachel, 59, 100
Chez Panisse, 9, 91, 94
Child, Julia, 59, 80–81, 92, 179; Thomas and, 90
Chocolate to Morphine (Weil), 139
Cold War, 3, 101; nuclear fallout and, 9; pollution and, 59, 99, 103; "somatic vulnerability" and, 96; supermarkets and, 17
Coming to My Senses (Waters), 9
Commune Cookbook, The, 64
community-supported agriculture (CSA), 10, 46, 94, 197, 200
Conscious Capitalism (Mackey), 184–85, 192
conservatism, 42; antistatism, 170; Barry Goldwater and, 170; capitalism and, 171; Christians and, 171, 182, 193–94; government growth and, 112; New Right and, 170–73; Ronald Reagan and, x, 42, 112, 117, 170–72
consumerism: counterculture and, 10, 20, 129; green, 133; health and, 136; new-century and, 46, 125, 190; 1980s resurgence of, 112, 117, 129; postwar ascendance of, 6
Consumers Cooperative of Berkeley (CCB), 20–23; conservatism of, 22–23; demise of, 42, 208–9n34; New Deal and, 22; politics in, 22
cookbooks, 4, 6, 17; commercial sponsors and, 58; counterculture and, 54–56; feminine ideals in, 58–59; Great Depression and, 56; natural foods and, 60, 71, 85–86; 1950s and, 56–59, 204n11; World War II and, 56
Cooked (Pollan), 198
counterculture, ix, 5; antiestablishment of, 140; antistatism of, x, 169–70; Christianity and, 172–75; collectives of, 15–16; consciousness and, 134; decentralization ideology of, 112; free markets/consumerism and, 6, 19, 93, 172, 187; libertarianism and, 135; 1960s vs. 1970s, 15, 107–9; psychedelics and, 134; "right livelihood" of, 11, 15, 68; sexism in, 66; spirituality and, 84, 172; traditionalism of, 171; whiteness of, 10, 11, 63. *See also* hippies
Counterculture Green (Kirk), 10, 186–87
counterinstitution, 10, 11, 23, 27, 38–39, 130, 172, 206n36
Crawford, Robert, 96, 148, 149
Crunchy Cons (Dreher), 192, 194
Culinary Arts Institute Encyclopedic Cookbook, The, 57–58

Davis, Adelle, 55, 99
Davis, Joshua Clark, 10, 172
DDT, 99, 100
Debra's Natural Gourmet, 188–89
dietary health, 7, 9, 46, 87, 98, 106, 147–48, 159, 185
Diet for a Small Planet (Lappé), 35, 53, 55, 62, 86, 94, 152, 178; personal politics and, 55
Dreher, Rod, 191; antistatism of, 194, 200; authenticity, ideas of, 192; Christianity and, 193; conservatism of, 192, 194; counterculture and, 192; farmers and, 192–93; gender traditionalism of, 194
Dupuis, E. Melanie, 7

Eden Foods, 187–91; Affordable Care Act lawsuit, 187, 189; boycott of, 189–90; ecological branding of, 190; prescriptions and, 188
Enchanted Broccoli Forest, The (Katzen), 72–74
Equitable Pioneers of Rochdale, 21
exercise: 1970s running, 113–15; Rodale Press and, 119–20; spirituality and, 114–15

Falwell, Jerry, 171
Farber, David, xiii, 172
Fast Food Nation (Schlosser), 178

Fear of Food (Levenstein), 161–62
Feminist Mystique, The (Friedan), 179–80
Flinders, Carol, 1–4, 8, 62–67, 86–88
food co-ops, x, 4, 6, 11, 13, 16–17
Food Co-ops (Ronco), 20
food deserts, 47, 48, 206n40
food revolution, x, 46; antistatism of, 200; bread baking, 160; cooking critique of, 178; counterculture and, 200; critique of feminism in, 179, 181; elitism in, 48, 50, 185, 197–98; origin of, 228n34; pro-capitalism of, 50, 200; social justice and, 199; traditionalism of, 177–78, 180–81
food purity, 59, 106, 191
Food Rules (Pollan), 197–98
Frank, Thomas, 131
French Chef, The, 179
Friedan, Betty, 179, 180
Furie, Noel, 67, 69, 70, 71, 88

Gardenburger, 154–57
gastropolitics, 7, 8, 9, 198
Germantown Ecology Co-op, 34–35
Ginsberg, Allen, 8
Gitlin, Todd, 39, 204n14, 210n80
Gosse, Van, 38, 170, 210n76
Green Gulch Farm, 5, 85
Greening of America, The (Reich), 2
Greens Cookbook (Madison & Brown), 85
Greens Restaurant, 85
Guthman, Julie, 118–19, 166, 201, 206n38

Happy People Rarely Get Cancer (J. I. Rodale), 103
haute cuisine, 59, 80–81
Health and Healing (Weil), 135, 140
health food, 10, 34, 35, 37, 41, 55, 97, 106, 158
Heart of the Plate, The (Katzen), 93
hippies: class status of, 12; do-it-yourself ethic of, x; drugs and, 109, 134, 135, 172; Hoffman, 168–69; mainstreaming of, 117, 200–201; Rubin, 168–69; spirituality and, 148–49, 172. *See also* counterculture
Hirshberg, Gary, 160, 164–65
Hoffman, Abbie, 168–69

holistic health, 87, 120, 135, 144, 149
homemade/homemaking, 2, 3, 4, 61–64, 77, 87, 112, 161, 180
Howard, Albert, 98

identity politics, 38, 52, 201n76

Jesus movement, 172–73
Johnson, Lyndon B., 170
Joy of Cooking, The (Rombauer), 58–59
junk food, 19, 35, 72, 166, 206n40

Katzen, Mollie, ix, 5; artistry of, 73, 74; bread baking and, 76; childhood and, 8, 75; counterculture and, 73; cultural elite and, 92; gastronomy of, 72; gender traditionalism in, 213n41; Moosewood Restaurant and, 73, 76; popularity of, 92; on soufflé, 75; tofu and, 75; vegetarianism and, 76, 93
Kennedy, John F., 100
King, Martin Luther, Jr., 37, 38
Kingsolver, Barbara, 178, 180–82
Kirk, Andrew, 10, 186

Lappé, Frances Moore, 35, 53–54, 55, 86, 93, 152, 178
Laurel's Kitchen (Robertson, Flinders & Godfrey): antiwar activism and, 1, 62, 67; Berkeley's Organic Foods Co-op and, 62; bread baking in, 64–65; counterculture and, 2–3; domestic politics of, 61, 63, 65–66, 88; feminine ideals and, 60; popularity of, 55, 86; spirituality and, 65, 87; sugar and, 62; vegetarianism in, 2, 62, 67
Laurel's Kitchen Bread Book, The (Robertson, Flinders & Godfrey), 64, 65, 160
Laurel's Kitchen Caring (Robertson, Flinders & Godfrey), 86–87
Leary, Timothy, ix, 134, 137, 170, 174, 204n14
Levenstein, Harvey, 16, 161–62
localism, 9–10, 13, 19, 34, 46–48, 51, 85–86, 180, 197–99, 201
LSD, 5

Mackey, John: antiunionism of, 185–86; counterculture origins of, 183, 185; libertarianism of, 183–84, 185, 191; New Age and, 186; Obamacare, critique of, 182–83, 187; obesity and, 182–83
Madison, Deborah, 85, 91, 92
Mailer, Norman, 7–8, 96
Making of the Counterculture, The (Roszak), 134
Marriage of the Sun and the Moon, The (Weil), 137
meat: cardiovascular disease and, 59, 152–53; decline of, 153; grass-fed, 127; natural foods critique of, 59, 60, 62, 67, 193, 194; radical feminism and, 69; symbolism of, 56–57
Men's Health, 119–20
Mifflin Street Co-op, 17, 18, 50
milk, 59, 154, 161–62
Miriam, Selma, 67, 71, 88–89
modernity, 57–58
Moosewood Cookbook (Katzen), ix, 55, 72, 74, 92; bread baking and, 5; popularity of, 76; processed food and, 75, 76

natural foods movement: anticapitalism in, 160; antistatism and, 170, 196; Cold War and, 3, 60; conservatism of, 104–5, 169; consumerism in, 9, 13, 19, 130–31, 169, 200–201; counterinstitutions of, 160; cultural power of, 12, 17; definition of, x; endurance of, x–xi, 6; gastronomy in, 9, 72, 77; growth in 1970s, 105–7; incorporation of, 146; politics of, xi, 7; traditionalism in, 64, 66, 182; whiteness of, 5, 60
Natural Mind, The (Weil), 137
neoconservatism. *See* conservatism
neoliberalism, xi, 46, 130, 200
New Age spirituality, 65, 87, 91
New American cuisine, 12
New Left, x, 18, 38–39, 54, 130, 170, 173
New Vegetarian Epicure, The (Thomas), 89, 90
New Wave co-ops, 16–17; anticapitalism of, 20, 33, 44; anticonsumerism of, 52; business critique of, 27; buying clubs, 2, 24, 207n4; community and, 43, 51, 52; counterculture and, 19, 30–31; environmentalism in, 19; food boycotts in, 36–37; food revolution and, 51–52; management alternatives in, 28–29; meat debates in, 35; member control and, 37; natural foods debates of, 34–37; New Left influence on, 18; nutritional dogmatism of, 19; Old Wave and, 20; participatory democracy in, 31, 37, 49; personalism in, 27; race and class of, 37, 50; social justice and, 19; supermarkets and, 20, 62; work requirement in, 49, 50. *See also* Brattleboro Food Co-op; People's Food Co-op; Weavers Way Co-op
Nixon, Richard, 17, 106, 109, 112
nuclear weapons and energy, 3, 22–23, 32, 59, 96, 99, 101, 103–4, 109

Obama, Barack, 196–98, 200; Task Force on Childhood Obesity, 46
Obama, Michelle: "Let's Move" campaign of, 13–14, 46; organic garden of, 46, 196, 197
obesity epidemic, 11, 47, 48, 182
Old Wave co-ops, 2, 17, 20–23; consumerism of, 21, 22; New Deal and, 21–22; 1920s and, 208n25
Omnivore's Dilemma, The (Pollan): agribusiness critique in, 46; food revolution and, 178; gender traditionalism in, 181; hunting and, 181
organic: agriculture and, 106, 117–18; consumerism and, 94, 97, 118, 124; farming standardization of, 119; grassroots activism and, 162–63; health and, 133; industrialization/incorporation of, 163–65, 167; market populism and, 16; milk and, 161–62; twenty-first-century rise of, 46, 47, 50, 86, 161
Organic Foods Production Act (OFPA), 118–19; National Organic Standards Board of, 162–63
Organic Front, The (J. I. Rodale), 102, 104
Organic Gardening, 95; alternative energy and, 109; circulation of, 101,

105; decline of, 115, 120–21, 124; Maria Rodale and, 121–24; Mike McGrath and, 120–21; 1980s renovation of, 116
Organic Style: commercialism of, 124–29; environmentalism and, 126, 129–30; global food system and, 127–28; healthism and, 136

Park Slope Food Coop, 42–43
People's Food Co-op, 17; expansion of, 42; financial problems of, 31–33; management debates in, 31–33; Packard Avenue store, 32–33; People's Produce Co-op, 32; professionalization of, 33
Perennial Political Palate, The (Bloodroot Collective), 88
personalist politics, xi, 2, 7, 110
pesticides, 100, 130. *See also* DDT
Political Palate, The (Bloodroot Collective), 54, 70–73, 103
Pollan, Michael, 46; agribusiness and, 196–98; appeal to Obama administration, 196; consumer politics and, 200; feminism and, 179–80; food punditry of, 178; industrial organics and, 163; masculinity and, 181–82; response to Trump and, 201
pollution, 96, 100, 106, 129–30
Polyface Farm. *See* Salatin, Joel
Port Huron Statement, The (SDS), 38
Potter, Michael, 182; Catholicism of, 188; contraception and, 188; Eden Foods founding and, 187; genetically modified organisms and, 187–88; libertarianism of, 188–89, 191
Prevention, 95, 96; advertising changes of, 115; health ideology of, 111, 113; 1950s circulation, 101, 105, 120; sports and fitness and, 113
processed food: cake mixes, 58; counterculture and, 3, 59; early twentieth century and, 3; functional foods and, 149; organic and, 161; postwar and, 3, 57; white bread, 64; World War II and, 3

Ram Dass, Baba, 27
recession, 107, 109, 117

Reich, Charles A., 2
Robertson, Laurel, 1–2, 60, 62–66, 160, 178
Rodale, Ardath (Ardie), 119
Rodale, Jerome Irving (J. I.), 95, 97–98; AMA and, 101; Cold War and, 104; conservatism of, 101, 104; death of, 105; hippies and, 217n38; Howard and, 98; organic agriculture and, 98, 131; organic diet and, 104, 105, 111; Native Americans and, 103; "negroes" and, 103; popularity of, 105; primitivism and, 103; rural idealism of, 102; USDA and, 100
Rodale, Maria: counterculture and, 124–25; environmental consumerism of, 126–27; healing platform of, 122; leadership of, 121–22; organic vision of, 123, 131–32
Rodale, Robert, 100; antimodernism of, 107–8; antiurbanism of, 108; baby boomer identity of, 105; checkbook activism and, 117; Cornucopia Project of, 110, 116; death of, 116, 119; environmental ideas of, 113; exercise and, 113; globalism and, 110, 111; international organics of, 116; *Novii Fermer* and, 116; organic ideas of, 107, 128; regeneration project of, 111, 116; Schumacher and, 107; self-sufficiency and, 109, 128–29, 131
Rodale Institute (Health and Soil Institute), 109, 117
Rodale Press: Bob Teufel and, 122; book department changes of, 120; consumerism of, 97; financial turnaround of, 123; founding of, 95–96; *New Farm* magazine, 113; *New Shelter* magazine, 113, 127; renovation of, 116, 122–23; Stephen Pleshette Murphy and, 122–23
Ronco, William, 20
Roszak, Theodore, 134, 170
Rubin, Jerry, 168–69

Salatin, Joel, 194–95
Schlosser, Eric, 178
Schumacher, E. F., 107

science, 148–49
Second Seasonal Political Palate, The (Bloodroot Collective), 69, 70
Seeds of Change, 163–64
Sexual Politics of Meat, The (Adams), 69
Shapiro, Laura, 8
Small Is Beautiful (Schumacher), 107
soy, 146; agribusiness and, 159; countercultural associations of, 159; health claims and, 152; incorporation of, 157–58; meat substitute and, 152, 155–56; milk and, 154–55; processing of, 158; supermarkets and, 153; tofu and, 155
Stark, Debra, 188–89
Student Nonviolent Coordinating Committee (SNCC), 37–38
Students for a Democratic Society (SDS), 16, 38–39; Economic Research and Action Project of, 38; parasitism of, 39; Tom Hayden and, 38–39, 210n82
sugar, 57–58
supermarkets: access to, 166; critique of, 2, 7–8, 16, 55, 70, 78, 80, 84, 107; natural foods in, 10, 90, 94, 165–66; postwar growth and, 16–17, 57–58, 100, 207n6; suburbs and, 166

Tassajara Bread Book, The (Brown), 81, 85
Tassajara Cooking (Brown), 5, 55, 81; minimalism in, 83; vegetarianism and, 84, 152; Zen method in, 82
tea: antioxidants and, 148; Asia and, 146–47; health claims and, 148–51; orientalism and, 150–51; popularity of, 150
Thomas, Anna: authenticity and, 80; childhood and, 8, 77; counterculture and, 79, 81, 89–90; eurocentrism of, 77; gastronomy of, 72–73, 78, 90; internationalism of, 78–80; marijuana and, 81; primitivism of, 80, 89; processed food and, 77, 80; vegetarianism and, 76–77, 89–90
tofu, 10, 75, 86, 126, 151–52, 155
Tomato Blessings and Radish Teachings (Brown), 85, 91
Trump, Donald, 201

Turner, Fred, 10
Twelve Tribes, 173–77; biblical childrearing ideas of, 175; counterculture and, 174; Elbert Eugene (Gene) Spriggs, 173–74; gender traditionalism of, 175; Island Pond, Vermont, and, 175–76; Marsha Spriggs, 173–74; natural foods and, 176–77; theology of, 174–77; Yellow Deli of, 174, 176, 177

U.S. Department of Agriculture (USDA), 14, 47, 100, 198–99; Carter's Low-Input Sustainable Agriculture program, 118; organic and, 162–163, 198–99; Robert and J. I. Rodale and, 100–101, 118

Vegetarian Epicure, The (Thomas), 77–78, 81, 91
vegetarianism: consumer politics and, 53; environmentalism and, 53; health benefits of, 153–54; natural foods cookbooks and, 55, 93; new century rise of, 153
Vietnam War, 1, 110, 112

Waters, Alice: California cuisine and, 12, 77, 81, 85, 91; counterculture and, 9; "delicious revolution" and, 12; "edible schoolyard" and, 12; gastropolitics of, 9, 12–13; haute cuisine and, 81
Weathermen, 110
Weavers Way Co-op, 24, 28; antiestablishment sentiments in, 45–46; "beloved community" and, 41, 43, 52; Chestnut Hill co-op, 49; expansion of, 43, 46; financial crisis of, 44–46; food debates in, 34–35, 37; food justice in, 47; food reformism of, 47–49; founding of, 18, 24–25; grape boycott by, 37; Jules Timerman and, 18, 24, 26, 29; lack of diversity in, 37, 39–41; management of, 27–31; member infighting at, 48–49; mission of, 18; Mount Airy race politics and, 25; West Oak Lane co-op, 47–48; work requirement at, 28, 49–50

Weil, Andrew, 5, 144; altered states campaign of, 139; celebrity and, 143, 145; commercialism of, 133, 141–46, 159, 166–67; consciousness and, 134, 135, 137, 167; corporation of, 136, 142, 145; counterculture and, 145–46, 167; drugs and, 134–35, 137–40; green tea and, 141, 147–48, 151; Haight-Ashbury Medical Clinic and, 134, 137; *Harvard Crimson* article and, 134; Harvard Medical School and, 136–37; holistic/integrative health and, 135, 140, 141, 143, 146; indigenous people and, 138; Leary and, 134; micronutrition and, 148–49; mind-body theory of, 142; natural foods and, 146; tofu and, 152, 155; University of Arizona and, 139, 141; vegetarianism of, 153; Western vs. Eastern culture, 147, 152

Whole Earth Catalog, 10, 112

Whole Foods, 11, 106, 165, 191; Amazon and, 187; boycott of, 183; dietary reformism of, 184–85; employees of, 184; philanthropy of, 184–85; shopping experience and, 165–66; success of, 183; union busting of, 186, 228–29n54

whole grains, 64–65

Williams, Raymond, 159

Yippies, 168–169

Zen Buddhism, 5, 81, 84–85, 92, 147, 172

www.ingramcontent.com/pod-product-compliance
Lightning Source LLC
Chambersburg PA
CBHW032213230426
43672CB00011B/2538